P9-CRR-820

# Fighting for Your
# African American
# Marriage

Keith E. Whitfield
Howard J. Markman
Scott M. Stanley
Susan L. Blumberg

# Fighting for Your
# African American
# Marriage

JOSSEY-BASS
A Wiley Company
www.josseybass.com

Published by

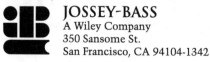

**JOSSEY-BASS**
A Wiley Company
350 Sansome St.
San Francisco, CA 94104-1342

www.josseybass.com

Copyright © 2001 by PREP Educational Products, Inc. and Keith E. Whitfield

Jossey-Bass is a registered trademark of John Wiley & Sons, Inc.

No part of this publication may be reproduced, stored in a retrieval system, or transmitted in any form or by any means, electronic, mechanical, photocopying, recording, scanning, or otherwise, except as permitted under Sections 107 or 108 of the 1976 United States Copyright Act, without either the prior written permission of the Publisher or authorization through payment of the appropriate per-copy fee to the Copyright Clearance Center, 222 Rosewood Drive, Danvers, MA 01923, (978) 750-8400, fax (978) 750-4744. Requests to the Publisher for permission should be addressed to the Permissions Department, John Wiley & Sons, Inc., 605 Third Avenue, New York, NY 10158-0012, (212) 850-6011, fax (212) 850-6008, e-mail: permreq@wiley.com.

Jossey-Bass books and products are available through most bookstores. To contact Jossey-Bass directly, call (888) 378-2537, fax to (800) 605-2665, or visit our website at www.josseybass.com.

Substantial discounts on bulk quantities of Jossey-Bass books are available to corporations, professional associations, and other organizations. For details and discount information, contact the special sales department at Jossey-Bass.

We at Jossey-Bass strive to use the most environmentally sensitive paper stocks available to us. Our publications are printed on acid-free recycled stock whenever possible, and our paper always meets or exceeds minimum GPO and EPA requirements.

**Library of Congress Cataloging-in-Publication Data**

Fighting for your African American marriage/Keith E. Whitfield . . . [et al.].
    p.  cm.
  Includes bibliographical references and index.
    ISBN 0-7879-5551-5 (alk. paper)
    1. Marriage—United States. 2. African Americans—marriage.
I. Whitfield, Keith E., 1962-
HQ536.F55   2001
306.85'089'96073—dc21                                              2001001340

FIRST EDITION
*PB Printing* 10  9  8  7  6  5  4  3  2  1

# Contents

102274

*Mom and Dad, here is to your loving spirits*
*and to your strong and rugged marriage.*

# Acknowledgments

My (Keith E. Whitfield's) parents' marriage of more than forty years is a testament to the indomitable African American spirit and a prime example of the strength of African American marriages and true teamwork. Now, as they see their children marry and raise families, they celebrate their successes together. They also have a good laugh when they see the trials that they overcame—and when they tell us that "You'll be fine with time."

I want to thank my wife, Linda Burton, professor of human development and family studies and sociology at the Pennsylvania State University, for the help she gave me almost every day as I worked on developing this book. She did not want to be a coauthor on this book, but her voice, her realism, and her perspective are represented in it nonetheless. She has been a constant companion and editor for much of my contribution. In some folks' eyes, we have only been married for a short time, but in that time we have seen at least two lifetimes together. Every day with Linda has been an experience. It was her loving encouragement that got me through my darkest days. As an African American scholar, I've seen almost every good idea I've ever had challenged and frequently belittled. My marriage to Linda has made me a better person and a better scholar and taught me to believe in myself. Hey Linda, you know, of course—now that the book is done—we have to keep practicing the PREP methods more than ever! Here's to you, Lindy.

All four of us coauthors would also like to recognize the more than thirty couples whose stories are portrayed in this book. The stories have been disguised so that no one will recognize them; you could say that the names have been changed to protect the helpful. These stories are about couples from the east coast to the west, and from north to south. Sharing their stories to try to help others is what makes this book so special.

Alan Rinzler was a constant devil's advocate in developing these themes to address the African American perspective. His energy and thought-provoking words were a driving force behind the hard choices in how to represent the African American experience in a way that is fair, not stereotypical, positive, and enlightening.

KEITH E. WHITFIELD
*April 2001*

# Introduction

# An African American Perspective

You might be asking yourself why we felt the need to write a special book just for African American couples. All four of us coauthors believe that, like other special groups with their own history and culture (Hispanics, Jews, Christians), African Americans have special issues and concerns that, frankly, no one else has. To listen to some of our friends and colleagues, we African Americans (Keith E. Whitfield, or KEW, speaking) really have *more* than our share because no other group, as we all know, has had to deal with the legacy of slavery in the United States—which ended 150 years ago—and the amazingly persistent cloud of relentless racism, which has continued ever since.

So there are special issues and concerns. We all know what they are, even if we don't always like to talk about them. We African Americans bring these issues and concerns into our marriages, whether we want to or not. This doesn't make us strange, and it doesn't mean we are victims; on the contrary, it's totally normal and understandable. Our struggle as Americans has made us strong and resilient. There's nobody else exactly like us.

Consequently, the four of us coauthors intend to provide a helping hand, to reach out and draw African American couples into our hearts and souls and say, "We understand, we know what you're feeling, we can give you some help." For example:

- We understand the special issues in raising, nurturing, and disciplining children in a society that often discriminates against them, fears them, stereotypes their behavior, and resists their healthy instincts to grow and flourish. We also understand how this, too, can come home to affect an African American marriage.

- We understand that African American couples have to deal with the pressures of racism on the job, in school, at the mall, and in the whole great big society at large; we know that daily encounters with this racism can have an impact on how husbands and wives get along.

- We understand how stereotyped gender roles—the powerful black woman who's supposed to hold everything together; the devalued black man who is assumed to remain victimized, angry, unavailable—can undermine and demoralize African American marriages.

- We certainly appreciate the difficulty of staying afloat economically in a society where high unemployment, inadequate incomes, and below-average educational opportunities are repeatedly the burden of African American couples. We know just how hard it is for blacks to benefit from the so-called booming economy that's supposed to be sweeping the country.

- We understand how the difficult question of color can play a role not only in assumptions and attitudes projected from the outside society, but within the African American marriage and family itself.

- We know that in-laws, the extended family of kin and non-blood relations, the neighborhood, and the community can all play a big role in the life of an African American couple.

- We very much appreciate the special role of the church and spirituality in African American marriages.

- We are sensitive to the concerns of African American couples, parents, and children regarding interracial intimacy, including dating and in some cases (about 4 percent) marriage.

This is why there is a need for a special book just for African Americans. We four wrote this book because we want to provide a useful, practical tool, honed through more than twenty-five years of research, to help you enhance your marriage, prevent divorce, and get along a whole lot better every day.

We live at a time of great advancements in comfort and convenience. We have weight loss pills, Internet shopping, and wireless phones. But regardless of technological advances, we still struggle to get along with one another. The struggle is nowhere more important than at home. As married African Americans, we see our worlds complicated by the same stressors other couples face: raising children, the needs of our parents and in-laws, and money problems. Further, and not necessarily like other couples, we struggle with outside forces in the form of racism as well as the particular issues and concerns we've already mentioned here. Amid all the turmoil, when is there time for our family and marital relationships? When is there time to take a look at our spouse and see the love that created a union of two?

Black families have always been quite varied. One estimate suggests that in 1997, of 8.6 million African American families, 46 percent were couples. Research shows that money issues are a key source of stress for nearly all couples, but money struggles seem to be a greater burden for African Americans than Caucasians, with more than one-quarter of all African American couples living at or below the poverty level. The stress from this kind of hardship is also likely to have a cumulative effect on couples of color. Yet despite the impression some people have gotten, the divorce rate among African Americans is only slightly higher than what is found among Caucasians (except after age sixty-five, when the rate rises significantly higher for African Americans). Frankly, we do not know why this is the case, but it may be that after sixty-five the children have moved out, work is less critical for survival, and the culmination of frustration from not dealing with problems effectively takes its toll.

It may also be that at this stage of life, there is less concern over religious sanctions against divorce. We are just not sure.

Ours is a constant struggle. The nature of our existence involves fighting—sometimes for basic rights—if we are to gain ground. We might have to fight with our bosses for our voice to be heard, or with salesclerks to be given equal treatment. We also have to fight for our relationships. It requires the same kind of effort we make for everything else in our lives. We have all heard that it takes work to maintain a relationship, but what about doing more than *maintaining* a relationship? What if we want to *excel* at a relationship? What does it take? How do we get there from where we are now? What does a great relationship look like? Are there a few things that make a big difference?

If you have picked up this book, it's likely that you're searching for answers to how you can develop better communication skills and a better relationship in general, whether you're thinking about marriage or already married. We have designed this book to boost your confidence in your ability to make your relationship work despite the various stresses and pressures in this society.

In this book, we want to give you three tools:

- A way to communicate with your spouse so that both of you are heard

- A framework for thinking about how to handle conflict

- Suggestions on how to balance dealing with issues in your marriage and the pressures from the world outside

We frame these useful tools within the daily life of African American couples: their lives, their stories, their ways of dealing with special issues and concerns.

My wife and I (KEW) have dealt with many of these special issues and concerns ourselves. We've been married for seven years and have four children. We've had to face issues of discrimination, economic hardship, and differences between us in our parenting styles and traditions. Although Linda is my soul mate, we have contrasting upbringings and differ in our life experiences. For example, she was raised in Compton, California, and her family is from Louisiana. She is book-smart and street-smart at the same time. She was taught lots of superstitions ("If you're a girl with hairy arms, you will have sons"; "Don't leave your hair in the garbage because someone might use it to get you"). I, on the other hand, am the son of an air force officer; my relatives are from Chicago. I was raised with an emphasis on rational thinking in every situation, using basic common sense, self-control at all times, and self-reflection.

My wife's parents had extended kin embedded in her family—aunts, uncles, and cousins living with them or nearby and participating in most every milestone of her upbringing. I always went to visit my relatives. I would be introduced to numerous cousins on every visit but almost never the same one twice in successive trips. My mother and father raised us with a loving but *firm* hand. Even though we grew up in the suburbs, my mother and father raised us as though we were in the city. We would constantly hear "Nothing good ever happens after dark" and "Be careful who you hang out with; they could get you in trouble." My wife, by contrast, lived the reality of those fears but really wasn't afraid most of the time.

These are just some of the differences between my wife and me. We have worked to make them strengths rather than difficulties. Linda and I have read self-help books and seen videos. What we found in those mainstream marriage products were the issues and situations that Caucasians have, and more important how they saw the world, their marriage, and the challenges to their marriage. We found some overlap with non-African American marriages, but not as much as we would have liked. Which brings us back to our earlier point about how important it is for African American couples to have their own point of view expressed in a book of this kind.

My wife and I are university researchers who deal with family issues, not only in our real lives but also in the work we do. We had the great fortune to work with one of the authors of this book, Howard J. Markman. Over time we have shared with him our interest in seeing something that African Americans could identify with in the struggle to create a solid marriage. We found that the work that he and his colleagues, Scott M. Stanley and Susan L. Blumberg, did boasted an excellent structure and research base, but it lacked "a particular kind of soul." So this book is built on the incredible success that Howard, Scott, Susan, and their colleagues have had with a system they call PREP (the Prevention and Relationship Enhancement Program). But it's also quite different. It's a unique book written specifically for African American couples. Their core book on PREP, *Fighting for Your Marriage*, has been immensely successful for helping all kinds of couples (including African Americans). But here, we plan to do something different. The four of us plan to take the strategies and principles that have made PREP's work so helpful to couples and tailor it to the specific needs of African American couples in today's society.

This book is based on research, group discussion with African American couples, and the experience of marriage educators and therapists who have used PREP with all kinds of couples. In preparing this work, I came to understand how much my parents' own marriage had personally influenced me. In fact, I have dedicated this book to them. Their children left home more than ten years ago, so we know they didn't stay together for the sake of the children. They found ways to resolve conflict, raise their children, save for the future, and show that they love each other.

My mother and father grew up on the south side of Chicago. They were married after a relatively short courtship and began their life of moving around the country. In the early 1960s, my father returned to school and became a military officer. These were, of course, challenging times for African Americans, and my father and mother had to deal with not only their marriage but also questions about their rank and status. Caucasians sometimes assumed my parents were uppity, while some African Americans assumed they were Uncle Toms at work and in social settings because of their success (by virtue of my father's rank). It was only through the inner strength of their marriage that they survived those years. It was through their respect for and commitment to one another that they demonstrated their unified perspective on child rearing, their ability to admit they were wrong, and the strength to step outside of themselves when they saw that the other needed support. These themes I saw so powerfully in their marriage are the very themes of this book: communication, problem solving, teamwork, commitment, friendship, and support.

## What Is PREP?

Based on twenty years of marital research, the Prevention and Relationship Enhancement Program approach focuses on specific attitudes and ways of acting that can make a powerful difference in a marriage over time. PREP incorporates principles based on couples research done in the United States and around the world. For example, there is a great deal of evidence that couples who are not doing well in their marriage differ significantly from happier couples in their ability to handle conflict. Such findings have led us to a number of specific strategies with which couples can handle issues constructively—the strategies that we teach you here. But this book is not just about communication and conflict. We also focus on topics such as commitment, forgiveness, spirituality, intimacy, friendship, sensuality, and fun—each with special application to an African American marriage.

Much of the research underlying key points and strategies in this book have been conducted at the University of Denver. Some of this research has been supported by the National Institute of Mental Health through grants awarded to coauthors Howard and Scott. Careful analysis of years of research—comparing couples who are having significant problems to couples who are happy together and solidly committed—resulted in PREP, and, now, many of the suggestions in this book.

We, and other researchers, have over the years conducted long-term studies looking at which couples thrive, which fail, and which limp along for years in misery. In studies of this kind, much has been learned about specific risk factors that we warn you about here while teaching you ways to protect your marriage into the years to come. Knowing how a marriage can fall apart gives us a clear idea where couples should focus their attention to make marriage all it can be. Here, we concentrate on things that are changeable, things you can really do something about to experience greater peace and openness in your marriage.

## How Are Things Going for You?

Here is a quiz that has been developed from numerous marriage studies (jointly by Scott, Howard, and Susan at the University of Denver and by many other marital researchers around the world). It can help you get a rough sense of how you are doing on some key dimensions. It doesn't cover everything that's important, by any means, but it does address key patterns that studies show are related to how a marriage will do over time.

Don't panic if you get a couple of yes answers; you can use them as a guide for areas to work on in your marriage. In the second half of this book, we go into detail about how to deal with the yeses. Everyone occasionally answers yes to some of these questions, but a persistent pattern of affirmative answers over time can be a warning signal that your relationship needs help—and you'll want to begin taking steps to turn things around.

You may find that you answer no to most of these questions. In this case, you should approach what we have to teach you as a matter of prevention. In other words, take the time to learn the kinds of strategy that can keep your marriage on track and growing over the years to come.

1. Little arguments escalate into ugly fights, with   yes   no
   accusation, criticism, name calling, or bringing
   up past hurts.

2. My partner criticizes or belittles my opinions,   yes   no
   feelings, or desires.

3. My partner seems to view my words or actions   yes   no
   more negatively than I mean them to be.

4. When we have a problem to solve, it is as   yes   no
   though we are on opposite teams.

5. I hold back from telling my partner what I   yes   no
   really think and feel.

6. I think seriously about what it would be like to   yes   no
   date or marry someone else.

7. I feel lonely in this relationship.   yes   no

8. When we argue, one of us withdraws—that is,   yes   no
   doesn't want to talk about it anymore, or leaves
   the scene.

9. I am fearful about what our future together will   yes   no
   be like.

As you read this book, you will understand not only why these questions are important but what you can do to build and maintain a great marriage that brings delight to both of you.

## Who Is This Book For?

The techniques in this book are for African American couples who want to solve problems or prevent them from happening, whether newlywed, married twenty years, or trying marriage for a second or third time. You may be having significant problems at this time in your marriage. Or you may have a sturdy relationship now but are interested in *preventing* problems of the kind encountered by all-too-many couples in our culture. In fact, PREP was originally devised as a program to help premarital couples prevent serious relationship problems from developing in the first place.

As we (HJM and SLB) have worked with many couples in the program, we've found that the techniques also prove effective for couples in distressed relationships. But whether or not you are having serious problems at this point, the information and specific techniques in this book are useful and beneficial for your relationship.

## How to Get the Most out of This Book

All four of us believe that learning how to have a good relationship is largely a skill, like any other skill; you can learn these skills together, as a couple, if you are motivated to do so. To help you learn the things we teach here, we include exercises at the end of each chapter that you can use to build your marriage.

We introduce a number of effective skills for handling conflict and disagreement. We also suggest strategies for building and maintaining friendship, commitment, and spiritual intimacy. Some of what we cover entails quite specific skills that you can learn. Like any new skills, with practice they become easier to use. With each skill or principle, we also tell you about the underlying theory and research so you understand why it works. You will find that these techniques are not really difficult to understand, but they do take work to master. We believe it is worth the effort to make what you learn here a part of your relationship.

In the first chapter, we focus on those unique issues and concerns that are of vital importance and have a powerful impact in African American marriages. Then we go on to present you with some assessment tools for self-evaluation of your marriage. This can sometimes be the hardest part of working on your marriage because you must try to be completely honest and admit your faults. You also have to bare your throat, as it were. You have to allow yourself to be vulnerable to your mate and be open to how he or she perceives you. This is a really hard process. We suggest that first you and your partner individually read each chapter before coming together to talk about it. You will probably have to read them again as you discuss your own issues, and that's OK. It is a good idea to pay particular attention to Chapters Three and Four on communication and problem solving. They present excellent ways to really hear what the other person is saying, communicate what your issues are, and find how you can work together to solve them.

We have tried to create a book based on empirical, academic research and thousands of hours with real couples from our clinical practice, and on our own experience and the wisdom of all the wonderful people who have contributed their personal stories about what worked best for them. Our team for this book consists of social scientists, teachers, and clinicians. As the lead writer and a black man, I (KEW) have walked the walk; been there, done that; and know what it's like to enhance and preserve an African American marriage in these times.

Above all, the four of us hope this proves to be for you a book that is, all at once, useful, practical, and inspiring.

# Fighting for Your African American Marriage

# 1

# What Makes Our World Go 'Round

The sun comes up and begins another day of work, kids, family, and the rest of life's slings and arrows. We take each day, add it to the ones before, and call it a life. But in each one of these days, where does our marriage, our relationship with our spouse rank in the long laundry list of responsibilities? For a relationship to work and stay healthy, we must take responsibility, pay attention, and make an effort—effort that is responsive to the needs of our spouse and the needs of the relationship.

Yeah, just what you need to hear, that in addition to everything else that goes on in your life you've go to work to fight for your marriage. But hold on. We're not trying to make things harder for you; not at all. Just the opposite in fact. The goal of this book is to try to help African Americans create a style of interacting with their spouses that promotes an easier life, not a harder one.

In this chapter, we briefly preview all the special issues and concerns that confront African American marriages: protecting our children, racism, stereotyped views of black women and men, money, accommodating different backgrounds, attitudes about color, in-laws and kin, the church, and interracial relationships. We also discuss how the chapters that follow offer skills to address these issues with your spouse.

# Racism

Marvin Gaye was one of the most influential musical poets of our time. His famous song "What's Goin' On" was a prophetic anthem, embodying the turbulent times of the seventies as well as the eighties, nineties, and even into the new millennium. He talked about the hate, which has produced a racial divide and affected our personal experience, our relationships, and our marriages every day of our lives. Although not every African American experiences racism in the same way or to the same extent, our recognition and acknowledgment of racism creates stress in our lives.

Racism is an important and often underestimated factor in the stress that can occur in relationships among African Americans. The very nature of this form of bigotry ranges from ignorance to unjust treatment to acts of violence against people of color, but this intolerance produces anger, hostility, and frustration in those who are on the receiving end of it. The stress of racism does not always take an obvious or insidious form. It can be much more subtle and, like water over a rock, wear away at your personhood. It can also leave you distrustful of the world and others—or worse, even distrustful of yourself.

How can all this happen? Because racism is not necessarily about someone calling you the N word. It can be subtle, it can be disguised, and it can be maddeningly hard to realize at times. Hence, you can examine interactions with people and wonder if it is a question of being black. How do you really know? The problem is that you often don't. You are left to wonder and assume based on previous experience.

The stress of racism can be exotic or mundane. An example of exotic stress is redlining. A couple looking for a house are "directed" by some real estate agents to certain communities, or presented with apparently insurmountable problems with getting a home loan. Mundane stress includes a situation like being followed around in a department store because they think you're going to steal something. Or racial profiling on the highway because you fit the supposed description of people who traffic in drugs or commit crimes (that is, you are black).

Another form of stress that can arise for African Americans is gender-based racism. Sometimes employers offer more opportunities for black women than men. Why? There are many theories. Three common ones are, first, fear of physical harm that whites sometimes feel toward all African American men. The second is the preconceived notion that black men do not work hard and are always late. A third is the belief that regardless of qualifications, if a man is to get the job he should be white.

Knowing that unfounded notions of this type exist in the workplace can be a painful challenge for African American men as they seek employment. It's natural that many black men develop feelings of hopelessness, anger, and frustration. When it's harder to get a job or to keep one because of some form of racism, this can have a profound effect on the person directly affected and his or her partner. For example, some black men may feel that they can't fulfill their responsibilities. They may also feel jealous and resentful that their wives can get a job but they can't. This can further damage self-esteem, and at times, the esteem of one's mate.

We know how tough it can get. We understand the doubts that can arise in one's mind. If you don't get that job that you are qualified for, is it because of a skill or quality that another applicant has, or is it because of the color of your skin? We can try to be objective and eliminate all other explanations, and sometimes all that is left to explain not getting the job is the color of your skin. If that's the reason, what do you do? Do you go to the EEO officer and submit a complaint? What backlash could arise?

All of these subtle or obvious situations build to produce frustration and uncertainty about the world around us. We carry this yoke about our shoulders, and then we go home. Home to our spouse and perhaps a family—both requiring time, patience, understanding, and love. But the world has just spit in your face; "I don't think that I can really feel love right now!"

Consider an example of how racism can influence a relationship. Levon and Shantee have been married for two years. Both work, Levon as an engineer and Shantee as a school teacher. Both started new jobs in the last month.

SHANTEE: Hey, babe, how was your day?

LEVON: The day was fine. I guess. My boss asked me why I was late getting back from lunch. He didn't seem to realize that I left thirty minutes late to lunch so that I could get a project done. He never questions others when they come in, but he always seems to have his eye on me.

SHANTEE: Is there some office policy on when you are supposed to take lunch?

LEVON: The point is that I'm the only black engineer for that company and I am being singled out. They're probably trying to find something to use to fire me.

SHANTEE: Do you do anything else they question? Do they say anything else?

LEVON: What else do they need to say for *you* to get the point? You know what it's like out there. (*walking off*) Never mind. You just ain't gettin' it.

Levon feels that not only his boss is questioning his motivation; his wife is too. That hurts. That leads to distance. Levon feels that Shantee's questions shouldn't be directed toward him, but rather about condemning his boss for his actions. In the absence of statements like that, he feels she isn't supporting him. Meanwhile, Shantee is left feeling that she doesn't understand why Levon doesn't think that she gets the point. Of course she knows what it's like; she's experienced it herself many times. But sometimes, in our effort to analyze things, we don't get what the other person really wants from us: that we need to be comforted and assured that our assumptions about the world may have grounding in reality. If this doesn't happen, the stress from the world comes right into the space between the marriage partners. In this book, we try to suggest how a couple can use the power of marriage to work as a team to fight against the stress of racism.

As African Americans, our strength as a people has always been driven through our families. Black men and women working together have always been a strength, no matter how the greater society has tried to pull us apart. In relationships, we need the strength to put the racist acts of the world into perspective. We have to take the attitude that no racist statements or actions are more important than our spouse is. We also must develop the ability to take our partner's perspective. This permits us to "be there" for our spouse. When both members of a couple can take the other's perspective, it's a powerful tool, one that makes us strong and able to fight the good fight, as teammates, against ignorance, unfairness, injustice, and stress!

Take a look at your marriage and ask whether racism affects it. Are either or both of you deeply affected by racism daily? What stress does this lead to between the two of you? How do you handle the stress?

Among the tools and techniques for enhancing and preserving African American marriages that we offer in this book are skills for being there for your spouse. Being there is the ability to have a sense of where he or she is and, without speaking a word, make your spouse feel supported. My wife and I (coauthor Keith E. Whitfield, or KEW) do this when we are at our best. When all is clicking, we're even able to finish each other's sentences. This kind of closeness has developed over the years in our marriage and comes from knowing each other deeply—often from talks between us that touch the depths of our souls. This is not to say we can do it all the time.

But we both try because we know how important it is, for us and our family.

Here is another discussion between Levon and Shantee, one that goes quite a bit better because the hurting one feels the care of the other.

LEVON: So how was your day?

SHANTEE: Nothing really happened.

LEVON: Nothing?

SHANTEE: Not much.

LEVON: What happened to that teaching assistant that you said wouldn't follow your lesson plans?

SHANTEE: Oh, I spoke to the principal and she was fired. Now some of her friends are talkin' to the principal about how I conduct my class.

LEVON: Fired! That sounds serious. I thought you said nothing happened? It sounds like the same kind of stuff I'm putting up with.

SHANTEE: Yeah, it bothers me, but I didn't want to trouble you with it.

LEVON: I'm very glad you did, though. That kind of thing can hurt a lot, and I want to know when you're going through things like that. Want to tell me more about it, and how you're dealing with it?

This also doesn't happen all the time. It happens when we step outside of our own worries and try to see the world through the other person's eyes. To do this, you have to put your feelings on hold. You have to know that the other person will do the same for you when you need it. In other words, it has to go both ways. It is an incredible pleasure to see the comfort that you can give when the other person knows that you understand and "have his/her back," that you are not someone out there in the world. This other person is part of another world that is safe, fair, just, and loving. A colleague of ours in the field of marital research has noted the importance of what couples do to repair the damage or distance when a conversation doesn't go very well. Of course, we all have conflicts; it's how we deal with them that counts. That's what fighting *for* your marriage is all about.

Here is more of Levon and Shantee later in the evening. This is a perfect example of great repair:

SHANTEE: I'm sorry I didn't understand how you felt about your boss. I've seen him. I know he has higher standards for you than for his other employees.

LEVON: I guess I look to you to make me realize that I'm not crazy.

SHANTEE: You're not crazy. We knew when you took that job that it would be tough being the only black engineer, and that they were going to take some time to get used to.

LEVON: I just don't want you to think that the issues I may have are more important than what you have to deal with.

SHANTEE: Well, if you have any more trouble, I may have to go down there and straighten him out, and that ain't what they want! Anyway, they'd be lost without you.

LEVON: That definitely ain't what they want! Thanks, baby!

Having good communication skills allows you to say what you really think and feel while helping your spouse understand where you are coming from. Developing good communication is the cornerstone for a good marriage; it helps to create sort of an inner world between the two of you. Without it, racism can make those who are alone feel lonely even if they are married. A relationship takes two, and the effort of keeping it healthy has to be shared.

## Stereotypical Views of Black Women and Men

We live in a culture that holds negatively defined ideas about African American men and women. Too often, these stereotypes infiltrate how we see our mates and influence how we interpret what they do and mean to do. On this point, it can be argued that black men may be portrayed in the most negative light of all, not just in the media (movies, TV shows, and popular fiction) but as well in the conventional wisdom of the society at large (with black women coming in a close second). Therefore, one of the greatest battles to be fought in creating a good marriage is to see your mate for who she or he is—not for what the latest situation comedy, rap video, or book by a racist white man or woman (or frustrated black man or woman) might say. Although we all tend to think we don't let these stereotypes affect our perception of African American loved ones, that's often not the case. Such is the culture we live in, and we have to watch out for how we can be affected. Therefore, look within yourself for stereotypes of what African American women or men will or won't do, and how they will or won't behave. Do you apply these notions to your spouse? Some very deep conflicts can start there.

Here is a conversation between Constance and Arron. Both are hard-working supervisors, Constance for a telephone company and Arron at a retail store. They were married at twenty-one, and five years later they still enjoy going out to clubs and keeping up with the latest music. But they do sometimes differ on what they see as appropriate attire.

ARRON: Aren't we suppose to go out tonight?

CONSTANCE: Yeah, we are, and look at the outfit I just picked up. Isn't it the bomb?

ARRON: Where did you get that from?

CONSTANCE: I picked it up from that new store on the east side.

ARRON: You need to take it back with a quickness. I can see through it, and those blue sequins don't hide anything.

CONSTANCE: I like it; I think it's funky.

ARRON: More like freaky. That looks like something Lil' Kim or one of those hoochies on MTV Raps would wear.

CONSTANCE: I like it, and I'm gonna wear it.

ARRON: You can wear it around the house, but not in public.

CONSTANCE: So, now you're my fashion warden? I don't think so. I'll wear what I please.


We have struggled for equality since being brought to this country in chains. We see many icons, myths, and characterizations that reflect poor ideas of African American men and women—for example, that all black men run out on their responsibilities if a woman gets pregnant, or that black women are hard on black men. The fact of the matter is that there are men who are involved in child care and black women who are supportive of their mates. These and similar stereotypes are views of black men and women that destroy oneness within relationships. Black men are admonished in the news as criminals, but in fact many black men have long been involved in their families as caregivers. The involvement of black men in the lives of their children needs to be celebrated by black women.

So in the case of Constance and Arron, it is not unreasonable that he might react to what he sees as her provocative dress. But we have to seek a balance in how we see the world and how it sees us. Perhaps more important, we must not let icons in the media allow us to change who we are or what we wear to appease others. At the same time, we should take our spouse's views into consideration. Perhaps Arron could ask Constance if she thinks the dress is provocative and then share, less domineeringly, that he has concerns about the dress.

Another popular stereotype is that in African American relationships the burden of upkeep in the relationship is on the woman, and that she has to make her man do this or that. If black women and men buy into this conventional misunderstanding, the resulting dynamic can lead to something far more like a parent-child relationship than a healthy marriage.

In Chapter Seven, we focus on helping you identify your beliefs and expectations for your marriage. There we help you attend to the impact of societal stereotypes of black women and men, and other beliefs that affect your marriage, so that you can decide how you want to handle things better. The bottom line: we want to help you think and act like a team. To do this, you must both have the same play book. One of the biggest daily issues or plays that a couple has to negotiate is money. In the next section, we discuss one of the biggest challenges for African American couples: spending money.

## Mo' Money, Mo' Problems

If you are like most African Americans, work occupies at least one-third of your waking hours during a normal week. Even if we don't like our work, we are in part defined and constrained by our jobs. Rarely do we hear—from any couple—that they make more money than they need. Many of us work not one but two jobs, and some even three or more in an effort to pay bills and live at the level we want.

Inevitably, we have less time for our families, and particularly our spouses. This is a catch-22 because if we are to help our families we must work more, but if we work more we are not with our families. Television shows us the great life and reports how everyone is making money in the stock market, retiring early, and vacationing every other month. But the path for us to obtain that kind of wealth is not always clear, nor does it even seem accessible.

Some of the obstruction is in the transition many African Americans have made from poverty or the working class to a middle-class life. We seem to assume quite readily middle-class values in relation to having things, but we don't do so well in focusing on savings. So every month we repeat a vicious cycle, working to have more but not having more money at the end of the month.

I (KEW) represent the first generation in my family to be raised beyond the inner city of Chicago. Other folks in the same circumstance as mine struggle with making sure they have money for what I call "putting out fires." This is the idea of having money in its most liquid form—in your hand—so that if an emergency arises you can handle the situation. Since there is always some fire or other to put out, some African Americans are reluctant to put money where we can't get hold of it. Savings and investments essentially represent this seeming lack of access. Many of my fellow first-generation "expatriates" also believe that we will not grow rich from slow, methodical saving; wealth will come from hitting it big in the lottery. The odds—in the millions to one—are against that, of course.

Let's hear more from Arron and Constance about how a money issue affects them: who spent how much on what.

ARRON: How much did that dress cost, anyway?

CONSTANCE: Not much. It definitely cost less than that cell phone of yours does each month.

ARRON: The difference is, I need that cell phone.

CONSTANCE: You need it? For what? To stay in touch with your boys?

ARRON: I use it for work when I'm in the car. And yes, I do use it to call the fellas. But I also call you.

CONSTANCE: Yeah, once in a blue moon. (*sarcastically*) That makes the phone absolutely necessary, huh?

ARRON: If you'd only put some of your salary away in our savings account, we might not have to worry so much about paying for things down the road.

CONSTANCE: That is just not my style. I like my cash in my hands. Then I always have it when I need it.

How can we minimize the impact of money worries in marriage? As African Americans, we bring varied perspectives to the table about how to get ahead economically. Many husbands and wives think they should spend money on the lottery because that's how they can strike it rich. Others think that as African Americans they will never be rich. Still others think that they have to end up in an accident and then sue somebody.

The ideas we have about financial success are in part tied to the history of racism in this country. Of course, many other African Americans feel that the road to prosperity works the same as it does for whites. Arron and Constance have to develop a style that brings the strength of both their ways of handling money so that each of them can enjoy the fruits of their labor. More important, they must work together and feel that each is heard and his or her needs met.

Differences within a couple about how financial success is to be achieved can fuel trouble. As African Americans, we know how it's not only hard to get a job and keep it but also to get a job with the same wages and opportunities for promotion as Caucasians in the same job. Although we are currently experiencing a thirty-year low in the unemployment rate, African Americans still endure unemployment at twice the rate of Caucasians. Also, labor statistics show that African Americans make less than Caucasians in every white-collar occupational category (clerical, technical, administrative, professional), with the difference ranging from a few hundred to several thousand dollars per year. In the struggle for equal compensation and employment opportunity, some couples experience conflict over money that eventually escalates into major battles. For some couples, conflict ends in withdrawal and distance from one another. We discuss how to deal with and avoid distancing from one another in Chapter Two.

It is interesting to observe how a couple handles money, and conflict over money, in their marriage. One person may be delegated as responsible for money management. Or they may have separate accounts and each contribute proportionally to the "community pot" to pay bills. Neither option is necessarily better than the other, but problems come up when spouses don't feel they have enough of a say in how the money is to be spent. We as a people need to develop a larger financial base in this country. We need to invest and save, and not rely on life insurance or hitting the lottery to become rich. Developing a plan to achieve this kind of financial goal allows two heads to find creative ways to build wealth and allows couples to see their hard work pay off.

Financial goals are hard to reach and aren't as meaningful if they are not shared goals. They also have to be goals that both people are working toward, together as a team. Tina is a travel agent and Bill works in software development. They have been married for six years and are trying to buy a new house. They embody the meaning of teamwork, as can be seen in this interaction:

TINA: I'm going to work overtime this weekend to make some more money. Do you mind?

BILL: I was hoping we could look at houses, but I know that every cent counts. I guess I married the hardest-working woman in town.

TINA: Y'know, I only work till three o'clock on Saturday, so if you want, you could pick me up and we could go look for houses from there.

BILL: That's cool with me. Hey, do you feel that our real estate agent is trying to limit our options to the Northeast part of town?

TINA: Yeah, I guess she thinks that's the only place blacks want to live in this town. We need to get her straight or get someone else. We're working too hard not to know all of our options in this town.

BILL: Yeah, we've saved a lot and sacrificed a lot, and we need to know all the options that might work out well for us. Since you're working extra, I'll have a talk with her before we meet you. Is that all right?

TINA: I like that plan. You're better at getting folks straight; I just lose it and tell them off. It's nice to have a man who handles business.

In Bill and Tina's interaction, they demonstrate that they have learned each other's strengths and aren't afraid of the other person handling situations he or she is good at doing. They also talk about the process of getting a house as "we" instead of two "I's." This kind of teamwork is critical to achieving success in the economic, practical, everyday aspects of a marriage. Later in this book, we have many suggestions to allow you both greater understanding of expectations you may have. We offer ideas on working together as a team on whatever life throws your way. We also talk about how to play and stay friends. It all matters in how your marriage goes. Money greatly affects so many things in our lives, but it's not the glue that holds a couple together. The love a couple shares is the glue that helps them make it through times of famine (and plenty). Some couples view prosperity in the form of children. Children are definitely a blessing, but if all is not right between the parents as a couple, the children don't benefit.

## How Parental Stress Can Influence a Marriage

One of the most important priorities in life is children. Of course, this also means that you are likely (if you have children) to put a lot of time into caring for them. Raising African American children requires keeping your eyes on the prize—which means there may be some special strains on your marriage. It takes vigilance to raise your children to grow up without drugs and violence and, more important, with self-esteem and opportunities so their lives will be better than yours. Here is an example of having differing perspectives on what to emphasize in rearing children. Sebrina is a physician's assistant and Dion is a data systems manager for an insurance firm. Both come from Los Angeles and have had great educational success. They have two boys, ages seventeen and thirteen, Shawn and Norman.

SEBRINA: Dion, I just spoke to Shawn and he told me that he was pulled over for turning on a yellow light.

DION: I told that boy to drive better. Do you know what that will do to our insurance rates?

SEBRINA: Who cares about insurance rates? You know how the police target black boys; you need to have a talk with him about how to talk to the police. I'm afraid he might give them an excuse to harass him.

DION: If he drives better, it won't be an issue.

SEBRINA: You are missing the point. Do you know what could happen to him if he's arrested? And what if Norman is with him?

DION: If he's arrested, we go and bail him out. But he needs to learn about driving better.

SEBRINA: You're missing the point as usual. Aren't you concerned about his safety? Does the name Rodney King mean anything to you? Remember? And my friend Lily's son, he was pulled over and harassed by some white police officers last month just because he was driving her new Mercedes.

DION: Don't accuse me of not caring about my own son. Of course, I care whether he's safe or not.

SEBRINA: You have a funny way of showing it.

You can see that there could be some hard feelings after a conversation like this. Both have the best interest of the child in mind, but they have starkly different ways of thinking as to how he should learn what he needs to know to navigate the world. Making parenting decisions together about discipline, school performance, dress, sex, drugs and alcohol, career expectations, and other hot-button issues can be especially difficult for African American parents, who are painfully aware of the hostility and discrimination their kids must overcome in the society around them.

## The Impact of Other Folks on Our Marriages

As with children, other folks are a piece of the puzzle as well. I recently attended a talk by Peggye Dilworth-Anderson on African American families. She gave a detailed description of how other kin have historically been integrated into the family. African families (African because they weren't really African Americans yet) were brought to this country and usually broken apart, as the mother was sold to one plantation and the father to another. Children were sometimes kept with the mother, but not always. To survive in this horrendous situation, parts of dislocated families joined together to survive, sharing child care and distributing meals and wisdom. When slavery ended, families were allowed to exist but had to struggle to establish some sort of economic base. Then, in the early 1900s, housing was granted in many northern cities on the grounds of a husband and wife. In this way, men became a retrieved piece of the puzzle of the African American family. Still, there were others who were not blood relatives but were considered kin. They too functioned as part of the family.

These other folk still exist in many African American families. All of us have experienced the "aunties" and "cousins" who were raised or brought up with us as members of the extended family, all throughout our childhood and adult lives. What can they mean for African American couples? Our research indicates that they can have either a positive or negative impact as we can see from an example.

Devon and Keena have been married five years and have a four-year-old daughter named Nicole. They have just moved into their first home and are getting used to balancing a marriage, a career, family, and the financial responsibility of a home. One of Devon's old family friends from the 'hood, "Cousin Ray-Ray," has fallen on hard times and asks to stay with them. Keena is not very enthusiastic about the idea but reluctantly agrees. A month after Ray-Ray moves in, the couple have this conversation:

KEENA: Hey baby, how was your day?

DEVON: Fine. What about yours?

KEENA: Fine. Where is baby girl?

DEVON: Ray-Ray took her to the circus.

KEENA: I said that Nicole couldn't go to the circus.

DEVON: Ray-Ray just kept begging and Nicole was begging, so I let them go.

KEENA: You always let him talk you into things.

DEVON: If you don't like what he does, I'll ask him to go.

KEENA: You know I can't ask you to do that.

DEVON: (angrily) I don't know anything. If all he does is get on your nerves, tell him to go yourself.

KEENA: *You* are the one getting on my nerves.

As we can see from this dialogue, the extended family can sometimes present problems for an African American couple who need to establish their own separate identity at times and make decisions that must ultimately be their own. The solution to problems is not always clear, nor is it clear where the boundaries of the relationship begin and end relative to their family. If a couple, or one member of the couple, is enmeshed in a broader family context, it may create difficulty for the two to work out problems or make decisions about their path as a couple. This can have implications for raising children, as well as managing money, celebrating holidays, taking vacations, and career decisions.

The cliché that too many cooks spoil the broth definitely applies to negotiating marriage. If you and your partner are having problems, you should "pull down the shades" so you can work out your problems together, without an audience. Kin have their own history, ideas, experiences, and perspectives; they bring outside pressures that make it hard for the two of you to work out your issues without interference.

## The Role of the Church and Spirituality

Some friends of mine were recently married. They had a fantastic wedding and at the end did the traditional African "jumping the broom." I thought how interesting it was that this very nineties couple included such a fine African American tradition in their wedding. It is always interesting to see the African American version of churches. My wife is Roman Catholic, and I have on occasion attended Catholic services with her. There is such a contrast between the white and black Catholic services. The black services are filled with a sort of heart and enthusiasm, while the white services tend to be much more formal. I used to hear my mother tell me that I could find a nice girl at church. I didn't find my wife at church, but her churchgoing was one of the many reasons I was so attracted to her. As with many African American men looking for a mate, the spiritual side of her was what made her the complete package. I knew that even though we didn't share the same religious affiliation, the basic aspect of faith was important to me, as it was to her.

In fighting for our African American marriages, however, we should also be aware that spirituality and religious practice vary among couples. Social scientists such as Robert Taylor and Linda Chatters have spent their careers studying the importance of the church in African American families. What they and others find is that attending church is only part of the equation for understanding African Americans. You must also know about the faith that goes along with going to church.

Spirituality is the glue that binds a marriage, from the time it is born at the altar, jumping over that broom, in front of friends and family. One way we demonstrate our spirituality is by attending church. However, the importance of attendance may not be shared, or understood to mean the same thing, or hold the same importance for two people within a marriage. Because we can be brought up with and develop during our adult years different ideas of the importance of attending church regularly, conflicts can arise. Let's hear another conversation between Keena and Devon.

KEENA: Aren't you going to church?

DEVON: I'm going to skip today.

KEENA: But it's the first of the month; you know the collection plate comes around twice.

DEVON: Well, you just take care of putting in two envelopes.

KEENA: But you know the reverend will be looking for the man to put the money in the plate.

DEVON: That's just what I don't like about that reverend of yours. He's so corny and old-fashioned. I'm not going if that's what you're trying to get me to do.

KEENA: Why are you staying home, anyway? Don't you care about the Lord? Don't you want to ask for forgiveness after a whole week of being so mean and stubborn?

DEVON: What do you know about my week of toil and labor? And I worked on Saturday, too. I'm tired from raking the leaves and mowing the grass all day yesterday.

KEENA: So, Nicole is supposed to learn about God from watching me, not her father, huh?

DEVON: It's one Sunday. Can you stop bugging me for just one Sunday?

KEENA: I'm so sorry that you're tired of hearing from me. I won't bother you again.

This interchange quickly grows from putting money into the basket to how your children learn about God. What Keena really wants is for Devon to be the leader of the family in spiritual matters, as her father was. Keena equates going to church with spirituality, but Devon doesn't. He was raised in a family that would go to church or listen to a service on the radio on Sunday, but not so much importance was placed on attendance.

When Keena returns from church with Nicole, the couple have another talk:

DEVON: How was church?

KEENA: It was a real good sermon about we all being the body of Christ and each of us are different, some are hands and some are feet.

DEVON: So I must be the butt?

KEENA: Naah, baby, I'm sorry about the earlier stuff. If you're tired, you should stay home.

DEVON: But I know it's important to you that your man is at church. I'll go next time. Tell you what. Tonight, I'll read her one of her Bible books for bedtime.

KEENA: I know Nicole would sure like that.

Sometimes we don't share with our spouse how we really feel or think about God. Our faith comes from the beliefs we have inside ourselves. Our spirituality comes from our practice of our faith. Sometimes we mistakenly wrap up the social dimension of going to church with the idea of spirituality. The church has been our spiritual connection with God, the gathering place for designing and leading our social evolution in this country, and a base for economic support in hard times. But the church is not faith, nor spirituality. It is where we can share our faith, express our spirituality, and celebrate our love for the Lord together as a community of believers. Each individual has his or her own faith and ideas of how to demonstrate spirituality. It is important for African American couples to acknowledge these differences and work toward building an understanding of how they come together. Understanding one another's perspective is the foundation for answering the challenges of our faith that we all experience during our life.

## Interracial Relationships

In a book about African American marriage, interracial relationships is a loaded topic, to say the least. Why is it loaded? There are many people who disapprove of interracial dating and marriage. From the perspective of some African Americans, it dilutes our African heritage. But really, how many of us don't have some mixture of ethnicity? We are all told stories of our lineage by our grandparents, and there is always some story of a marriage to someone from another ethnic group. I am supposed to have American Indian and German in my heritage. By the nature of the label, *African American* represents the diversity of backgrounds that we share, with African ancestry being a common factor. I guess everyone in this country is really an *African* American, if the anthropologists are right and all people originated from African.

Our goal here is to not dismiss the issues that mixed couples experience. If one person in the relationship is not African American, can it really be an African American marriage? I do, however, think that our culture (the African American culture) is always influential in an interracial marriage.

There is much taboo around interracial relationships, and even more around marriage between people of different ethnicities. I have always found it interesting that although the taboos exist, people from every segment of our society see the children of these unions as attractive. I can remember watching the Miss America contest with a bunch of friends the year Vanessa Williams was the winner. I remember one of my friends saying, "They had to find the lightest skinned black woman before they would give the crown to one of us," and another friend chimed in, "But she sure is fine."

Some of the issues for an interracial marriage are the same as those for an African American marriage—racism, rearing children, kin involvement—but each is exacerbated by the fact that there may be even bigger differences in individual history and perspective on the world. Not only are these individual histories and perspectives challenged from within the marriage, they are influenced by friends outside of the relationship as well. Take Laura and Markus. Markus comes from an African American family raised in the South with a family that was heavily involved in the civil rights movement of the 1960s. Laura comes from a middle-class white family who live on the West Coast, near San Diego. They met in college and are newlyweds of eight months. Here they discuss their friends.

LAURA: So, what are we doing this weekend?

MARKUS: I thought we could go to the company picnic on Saturday.

LAURA: Do we have to? I don't think your coworkers approve of me.

MARKUS: What do you mean?

LAURA: The women are always sucking their teeth when I walk by, and I hear that one of the guys calls me "Snowflake."

MARKUS: I think you're making too much of it.

LAURA: It really hurts my feelings that I'm not being judged on who I am rather than the color of my skin.

MARKUS: Now you know how I feel every time I go to your parents' house. I feel like they put the good silverware away because they think I'm gonna steal something.

LAURA: *Now* who's making too much of it? My parents like you!

MARKUS: So, we're not supposed to hang out with the people I work with?

LAURA: So, we're not supposed to visit my parents?

The perceptions of others can find their way into an interracial relationship and cause division. As much as in any African American relationship, an interracial relationship needs partners who are sensitive to how the other person sees the world—and to how they believe the world sees them. Only through unity can an interracial marriage survive. It is also true that you may not always understand how the other person feels, but making an effort to avoid invalidating his or her feeling is critical to a successful mixed marriage.

MARKUS: Of course we won't stop visiting your parents. I just wish I could feel more comfortable around them.

LAURA: Why don't we sit down with them and talk about how you sometimes feel when you're in their house? Maybe if you hear it from them you'll see that they like you. They're just a little weird sometimes.

MARKUS: I guess I would be willing to talk to them. I also know that my coworkers can be a little hard on you sometimes.

LAURA: It's not all of them, just a few.

MARKUS: What if I promise to stay with you the whole time during the picnic so you don't feel left out?

LAURA: That would really help. They seem to only make the smart comments when you aren't around.

MARKUS: Even if they do, you should know that I'm proud to be there with you.

Laura and Markus were together for four years during college, so they are familiar with the idea that not everyone approves of their relationship. This is, of course, just one issue interracial couples deal with regularly. They also have to be concerned with how others treat their children—teachers, family, and other children. There are similarities as well as differences between an interracial and an African American marriage in the kinds of challenges they experience. The cornerstones of this book, which are teamwork, unity, communication, respect, and love, apply equally regardless of the ethnic makeup of the couple. The common thread is that the struggle must be won with each member of the marriage being willing to work with the other and take into account his or her perspective.

## Conclusion

We have presented some common issues and concerns that face many African American marriages. Although we surely have not addressed everything that might come up, have we addressed some of your issues? We hope so.

Our goal in this chapter has been to help you think about issues to begin a dialogue with your spouse, even if not every issue is one you experience in your marriage. The remainder of the book offers you some powerful tools for use in your marriage. My wife and I (KEW) were introduced to the PREP (Prevention and Relationship Enhancement Program; see the Introduction) through reading some of the program's past publications. First I read a few chapters and saw how some of the ways that I was communicating might be taken differently from what I meant. I started to make some small changes in how I interacted with my wife. But she saw what I call small changes as big differences. They inspired her, too, to read some of the PREP materials. As a result, she got a better understanding of the efforts I was trying to make, and she made changes in the way she interacted with me.

This wonderful reciprocity of building on the efforts of the partner to make our relationship better continues to this day. We are both busy professionals; it seems that as soon as one of us gets over a hump, the other has a challenge to meet. We have always loved each other, but we both feel now that we truly enhance each other's life by knowing how to understand one another, handle conflict better, and establish ways to deal with what life throws at us. Just simply making an attempt to use the strategies in this book can be the start of making powerful changes in your marriage, since (unlike the previous PREP books) this one is designed specifically for African Americans. As you'll see, it offers solutions to our unique issues and situations.

# 2

# Four Key Patterns
# That Destroy Oneness

In this chapter, we focus on four specific patterns of conflictual interaction that often lead to or reflect marital problems. The patterns we describe here are not the only ones that have been found to predict divorce, but if you understand these four well, you can identify problem areas to work on in your African American marriage. The four patterns we highlight are:

1. Escalation

2. Invalidation

3. Withdrawal and avoidance

4. Negative interpretation

These patterns are like a darkness that destroys the very life of a relationship. They destroy the oneness that is the foundation of a solid relationship. Once you understand these patterns, you can learn to prevent them from taking over in your relationship.

## Some Research Findings

You might be thinking, *Why are all of these things negative?* This is a good point. Social scientists have found that the likelihood of divorce can be predicted to a surprisingly high degree. Keep in mind that, when we talk about research findings, we are always talking about things that *tend* to be true. This means that although things found to be important factors in successful or unsuccessful married life tend to have similarity across couples, there are also aspects that are unique for every couple.

We mean to say that research findings are important general ideas about what tends to happen, and they can be used as a starting point to take a closer look at your marriage. Some of the factors that make it likely a marriage will not make it are the divorce of a spouse's parents, having been young at the time of marriage, premarital cohabitation, differences in religious background, and neuroticism (or the tendency to react defensively). There are others, but the strongest predictors of how a couple will fare in the future have to do with how they interact and handle conflict. The danger signs we discuss here have most to do with how you treat one another in everyday life situations.

We focus on the negative here because it is very clear that how you treat one another when in conflict says a great deal about how your marriage will be in the years to come. The kinds of negative pattern we describe here can wipe out positive aspects of your marriage. In fact, some researchers have estimated that one negative in how you interact can overwhelm the effect of five or as many as twenty positives. Beginning in Chapter Three, we teach you positive strategies for eliminating negative patterns. By doing that, we believe you can give your marriage the greatest chance to fully develop the mystery of oneness.

We want to help you fully enter into all the blessings of life. Let's begin by looking at patterns that you would be wise to avoid.

## Escalation: What Goes Around Comes Around

*Escalation* occurs when partners respond negatively to each other, continuously one-upping the other person's negative with hateful comments and actions. The comments often spiral into increasing anger and frustration. Couples who are happy now and likely to stay that way are less prone to escalation; if they begin escalating, they are able to stop the negative process before it erupts into a full blown, nasty fight.

Delancy, a thirty-year-old human resource manager, and Nicole, who is twenty-seven and runs a small clothing boutique, were married for three years when we first saw them. Like many couples, their fights started over small issues. Here, Nicole is straightening up their bedroom (again) and feels pressed because she is trying to get out the door to get to work. Delancy comes to kiss her and gets an unexpected reception:

NICOLE: *(sarcastically)* Can't you put your nasty underwear in the bin?

DELANCY: *(hurt, and equally sarcastically)* I forgot how organized and neat you are. Sorry, Princess.

NICOLE: I always put them away because you're such a pig about your clothes.

DELANCY: Oh, I forgot just how lucky I am to have you. Thank you, thank you, thank you!

NICOLE: You're gonna push me too far one day.

DELANCY: And what then? You'll leave me? Hey, don't let the door hit you where the good Lord split you.

NICOLE: *(under her breath)* I don't know why I put up with that man.

One of the most damaging elements about an argument that escalates out of control is that the partners tend to say things that threaten the very lifeblood of their marriage. As frustration and hostility mount, partners often try to hurt each other by hurling verbal (and sometimes even physical) weapons. You can see this pattern with Delancy and Nicole, where the stakes quickly rise to include the threat of ending the relationship. Once negative comments are made, they are hard to take back; these reckless words do a lot to damage any sense of oneness and intimacy.

Partners can say the nastiest things during an escalating argument, but such recklessness does not usually reflect what one generally feels about the other. You may think people reveal their true feelings in the midst of a fierce fight, but we do not believe this is usually the case. Instead, what is said is designed mostly to pierce the other and create a barrier to defend oneself.

In Delancy and Nicole's argument, for example, he mentions her desire for perfection because he really wants to hit her below the belt. At an earlier, tender moment between them, we were told, she shared her concerns about being so driven, and that in growing up she had learned this style to please her stepfather. Although Delancy may have been provoked in this argument, the escalation led him to use intimate knowledge against her to try to win the battle. When escalation leads to using intimate knowledge as a weapon, the damage to the likelihood of any future tender moments is great. Who is going to share deep information if it may be used later when conflict is out of control?

Now, in a calmer moment, this couple agree that when they have such a battle no one wins and the relationship loses. Another couple we spoke with decided that in the heat of such an argument one would try to say "surrender" at the moment he or she would usually go on the offensive; this would remind them that they need to stop and talk about it later when cooler heads prevail. Every couple have to create their own way to stop the madness, get back on track, and communicate effectively.

You may be thinking, *We don't fight like cats and dogs; how does this apply to us?* Escalation actually can be subtle. Voices don't have to be raised for you to get into the cycle of returning negative for negative. Research shows how even subtle patterns of escalation can lead to divorce or unhappiness down the road. Consider this conversation between David and Crystal, newlyweds in their twen-ties who are just starting out in an apartment in Baltimore.

DAVID: Did you get the rent paid on time?
CRYSTAL: That was going to be your job.
DAVID: No, you were supposed to do it.
CRYSTAL: No, you were.
DAVID: Did it get done?
CRYSTAL: No. And, I'm not gonna.
DAVID: *(muttering)* Great. Just great.

Being newlyweds, David and Crystal are very happy with their marriage. Imagine, however, years of small arguments like this one taking a toll on their marriage, eroding the positive things that they now share.

It is very important for the future health of your relationship to learn to counteract whatever tendency you have as a couple to esca-late. If in general terms the two of you don't escalate much, great! Your goal is to learn to keep things that way. If you do escalate a fair amount, your goal is to recognize it and stop it. You might want to take a second and look again at your results in the quiz of danger signs, at the end of the Introduction, to see the kind of issues you say you are dealing with in your marriage.

Escalation can be short-circuited. All couples escalate from time to time, but some couples steer out of the pattern quickly and pos-itively. Compare Nicole and Delancy's argument, earlier, with San-dra and Kevin's. Sandra, a forty-two-year-old salesclerk for a jewelry store, and Kevin, a forty-four-year-old attorney who works in pri-vate practice, have been married twenty years. As with most cou-ples, many of their arguments are about everyday events.

SANDRA: *(annoyed)* You left the back door unlocked again.

KEVIN: *(irritated)* Why are little things so important to you? Just lock it.

SANDRA: *(softening her tone)* I'm afraid someone will break in and take all the things we've worked so hard to get.

KEVIN: *(calmer)* I'm sorry. I won't forget again.

Notice the difference. Like Crystal and David's, Kevin and Sandra's argument shows escalation, but they quickly steer out of it. If the sequence is short-circuited, it is usually because one partner backs off and says something to deescalate the argument, thus breaking the negative cycle. This often takes simple humility, choosing to soften the tone and put down one's shield. For her part, Sandra softens her tone rather than getting defensive. For his part, Kevin makes the decision to back off and acknowledge Sandra's point of view.

Softening your tone and acknowledging your partner's point of view are powerful tools you can employ to defuse tension and end escalation. Often, that's all it takes. In addition to softening the tone, we will teach you a number of ways to keep escalation in check.

## Invalidation: Painful Put-Downs

*Invalidation* is a pattern in which one partner subtly or directly puts down the thoughts, feelings, or character of the other. Let's take a closer look at this pattern, which can take many forms. Here are two arguments, the first between Nicole and Delancy and then between Sandra and Kevin.

NICOLE: *(very angrily)* You missed your doctor's appointment again! You are so irresponsible. I don't know why you won't take care of yourself.

DELANCY: Look, I don't need to go to the doctor for every little ache and pain.

NICOLE: You're not a doctor, and this high blood pressure of yours might be serious. But you're too stupid to go and find out what's wrong.

DELANCY: *(dripping with sarcasm)* I'm sorry. I forgot my good fortune to be married to Doctor Know-It-All.

NICOLE: At least I take care of myself and don't abuse my body.

DELANCY: You are so arrogant.


SANDRA: *(with tears)* You know, I'm really mad at the way that banker didn't even want me to ask questions about getting a second mortgage on the house.

KEVIN: I don't think he was trying to keep you quiet. I think he was just in too much of a hurry to get to lunch.

SANDRA: *(with a sigh and turning away)* You don't get it. It upset me.

KEVIN: Yeah, I see that, but I still think you're overreacting.


These examples are as different as night and day. Both show invalidation, but the first example is much more caustic, and hence damaging to the relationship, than the second. With Nicole and Delancy, you can feel the *contempt* seeping through. The argument has settled into an attack on character.

Although Sandra and Kevin do not show the contempt displayed by the other two, Kevin is subtly putting down Sandra for the way she is feeling. He may even think that he is being constructive or trying to cheer her up by saying, in so many words, "It's not so bad." Nevertheless, this kind of communication is also invalidating. Sandra feels hurt now because he has let her know that her feelings of sadness and frustration are inappropriate.

The contemptuous invalidation displayed by Nicole and Delancy in the first example is more obviously destructive than the subtle form of invalidation in the second case. But any kind of invalidation sets up barriers in a relationship. Invalidation hurts. It leads naturally to covering up who you are and what you think because it's just too risky to do otherwise. What couple can maintain the ability to be open and intimate when invalidation is regularly present?

In either argument, both of these couples would do better by preventing invalidation in the first place. Each partner can show respect for and acknowledge the viewpoint of the other. Note the difference in how conversations of this kind could go.

NICOLE: (*very angry*) I'm so mad at you. You missed your doctor's appointment again. I worry about you being around for me in the future.

DELANCY: I'm sorry, Baby. This really upset you, didn't it?

NICOLE: Your father died of a heart attack and left your mother all alone. I want to know that you're going to be there for me, and when you miss those appointments I get worried that there may be something wrong.

DELANCY: I understand why it would make you worried when I don't take care of myself.

SANDRA: (*with tears*) You know, I'm really mad at the way that banker didn't even want me to ask questions about getting a second mortgage on the house.

KEVIN: I know how you feel. It was like we weren't important enough for him to spend time making sure we understood what was going on.

SANDRA: Yeah. I've been tricked before and signed things that have a lot of small print that get you in trouble.

KEVIN: I didn't know you were so worried about this. Well, we'll take our time and look at everything twice before signing on the dotted line.

In these examples, we replay the issues but with quite different outcomes. Now, there is ownership of feelings, respect for each other's character, and emphasis on validation. By that, we mean the one raising the concern is respected and heard. You don't have to *agree* with your partner to validate his or her feelings. Our research shows that invalidation is one of the best predictors of future problems and divorce. But the amount of validation doesn't say as much about the health of a relationship as the amount of invalidation does. Does this mean validation is not so important? Not really, but it does tell us that stopping invalidation is crucial. Respectful validation happens to be a powerful way to inhibit invalidation when you are trying to stay on the high road. But it takes discipline, especially when you are really frustrated or angry. In later chapters, we teach you some effective ways to limit invalidation and enhance validation.

## Negative Interpretation: When Perception Is Worse Than Reality

*Negative interpretation* occurs when one partner consistently believes that the motives of the other are more negative than is really the case. This can be a destructive pattern in any relationship, and it makes any conflict or disagreement hard to deal with constructively.

Cherrell and Donny have been married twelve years. They have two children, Jamie, ten, and Quincy, eight. Although they are generally happy with their relationship, their discussion at times has been plagued by one particular and recurring negative interpretation: every December they have trouble deciding whether or not to travel to her parents' home for the holidays. Cherrell believes that Donny dislikes her parents, but in fact he is quite fond of them in his own way. She holds this mistaken belief because of a few incidents early in the marriage that Donny had long forgotten but she hasn't. Here's how a typical discussion around their issue of Christmas travel plans goes:

CHERRELL: We should start looking into plane tickets to go visit my parents this Christmas.

DONNY: *(thinking about their budget problem)* I was wondering if we can really afford it this year. The kids want a lot of stuff, and aren't they in the play at church?

CHERRELL: *(becoming angry)* My parents are very important to me, even if you don't like them. Don't use the kids as an excuse. Me and the kids are going.

DONNY: I want to go. I just don't see how we can afford $1,500 for plane tickets and pay the bill for Jamie's orthodontist, too.

CHERRELL: You just can't be honest and admit you just don't want to go, can you? You don't like my parents.

DONNY: There is nothing to admit. I enjoy visiting your parents. They're good, God-fearing Christians. I'm thinking about money here, not your parents.

CHERRELL: That's a convenient excuse. *(storms out of the room)*

Given that we know Donny really does like to go to her parents, can you see how powerful her negative interpretation has become? He cannot penetrate it. What can he say or do to make a difference as long as her belief that he dislikes them is so strong? If a negative interpretation is entrenched enough, almost nothing will change it. In this case, Donny wants to address the decision they must make from the standpoint of the budget, but her interpretation overpowers their ability to communicate effectively and come to a decision that makes both of them happy. Fortunately for them, this problem is relatively isolated and not a consistent pattern in their marriage.

As a relationship becomes distressed, the negative interpretations mount and help create an environment of hopelessness and demoralization. Elaine and Benny are a couple who were high school sweethearts, have been married eighteen years, and have three children, but they have been very unhappy in their marriage for more than seven years—in part thanks to the corrosive effect of strong, negative interpretations. There are positive things in their marriage, but almost nothing that each one does is recognized positively by the other, as seen by this recent conversation about turning off the TV.

BENNY: You left the TV on again.

ELAINE: Oh. I guess I forgot to turn it off when I went to Sharon's.

BENNY: *(with a bit of a sneer)* I guess you did. You know how much that irritates me.

ELAINE: *(exasperated)* Look, I forgot. Do you think I leave it on just to irritate you?

BENNY: *(coldly)* Actually, that is exactly what I think. I have told you so many times that we can't afford to be wasting money on the power bill.

ELAINE: Yes, you have. But, I don't leave it on just to piss you off. I just forget.

BENNY: If you cared what I thought about things, you'd remember.

ELAINE: You know that I turn off the TV nine times out of ten.

BENNY: More like half the time, and I have to turn if off the other half.

ELAINE: Have it your way. It doesn't matter what reality is; you'll just see it your way.

This may sound like a minor argument, but it is not. It represents a long-standing tendency for Benny to interpret Elaine's behavior in the most negative light possible. For the sake of argument, assume that she is absolutely correct when she says that she simply forgot to turn off the TV and that this only happens about one in ten times. Benny sees it differently, especially in his interpretation that she leaves the TV on mostly to upset him.

Negative interpretation is a good example of mind reading. This occurs when you assume you know what your partner is thinking, or why he or she does something. If you do mind reading positively, it does not tend to cause any harm. But when your mind reading includes negative judgment about your spouse's thoughts and motives, you are in real trouble.

It's important to be on guard for the tendency to view others harshly. After all, a marriage is truly in terrible shape if either partner routinely and intentionally acts just to frustrate the other. Much more frequently, the actions of one partner are interpreted negatively and unfairly. This is a sign of a relationship heading for big trouble in the future. Negative interpretation is quite destructive, in part because it is hard to detect and counteract. It easily becomes cemented into the fabric of a relationship because we have a strong tendency toward "confirmation bias," the tendency to look for evidence that confirms what we already think is true about others or in a given situation. In other words, once formed, negative interpretations do not change easily.

Even though you can be wrong in your assumptions, you tend to see what you expect to see. If you believe that your neighbor can never say anything nice to you, then no matter what he actually may say you will interpret his comments in light of your expectations. He could say, "You did a nice job on your yard" and you might think to yourself, *What does he want now? He's always complaining about my yard.* If he is being sincere, your strong assumption wipes out his good intent. No one is immune from looking for information to confirm expectations about others.

In the earlier example, Benny has the expectation that Elaine doesn't care one bit about anything that's important to him. This assumption colors the good things that do happen. In a distressed relationship, there is a tendency for a partner to discount the positive things he or she does see, attributing them to causes such as chance rather than to positive characteristics of the other. Because of Benny's negative interpretation, he attributes how frequently Elaine does turn the TV off to his own action of being mindful of the electric bill, and not to her intention to turn it off. She can't win this argument, and they will not be able to come to an acceptable resolution with his negative mind-set.

We are not advocating some kind of unrealistic positive thinking; we are simply encouraging you to do battle against negative interpretations. You can't just sit around and wish that your partner will change truly negative behavior, but you may need to consider that your partner's motives are more positive than you are acknowledging. Negative interpretation is something you have to confront within yourself. Only you can control how you interpret your partner's behavior. You have to take responsibility for your own behavior to be the best partner you can.

First, you have to ask yourself if you might be overly negative in your interpretation of your partner's actions. Second—and this is hard—you must push yourself to look for evidence that is contrary to the negative interpretation you usually take. For example, if you believe that your partner is uncaring and you generally see most of what he or she does in that light, you need to look for evidence to the contrary. Does your spouse do things for you that you like? Could he or she be doing nice things to try to keep the relationship strong? It's up to you to consider your interpretation of someone's behavior since the other person surely sees it as positive.

As you work through this book and consider many positive changes in your relationship, make sure you try to give your partner the benefit of the doubt in wanting to make things better. Don't allow inaccurate interpretation to sabotage the work you are trying to accomplish. You can control *your interpretation* of your partner, but not his or her behavior. If you start thinking positively about your partner, your investment will likely pay off in terms of how you want him or her to see you.

## Withdrawal and Avoidance: Hide and Seek

*Withdrawal* and *avoidance* are different manifestations of a pattern in which one partner shows an unwillingness to get into or stay with an important discussion. *Withdrawal* can be as obvious as getting up and leaving the room, or as subtle as tuning out or shutting down during an argument. The withdrawer often tends to grow quiet during an argument, or agree quickly to some suggestion just to end the conversation with no real intention of following through.

*Avoidance* reflects the same attitude of reluctance toward certain discussions, but with emphasis on the attempt to not let the conversation happen in the first place. A person prone to avoidance prefers that the topic not come up, and if it does, he or she may manifest the signs of withdrawal that we have described.

Let's look at this pattern as played out in a discussion between Paula, a twenty-eight-year-old real estate agent, and Jeff, a thirty-two-year-old loan officer. Married for three years, they have a two-year-old baby girl, Tanya, whom they adore. They are concerned that the tension in their relationship is starting to affect their daughter.

PAULA: When are we going to talk about how you're handling your anger?

JEFF: Can't this wait? I have to get these taxes done.

PAULA: I've brought this up at least five times already. No, it can't wait!

JEFF: (*tensing*) What's to talk about, anyway? It's none of your business.

PAULA: (*frustrated and looking right at Jeff*) Tanya is my business. I'm afraid you'll lose your temper and hurt her, and you won't do a damn thing to learn to deal better with your anger.

JEFF: (*turning away, looking out the window*) I love Tanya. There's no problem here. (*leaving the room as he talks*)

PAULA: (*very angry now and following Jeff into the next room*) You have to get some help. You can't just stick your head in the sand.

JEFF: I'm not going to discuss anything with you when you're like this.

PAULA: Like what? It doesn't matter if I'm calm or frustrated, you won't talk to me about anything important. Tanya is having problems and you have to face that.

JEFF: (*remains quiet, tense, fidgeting*)

PAULA: Well?

JEFF: (*going to the closet and grabbing a sweater*) I'm going out to have a drink and get some peace and quiet.

PAULA: (*voice raised, angrily*) Talk to me—now. I'm tired of you leaving when we're talking about something important.

JEFF: (*looking away, walking toward the door*) I'm not talking, you are; actually, you're yelling. See you later.

Many couples do this kind of dance when it comes to dealing with difficult issues. One partner *pursues* dealing with issues (Paula) and one avoids or withdraws from dealing with issues (Jeff). Although common, this scenario is definitely destructive. As with the other patterns we have presented, it does not have to be this dramatic to predict problems to come. It is one of the most powerful predictors of future unhappiness and divorce.

# Pursuing and Withdrawing Dynamics: The Gender Dance

The pursuer is the one in the relationship who most often brings issues up for discussion or calls attention to the need to make a decision about something. The withdrawer is the person who tends to avoid these discussions or pull away during them. Studies show that men tend to be in the withdrawing role, with women tending to pursue. However, there are many relationships where this pattern is reversed. In some relationships, the partners switch roles depending on the topic. Simply reverse the points we make here if the pattern is reversed between the two of you in your marriage.

Why do men tend to withdraw? Some say it's because they are less interested in change and pull away to avoid dealing with the issues. Some people think that African American women's strong personalities don't allow room for African American men to have any other choice. This may be the case for some men and women, but we believe that most of the time the one who withdraws tends to do so because it does not feel safe to stay in the argument— meaning, it's not emotionally safe, or one even fears the conflict will turn physical. (If you have concerns about physical conflict and aggression in your relationship, please see the appendix on that subject for important information.)

When this pattern gets going, it tends to be frustrating for both men and women. If married to a man who withdraws, a woman usually feels shut out and begins to think her husband doesn't care about the relationship. For many women, lack of talking equals lack of caring. But this is usually a negative interpretation of what the withdrawer is about—which has more to do with trying to stop the conflict than not caring about the relationship. Likewise, men often complain that their pursuing wives get upset too much of the time, griping about this or that and picking fights, as if their wives like to fight. This is also a negative interpretation, because what pursuers really want is to stay connected or resolve issues. Those are not negative motives, either.

It is important to learn how to stay out of the pursuer-withdrawer pattern. This takes some working together. Refrain from taking the most negative interpretation of what your partner does when you are doing your dance of conflict. Research we (Scott M. Stanley, SMS; and Howard J. Markman, HJM) have done suggests that the couples that are the happiest, most relaxed together, and the most open are those who do the best job of not falling into this pursuer-withdrawer pattern. We will give you some tips here for reducing withdrawal, and many more strategies as we go on, to help you avoid these destructive patterns in your marriage.

If you see this pattern in your relationship, keep in mind that it is likely to get worse if you allow it to continue. This is because as pursuers push more, withdrawers withdraw more. As withdrawers pull back, pursuers push harder. Furthermore, when issues are important, it should be obvious that trying to avoid dealing with them only leads to damaging consequences. You can't stick your head in the sand and pretend important or bothersome problems are not really there.

In the case of withdrawal and avoidance, the first and best step you can take right now is to realize that you are not independent of one another. Your actions cause reactions, and vice versa. For this reason, you will have much greater success if you work together to change or prevent the kind of negative pattern we discuss here. A withdrawer is not likely to reduce avoidance unless the pursuer pursues less (or more constructively). A pursuer is going to find it hard to cut back on pursuing unless the withdrawer deals directly with the issues at hand.

In your marriage, you need to keep the lines of communication open, but do so in such a way that neither of you feels the urge to withdraw. In the next few chapters, we are much more specific on how to combat these patterns. For now, try to agree that if you are having trouble with pursuit or withdrawal, you will work together to change the pattern. Working together doesn't mean that both people are always working at the same level. Think of the familiar poem about two sets of footprints in the sand and know that there will be times when you only see one set. Those are the times when one of you is doing more than the other. (Hopefully, most of the time there are two sets.) Far too often, we wait for the other person to do the right thing. Ask yourself, *If not now, when? If not me, then who will try to work to make a change?*

## How Positive Feelings Erode: Long-Term Effects of Negative Patterns

Contrary to popular belief, positives in marriage do not slowly fade away for no reason in particular. We believe that the chief reason marriages fail at an alarmingly high rate is that conflict is handled poorly, as evidenced by such patterns as those described in this chapter. Over time, these patterns steadily erode all the good things in the relationship.

For example, if a couple routinely escalates when issues arise, both people may come to the conclusion that it is just as easy not to talk at all. After all, talking leads to fighting, right? Or, as issues arise, the partners become concerned with getting their own way, and invalidation becomes a weapon easily taken in hand. Over time, no issue seems safe.

Many couples handle issues poorly, and they do not succeed at setting aside a particular time or agreeing on how these issues will be handled. Even in what starts out as a great marriage, these factors can lead to growing distance and lack of confidence in the relationship. Remember Jeff and Paula, earlier in this chapter. Though a genuinely caring couple, their inability to discuss tough issues—in this case, his anger—has caused a rift that will widen and perhaps destroy the marriage if nothing is done.

As real intimacy and a sense of connection die out, a couple settles for frustrated loneliness and isolation. If you want to keep your relationship strong, or renew one that is lagging, you must learn to counteract destructive patterns such as those we have described.

Fortunately, this can be done. You can prevent the erosion of happiness in your relationship for the years to come.

In this chapter we have described four patterns in handling conflict that predict future marital discord and divorce. We've made the point that certain patterns of dealing with conflict are particularly destructive in a relationship. How can a couple manage their tendency toward destructive patterns and limit the damage caused by them? Later in this book, we suggest a specific set of agreed-upon rules and strategies for handling conflict and difficult issues in your relationship.

Keep in mind that most couples show some of these patterns, to some degree. It is not as important whether you currently exhibit these patterns as it is to decide to do something to protect your relationship from them. The exercises that follow are a first step toward protecting your relationship from these patterns.

In the next chapter, we deepen our discussion of how couples handle conflict and show that the major difference between men and women in marriage is not how they handle intimacy, or how they make love, but how they make war.

## Exercises

At the end of each remaining chapter in this book, we ask you to consider some questions or practice some skills to strengthen your relationship. For this chapter, we want you each to consider these questions and then talk with your partner about your perceptions. We will ask you if you see the patterns we have presented in your relationship.

Please take a pad of paper and write your answers to these questions independently from your partner. After you have finished, we suggest you share your perceptions. However, if this raises conflict, put off further discussion on your answers until you have learned in the next few chapters how to talk safely on tough topics. Before getting into specifics about the four negative patterns, consider this question about your overall impression of how you handle conflict together:

- When you have a disagreement or argument, what typically happens? To answer, think about the patterns described in this chapter.

## Escalation

Escalation occurs when you say or do something negative, your partner responds with something negative, and off you go into a real battle. It's the snowball effect, where you grow increasingly angry and hostile as the argument continues.

1. How often do you think you escalate as a couple?
2. Do you get hostile with each other during escalation?
3. What or who usually brings an end to the fight?
4. Do one or the other of you sometimes threaten to end the relationship when angry?
5. How do each of you *feel* when you are escalating as a couple? Do you feel tense, anxious, scared, angry, or something else?

## Invalidation

Invalidation occurs when you subtly or directly put down the thoughts, feelings, actions, or worth of your partner. This is different from simply disagreeing with your partner or not liking something he or she has done. Invalidation includes an element of belittling or disregarding what is important to your partner, either out of insensitivity or outright contempt.

1. Do you often feel invalidated in your relationship? When and how does this happen?
2. What is the effect on you?

3. Do you often invalidate your partner? When and how does this happen?

4. What do you think the effect is on him or her? On the relationship? What are you trying to accomplish when you do this? Is this what happens?

## Withdrawal and Avoidance

As discussed earlier, men and women often deal quite differently with conflict in a relationship. Most often, men are more prone to withdraw from, and women more prone to pursue, discussion of issues in the relationship.

1. Is one of you likely to be in the pursuer role? Is one of you likely to be in the withdrawer role?

2. How does the withdrawer usually withdraw? How does the pursuer usually pursue? What happens then?

3. When are you most likely to fall into this pattern as a couple? Are there particular issues or situations that bring out this pattern?

4. How are you affected by this pattern?

5. With some couples, both tend to pursue or withdraw. Is this true for your relationship? Why do you think this happens?

## Negative Interpretation

Negative interpretation occurs when you interpret the behavior of your spouse much more negatively than he or she intends the action. It is critical that you open yourself up to seeing the possibility that your view could be unfair in some areas. These questions help you reflect on this.

1. Can you think of some areas where you consistently see your partner's behavior as negative?

2. Reflect on this for a moment. Do you really think that your negative view of your spouse's behavior is justified?

3. Are there some areas where you have a negative interpretation but are open to considering that you may be missing evidence to the contrary?

4. List two or so issues where you are willing to push yourself to look for the possibility that your partner has motivations that are more positive than you have been thinking he or she has. Next, look for the evidence that this is contrary to your interpretation.

We hope that these questions have shed further light on how your relationship is affected by these patterns. You should now have a good understanding of these destructive patterns. This helps you know what patterns to try to counteract, which in turn helps you replace the patterns with the positive behaviors and attitudes we are teaching you.

Sometimes, considering questions such as the ones here can cause anxiety or sadness, as you reflect on where your relationship stands at this point. It may not be pleasant to think about negative patterns, but we believe it will help you as you move ahead in this book and learn constructive ways to keep your marriage strong. Now let's turn to laying more groundwork by presenting ways to understand the differences in how men and women handle conflict and intimacy.

# 3

# Communicating Safely and Clearly
## *The Speaker-Listener Technique*

Do you really want to communicate well? Most African American couples do, but many have never learned to communicate well when it counts most—in conflict and in talking about the key themes raised in Chapter One. As you learned in the first two chapters, handling conflict well is critical to the future of your marriage, and communicating well is critical to handling conflict. There are two keys: making it clear and making it safe.

## Making It Clear: The Problem of Filters

Have you ever noticed that what you are trying to say to your partner can be very different from what he or she hears? You may say something you think is harmless and suddenly your spouse is mad at you. Or you may ask "What do you want for dinner?" and your partner starts complaining about you not doing your share of the work.

We have all experienced the frustration of being misunderstood. You think you are being clear, but your partner just doesn't seem to get it. Or you are just sure you know what she said yesterday, but today she says something that seems completely different.

Like the rest of us, Tera and Wellington can relate to this common problem. They married five years ago. Tera works as a reservation agent for an airline and Wellington is an accountant for a major firm. Their jobs leave them exhausted at the end of the day. There are no kids yet, so they can usually crash when they get home.

One Thursday night, Wellington comes home first and reads the paper while waiting for Tera. He's thinking, *I sure am wiped. I bet Tera is, too. I'd really like to go out to eat and just relax with her tonight.* Good idea, right? This is what happens with his idea (what they are thinking or hearing is in parentheses):

WELLINGTON: *(thinking he'd like to go out to dinner with Tera, as she comes in the door)* What should we do for dinner tonight?

TERA: *(hearing "When will dinner be ready?")* Why is it always my job to make dinner?

WELLINGTON: *(hearing her response as an attack and thinking, Why is she always so negative?)* It's not *always* your job to make dinner. I made dinner once last week!

TERA: *(negative cycle continuing, with Tera feeling she does everything around the house)* Bringing home hamburgers and fries is *not* making dinner, Wellington.

WELLINGTON: *(with frustration mounting, gives up)* Just forget it. I didn't want to go out with you anyway.

TERA: *(confused; she can't remember him saying anything about going out)* You never said anything about wanting to go out.

WELLINGTON: *(feels really angry)* Yes I did! I asked you where you wanted to go out to dinner, and you got really nasty.

TERA: I got nasty? You never said anything about going out.

WELLINGTON: Did too!

TERA: You're never wrong, are you?

Sound familiar? We can easily see where things go wrong for them this evening. Wellington has a great idea, a positive idea, and yet conflict blows out the evening. He is not as clear as he could be in telling Tera what he is thinking. This leaves a lot of room for interpretation, and interpret she does. She assumes he is asking—no, telling—her to get dinner on the table, and she has hardly even walked in the door.

This kind of miscommunication happens in relationships all the time. Many of the biggest arguments you have together begin with failing to understand what your partner is saying, in a way that fosters anger. What gets in the way? *Filters*.

Filters change what goes through them. A furnace filter takes dust and dirt out of the air. A filter on a camera lens alters the properties of the light filtering through. A coffee filter lets the flavor through and leaves the gunk behind. As with any other filter, what goes in to our communication filters is different from what comes out.

We all have many kinds of filters packed into our heads. They affect what we hear, what we say, and how we interpret things. They are based on how we feel, what we think, what we have experienced in our life, family and cultural backgrounds, and so on. For this discussion, we emphasize five types of filters that can affect couples as they struggle for clear communication:

1. Inattention

2. Emotional state

3. Belief and expectation

4. Difference in style

5. Self-protection

## Inattention

The first basic kind of filter has to do with whether you have the attention of the person with whom you are trying to speak. Both external and internal factors can affect attention. External factors are noisy kids, a hearing problem, a bad phone line, the background noise at a party, and so on. Internal factors affecting attention include feeling tired, thinking about something else, feeling bored, and mentally forming a rebuttal. The keys are to make sure you have your partner's attention and to give your attention when it really counts most. For an important talk, find a quiet place if you can. Don't answer the phone. Make it easy to pay attention to one another, and try not to assume that your partner is ready to listen right now just because you are ready to talk. Ask.

## Emotional State

An emotional state or mood becomes a filter affecting communication. A number of studies demonstrate that we tend to give people the benefit of the doubt when in a good mood, less so when in a bad mood. If you are in a bad mood, you are likely to perceive whatever your partner says or does negatively, no matter how positive he or she is trying to be. Have you noticed that sometimes, when your spouse is in a bad mood, you get jumped on no matter how nicely you say something?

The best defense against a filter of this kind damaging your relationship is to acknowledge it as soon you are aware that one is operating.

Here is an example. It's dinner time. Jabrill and Lynn have just gotten home and read the mail. Lynn goes to the kitchen to start dinner.

JABRILL: Hey, there's a letter here from your alma mater. Do you want to read it?

LYNN: *(snapping with anger)* Can't you see I have my hands full? Can't you do something helpful?

JABRILL: I'm sorry. I should have seen you were busy. Rough day?

LYNN: Yes. I had a very frustrating day. I don't mean to snap at you, but I've had it up to here. If I'm touchy, it's not really anything you've done.

JABRILL: Let's talk about what's going on.

LYNN: OK. Thanks.

Without using the term *filter*, Jabrill and Lynn are acknowledging that one is there. Lynn had a bad day and is on edge. They could let this conversation escalate into an argument, but he has the good sense to see he has raised an issue at the wrong time. He decides not to get defensive and chooses to become gentle with Lynn in her frustration. She responds by telling Jabrill, in essence, that she has a filter going—her bad mood. Knowing this helps him be less defensive in reacting to her mood.

Many kinds of emotional filters can coexist in a person. If you are angry, worried, sad, or upset about anything, it colors your interpretation of and response to what your partner says. Jabrill's response is helpful because it opens the door for Lynn to clarify her emotional filter and allows them to deescalate and be clear with one another.

## The Belief-and-Expectation Filter

Important filters arise from how you think and what you expect in your relationship. As we mentioned in the first chapter, research and experience show the tendency to see what is expected in other people and situations. You are not immune to the tendency to look for or hear in others what you are expecting. This kind of expectation becomes a filter that distorts communication. Studies show that expectations not only affect what we perceive but also influence the actual behavior of others. For example, if you believe that someone is an extrovert, she is likely to sound like an extrovert when talking with you, even if in fact she is introverted. We interpret others' behavior based on what we expect.

The next dialogue shows how difficult it can be to get around a mental filter. Carmen and Gerald have come to us with a number of problems, one of which is deciding what to do for fun whenever they have free time. With three kids in elementary school, free time without the kids is valuable. But they rarely get their act together to get out and do something, so both are frustrated. This conversation is typical for them. Note how each acts as if he or she can read the other's mind.

GERALD: (*really wanting to go to the club, but thinking that Carmen is not interested in going out and doing anything*) We have some free time tonight. I wonder if we should try to do something.

CARMEN: (*thinking that she'd like to get out, but hearing the tentativeness in his voice, and thinking he really does not want to go out*) Oh, I don't know. What do you think?

GERALD: Well, we could go to the club, but it might be too crowded and we might not get in anyway. Maybe we should just stay in and watch "Jamie Fox."

CARMEN: (*thinking A-ha, that's what he really wants to do*) That's sounds good to me. Why don't we make some popcorn and watch some tube?

GERALD: (*disappointed, thinking I knew it. She really doesn't like to get out and do things that are fun*) All right.

In this conversation, there is no escalation, invalidation, or withdrawal. Nevertheless, they do not communicate well because of the belief-and-expectation filters involved. Gerald's belief that Carmen doesn't like to go out distorts the entire conversation—so much so that how he asks her to go out leads her to think he wants to stay in. He "knows" that she really does not want to go, which constitutes mind reading. As we have already suggested, mind reading occurs when you assume you believe you know what your partner is thinking or feeling; it is a specific form of negative interpretation.

In Gerald's eyes, he can only see that they are staying in once again because that's what she wants. His mental filter pulls the conversation in this direction and becomes a self-fulfilling prophecy. Carmen too does a good deal of mind reading. In this conversation, she assumes she knows Gerald really wants to stay in and participates in a distorted conversation in which neither says what he or she wants. If they were able to communicate clearly, without any filters, they would conclude that both want to get out and would probably try the club idea first.

## The Difference-in-Style Filter

Everyone has a style of communicating, and differing styles can lead to filtering. Perhaps one of you is expressive and the other is more reserved. You may have some trouble understanding each other because you use such different styles.

Styles are determined by many influences, including gender and upbringing. Sometimes, difference in style, rooted in family backgrounds, can cause great misunderstanding, becoming a powerful filter that distorts communication.

Pam and Thomas come from contrasting families. His has always been very expressive of all manner of emotion; they show their love and don't care where they are when they do it. It's just their way. Pam's family is much more conservative. There is a place and time to be emotional, and it is not in public. As a result, a slight raising of the voice could mean great anger in her family, whereas in his family that is when the conversation is just getting started. In many conversations, therefore, she overinterprets the intensity of his feelings, and he underestimates her feelings.

THOMAS: What did it cost to get the muffler fixed?

PAM: Four hundred and twenty-eight bucks.

THOMAS: (intensely) What? How could they possibly charge that much? That's outrageous.

PAM: (lashing out) I wish you would stop yelling at me! I've told you over and over that I cannot listen to you when you're yelling!

THOMAS: I am not yelling at you. I just can't believe that it could cost that much.

PAM: Why can't we have a quiet conversation like other people? My sister and brother-in-law never yell at each other.

THOMAS: They don't talk about anything, either. Look, $428 is too much to pay, that's all I'm reacting to.

PAM: Why don't you take the car in next time? I'm tired of being yelled at for things like this.

THOMAS: Honey, look. I'm not upset at you. I'm upset at them. And you know I can get pretty hot, but I'm not trying to say you did anything wrong.

PAM: (calming down) Well, it seems that way sometimes.

THOMAS: Well, I'm not upset at you. Let me give that place a call. Where's the number?

They are caught up in a misunderstanding based on difference in style. But in this conversation, they do a great job of not allowing things to escalate. As in preceding examples in which the conversation gets back on track, one partner figures out there is a filter distorting the intended message and takes corrective action. Here, Thomas forcefully clarifies that he is not mad at Pam.

Being aware of the effect your differing styles have on your communication can go a long way toward preventing misunderstanding. We recommend that you give some thought to these differences between the two of you.

## Self-Protection

The fifth kind of filter comes right from the fear of rejection that we all struggle with in some way. Basically, what we really want or feel does not get said out of fear of rejection. Even something as simple as "Wouldn't *you* like to go see that new movie with me?" can reflect this. Instead of saying it directly ("I'd like to see that new movie; want to go?"), we often hide our desire because to speak it clearly reveals who we are—raising the risk of rejection. This may not matter a lot when it comes to movies, but when it comes to the real day-to-day issue of marriage—feelings, desires, expectations—the tendency can lead to a lot of miscommunication. More on this when we get to hidden issues in Chapter Six.

## Filters and Memory: That's Not What You Heard!

Some of the biggest arguments couples have are about what was actually said in the past. How often have you wished you had a tape recording of a previous conversation? This happens to all of us. These differences in memory occur in great measure because of the variety of filters that operate in any relationship. Any of the filters discussed here can lead to difference in (and argument about) what was actually said or done in the past.

Reread the conversation earlier in this chapter between Wellington and Tera. Notice that they end up arguing about what was actually said at the start of the conversation. He truly thinks he asked her out to dinner, but what he said was vague. She truly thinks he told her to get dinner on the table, which also is not what he said. Without a tape recording, no amount of convincing can get either one to back off from that version of the story.

We recommend two things that can save your relationship from such fruitless arguments about the past. First, don't assume your memory is perfect. Have the humility to accept that it is not. There are countless studies in the field of psychology that show how fragile human memory is, how susceptible to motivation and belief. Accept that you both have filters and that there is plenty of room for things to be said or heard differently from what was intended.

Second, when you disagree, don't persist in arguing about what was actually said in the past. You will get nowhere. For example, Perry and Veronica are discussing how to ask her parents for a loan to get a car. They are struggling because Perry keeps referring back to how in the past his parents didn't ask them to pay money back but Veronica's parents would. This, of course, upsets her. Every time they try to discuss the issue, he reminds her of how his parents are easier to deal with in terms of borrowing money. His reference to the past is getting them nowhere. Don't get stuck in the past—even if it was five minutes ago. Shift the topic to what you each think and feel in the present.

We hope you understand how important it is to be aware of filters in your communication with one another. We all have filters. Either we react to them with little awareness, which can cause damage to the relationship, or we learn to look for them when a conversation go awry. Try to get in the habit of "announcing your filter" as soon as you are aware that you might have one. ("I know I'm sensitive about sex, so I may not be real clear in what I'm trying to tell you right now.")

We all have moods, levels of attention, and various beliefs. We also have different experiences and upbringing, which can result in filters working against clear communication. After discussing the importance of safety in your relationship, we teach you an effective communication technique for reducing the effect of filters on your important discussions.

# Making It Safe: The Value of Structure

To have a great marriage, both of you must be able to express your beliefs, concerns, and preferences clearly, without damaging the relationship in the process. The patterns we discussed in Chapters One and Two can make it unsafe to express your views about what is most important to you—and you can't be naked and unashamed unless it is safe to express important thoughts and ideas together. People generally do not share openly with anyone (including a spouse) without there being some feeling of safety. Filters compound the problem, making it a wonder that couples can communicate about anything truly important.

Is a marriage necessarily safe? No. Most people want the safe haven of a friendly relationship, but many couples just don't get or remain there. By *safe* we do not mean risk-free. If you are going to share what you are concerned with, hurt by, or hoping for, you are going to take risks. There is a direct relationship between risk and reward in much of life. You cannot be accepted deeply without offering something deep for your partner to accept. Conversely, you can also take the risk, share deeply, and be rejected. This hurts a lot, because you have chosen to risk a deep part of yourself in the relationship. If it goes well, you find deep, soul-satisfying acceptance of who you are, imperfections and all.

When you disagree, or think you do, more is at stake and more can go wrong. For your relationship to grow through conflict, instead of being damaged by it, you need to work at keeping things such as escalation, invalidation, withdrawal, and negative interpretation from happening.

One way to do this is to use agreed-upon strategies and techniques to help you in an important conversation. We call this adding structure to your interaction. This is exactly what is done all the time in work and political settings. Consider for a moment what a typical session of the congressional black caucus would look like if the members did not agree on the rules for how and when things can be shared. With adequate structure, you can manage conflict with less chance of damage to relationships. When less is at stake, or you are not in conflict, you don't need much structure. Just communicate in whatever way you are most comfortable. But at other times, a bit of structure can get you through without damage, and maybe with greater closeness.

## The Speaker-Listener Technique

The speaker-listener technique offers couples an alternative way of communicating when issues are hot or sensitive, or likely to turn out that way. Any conversation in which you want to enhance clarity and safety can benefit from this technique. Most (although not all) couples can decide whether to go out for Chinese food without using this technique, but few can handle emotionally sensitive issues around, say, money, sex, or in-laws without the safety net that such a technique can provide.

We have found particular success with the speaker-listener technique because it is so simple and effective. Most couples seem to really appreciate this technique; some do not. The key really is this: you need a way of communicating well when you really must do a good job of it. This technique works because you both follow certain rules, which we now describe.

Rules for both of you:

1. *The speaker has the floor.* Use a real object to designate "the floor." In our seminars, we actually hand out small pieces of linoleum or carpet for couples to use as the floor. You can use anything, though: the TV remote, a small piece of paper, a book, anything at all. If you do not have the floor, you are the listener. As speaker and listener you follow the rules for each role.

2. *Share the floor.* The two of you share the floor over the course of a conversation. One has it to start and may say a number of

things. At some point, you switch roles and continue as the floor changes hands.

3. *No problem solving.* In using this technique, focus on having a good discussion without trying prematurely to come to a solution.

Rules for the speaker:

1. *Speak for yourself. Don't do mind reading.* Talk about your thoughts, feelings, and concerns, not your perception of the listener's point of view or motive. Try to use *I* statements, and talk about your own point of view. (By the way: "I think you're a jerk" is not an *I* statement. "I was upset when you forgot our date" is an *I* statement.)

2. *Don't go on and on.* You will have plenty of opportunity to say all you need to say. To help the listener listen actively, it is very important to limit what you say to manageable pieces. If you are in the habit of giving monologues, remember that having the floor protects you from interruption, so you can afford to pause to be sure your partner understands you.

3. *Stop and let the listener paraphrase.* If the paraphrase is not quite accurate, you should politely restate what was not heard in the way it was intended to be heard. Your goal is to help the listener hear and understand your point of view.

Rules for the listener:

1. *Paraphrase what you hear.* You must paraphrase what the speaker is saying. Briefly repeat back what you heard the speaker say, using your own words if you like, and make sure you understand what was said. The key is to show your partner that you are listening and to restate what you heard. If the paraphrase is not quite right (which happens often), the speaker should gently clarify the point being made. If you truly don't understand some phrase or example, you may ask the speaker to clarify, but you may not

ask questions on any other aspect of the conflict, unless you have the floor.

2. *Don't rebut. Focus on the speaker's message.* While in the listener role, you may not offer your opinion or thoughts. This is the hardest part of being a good listener. If what your partner says upsets you, you need to edit out any response you may want to give, and *pay attention* to what your partner is saying. Wait until you get the floor to make your response. As listener, your job is to speak only in the service of understanding your partner. Any words or gestures to show your opinion are not allowed, including making faces!

Before showing how this works in a conversation, we want to give you some ideas about what a good paraphrase sounds like. Suppose your spouse says to you, "I really had a hard day. Mama got on my case about how I handled the arrangements for Dad's retirement party at the church this weekend!" Any of these might be an excellent paraphrase:

> "Sounds like you had a really tough day."
>
> "So, Mama was critical of how you handled the party and really got on you about it."
>
> "It sounds like you had a bad day, Baby."

Any one of these responses conveys that you have listened and displays what you have understood. A good paraphrase can be short or long, detailed or general. At times, if you are uncertain how to get a paraphrase started, it can help to begin with "What I hear you saying is. . . ." Then you fill in what you just heard your partner say. Another way to begin a paraphrase is with the words "Sounds like . . . ."

When using the speaker-listener technique, *the speaker* is always the one who determines if the listener's paraphrase is on target. Only the speaker knows what the intended message is. If the paraphrase is not quite on target, it is very important that the speaker gently clarify or restate the point—not respond angrily or critically. One more key point. When in the listener role, be sincere in your effort to show you are listening carefully and respectfully. Even if you disagree with the point being made by your partner, your goal is to show respect for—and validation of—his or her perspective. This means waiting your turn and not making faces or looking bored. Rather, showing real respect is the key. You can disagree completely with your mate on a matter and still show respect. Just wait until you have the floor to make your points.

## Using the Speaker-Listener Technique

Here is an example of how this technique can change a conversation that is going nowhere into a real opportunity for communication. Paul and Sadie are in their mid-thirties, with four kids ages two to ten. For years, the couple have had a problem dealing with issues. Paul consistently avoids discussing problem areas, and if cornered by Sadie he withdraws into himself. They know they need to communicate more clearly and safely on tough topics, and they have agreed that the structure of the speaker-listener technique can help.

In this case, Paul and Sadie have been locked in the pursuer-withdrawer cycle over the issue of their son Malcolm's behavior in Sunday school. However, they have been practicing the speaker-listener technique and are ready to try something different. Let's see what happens.

SADIE: I want to talk about what to do about Malcolm acting up in Sunday school. We have got to deal with this, now.

PAUL: (*not looking up from the TV*) Oh?

SADIE: (*walking over and standing in front of the TV*) Paul, we can't just ignore this. I'm getting really upset about you putting it off.

PAUL: (*recognizing this would be a wise time to act constructively and not withdraw*) Yo, time out. I can tell we need to talk, but I have been avoiding it because it seems that talking just leads to fighting. Let's try that speaker-listener technique we have been practicing.

This is, of course, not the normal way people communicate. But it is a relatively safe way to communicate on difficult issues. Each gets to talk, each is heard, and both show commitment to discussing the problems constructively. If the person who usually withdraws moves constructively toward the pursuer in this manner, the effect on the relationship is surprisingly positive. It attacks the foundation of the pursuer's belief that the withdrawer does not care about the relationship.

The conversation proceeds, with Paul picking up a small square of carpet they use to denote who has the floor.

PAUL (SPEAKER): I've also been pretty concerned about how Malcolm has been acting in Sunday school, but I'm not sure what to do about it.

SADIE (LISTENER): So you've been concerned, too, and you're not sure what to do either?

PAUL (SPEAKER): Yeah. We know that he's a little hyper, but Sunday school is important for his spiritual development.

[Note how he acknowledges that her summary is on the mark, before moving on to another point.]

SADIE (LISTENER): You're worried that he wouldn't get a good spiritual grounding without attending Sunday school, right? [Sadie is rephrasing to make sure they are on the same page.]

PAUL (SPEAKER): Mostly I worry that he won't learn about how to get along with other kids in a classroom. Next year he's supposed to go to kindergarten. Black boys are targeted for special ed and labeled as behavior problems. [Note how Paul gently clarifies. He's moving forward in the conversation, rather than backward. In general, whenever the listener feels that clarification is needed, use your next statement to restate or expand upon what you're trying to get across.]

SADIE (LISTENER): So, you're feeling that his future might be at risk if we don't do the right thing now.

PAUL (SPEAKER): That's right. Here, you take the floor. [They pass the floor.]

SADIE (NOW THE SPEAKER): Well, I feel the same way you do. Actually, I didn't realize you'd thought this much about it. I was worried that you didn't see this as a serious problem. [As the speaker now, Sadie validates Paul in the comments he has made.]

PAUL (LISTENER): Sounds like you're glad to hear that I'm concerned.

SADIE (SPEAKER): Yes. I agree that this is an important issue and we need to really think about how to teach him the importance of behaving when he's not with us.

PAUL (LISTENER): You're saying that we have to teach him proper manners and how to behave in this special setting.

SADIE (SPEAKER): Exactly. I think it might be worth having a long talk with him and trying some new ways to reward his good behavior. [Sadie feels good with Paul listening so carefully, and she lets him know it.]

PAUL (LISTENER): So, you want us to work with him.

SADIE (SPEAKER): Yeah, and I'm glad that you want to be involved, because he tries to mimic you.

PAUL (LISTENER): So, you want me to play an important role in helping him change the way he acts in Sunday school.

SADIE (SPEAKER): Exactly. Here, you take the floor again. [They pass the floor again.]

As you can tell, they have been practicing quite a bit. They are both doing an excellent job following the rules and showing concern and respect for each other's viewpoints. Couples can have discussions like this on a difficult topic, even if they disagree. The key is to make it safe, and to show respect for your partner's thoughts, feelings, and opinions.

## Advantages of the Speaker-Listener Technique

The speaker-listener technique has many advantages over unstructured conversation in discussing a difficult issue. Most important, it counteracts the destructive style of communication described in Chapters One and Two. The technique makes it hard to escalate because you are slowing things down. It helps cut invalidation by each one listening carefully to the other. It makes a tough talk feel safe, which cuts the desire for withdrawal. It makes it less likely that a filter gets in the way of understanding because things are being carefully checked out.

## For the Skeptical: Common Questions or Objections

We anticipate a number of objections or criticisms of this approach.

### "It's So Artificial"

Probably the number one criticism we hear about this technique is that it's artificial and just not natural. Very true. Note, however, the assumption that is embedded in this criticism: that how we naturally talk to one another is usually superior to ways we can consciously learn to talk with one another. If you have children, you already know how often you show that you don't really believe this assumption. There are many "natural" ways children communicate with others—ways that you try to help them overcome by teaching them principles and rules for how to treat others. If you and your partner naturally use what we call danger signs when discussing conflicts and problems, what's so hot about being natural?

## "It Goes So Slowly Talking This Way"

It does go slowly. This is one of the chief benefits of the technique. Stop to think about all the time couples waste in fighting over and over again about the same issues, without the partners really hearing one another. This is sad and unproductive. Sometimes, if you want to get somewhere the fastest route is the slow lane.

## "We Have Trouble Sharing the Floor"

Suppose one or both of you tend to want to hang onto the floor once you have it. We have a simple suggestion to solve this. Add a rule: you will switch the floor after every three or four speaker statements are paraphrased by the listener, regardless. This ensures that each of you knows your turn to talk is coming up soon. You are a better listener when you know you will soon have a chance to respond with your point of view.

Although it may be frustrating to have to pass the floor when you are in the middle of building a point, rest assured you will get the floor back quite soon. People often feel that, now that the partner is finally listening, they have to get everything in before the door shuts. Don't try to get so much through each open door that you make it unpleasant for your partner to keep the door open. Share. Take turns.

## "I Really Hate Rules"

Some people dislike structure more than others. Some people feel confined when trying to follow rules of this kind. We value that input. Keep in mind something we cannot stress enough: we do not recommend talking like this when you are just being together as friends and not talking about things that are difficult. This would be unnatural and constraining in ways that we do not think would benefit your relationship.

The primary point in this chapter is that any and every couple needs to have a way to talk about the most difficult things. If you have another way, or develop another way, you'll do fine. You can safely ignore our ideas in this chapter and move on to the next—as long as the two of you agree that you have another way to talk safely, and that you both agree what the other way is.

We've noted that if one partner is not so wild about trying this and working at it, it's usually the one who is otherwise most comfortable with conflict. If this sounds like you, give it a lot of thought. *You* might not feel intimidated by talks about anything without structure. But if only one of you clearly benefits from using structure to make it safe, both of you gain in your relationship.

### "I've Heard 'Active Listening' Doesn't Work"

In part, the speaker-listener technique is based on what some call active listening. Paraphrasing is a key example of being active in the listening role. As some of you may have heard, we disagree a bit with a longtime colleague in this field. John Gottman and his associates have suggested that, since couples do not naturally talk in this way, it's not worth trying to teach any couple to do so. Further, he's suggested that asking people to communicate in this way when they are upset about things is emotional gymnastics—something that's just plain hard to do. We want to reply to such thoughts.

First, to be clear, for many years we've been doing kinds of research similar to (and also different from) Dr. Gottman's. There is far more agreement on what hurts and helps couples than the debate about active listening conveys. Second, as we've said above, we don't think the fact that people do not naturally communicate in this way is much of a criticism at all. You have already done many useful things today that were not natural to you at some earlier point in life.

Third, we agree with John that couples cannot do this well when they are upset and negatively aroused. If you are so upset that you cannot talk respectfully to one another, even in trying to follow a few agreed-upon rules, you need to have a time out rather than talk.

Fourth, our confidence in the value of this technique for most, not all, couples comes from many years of research, in which we find several things: (1) couples can learn how to do this; (2) couples who practice this for some period of time (our recommendations follow) can show improvement in communication up to five years later; and (3) couples say this technique is the most valuable thing they learn in PREP workshops, suggesting that couples themselves see great value in this model.

Don't take our word for it. Don't take Dr. Gottman's. Find out for yourselves what works for the two of you. As we said before, the real key here is that you both need some way that works to talk well about those things that are not so easy to talk about. This is one powerful, relatively simple, way; there are others. You need only one. If you don't have one already, try ours.

## A Final Word on the Importance of Practice

Practice is everything here. Practicing this technique regularly for some time can help all of your communication in your marriage—not just when you are using the rules of the technique. We think this is partly due to the fact that what you are practicing with the speaker-listener technique is inhibiting the danger signs. You are also practicing respect, in that there are two viewpoints in any important talk, and both need to be heard.

Some couples who practice this technique become what we call "floor on the fridge" couples. They get used to it. It works well for them, and they agree to use the model when things get hot, sensitive, or simply important. They keep "floor magnets" (on which we've printed the rules) on the refrigerator so that the rules and the floor object itself are handy when desired.

Other couples practice enough so that they incorporate the key aspects of the rules into their style of talking generally. For them, there is a mutual sensing of when a conversation is getting touchy, and they learn to shift into a modified version of the technique. For example, they might not use an object for the floor but begin something of a careful, turn-taking process. This only happens because they've practiced this. So even if you don't think you want to communicate this way very often, practicing these skills for some time can produce big benefits.

It is true that the exercises for most of the chapters of this book can *potentially* help you learn the material, but doing the exercises for this chapter is absolutely essential.

## Exercises

The speaker-listener technique does not work miracles, but it does work well. If it is going to be useful, you have to practice. Like any new skill, you're likely to be a bit unsure at the start. You need to learn this technique so well *together* that the rules are automatic when you have something really difficult to discuss.

If you were learning to play tennis, you would not try to perfect your backhand at center court in Wimbledon. Instead, you would hit backhands against a wall for hours to get it just right. Trying to learn a new skill under a high-stress situation is not advisable. Hence, we suggest you follow these suggestions to learn the speaker-listener technique.

1. Practice this technique *several* times a week for fifteen minutes or so each time. If you do not set aside the time to practice, you will never find this powerful technique helpful.

2. For the first week, try the technique with only nonconflictual topics. Talk about anything of interest to either of you: your favorite vacation, news, sports, dreams for the future, concerns you have at work, and so on. Your goal here is not to resolve any problem but to practice new skills.

3. After you have had three successful practice sessions about nonconflictual topics, choose minor conflict areas to discuss. Some-

times couples are poor at knowing what will and will not trigger a fight. If things get heated on a topic you choose, drop it. (It won't go away, but you can deal with it after you have practiced more together.) Practice several discussions in which you both exchange some thoughts and feelings on these issues. Don't try to solve problems; just have a good discussion. This means your goal is to understand each other's point of view as clearly and completely as possible. Problems are sometimes solved in the process because all that is needed is to understand where the other is coming from. That's OK, but don't set out or intentionally try for a solution. You are focusing on good discussion right now. You learn and practice problem solving in the next chapter.

4. As you find yourselves doing well on the third exercise, move up to tougher and tougher issues. Remember to work at sticking to the rules. It works if you work at it.

As the technique becomes comfortable, you'll be able to take full advantage of many other ideas presented in this book.

In the next chapter, we teach you a structured model for solving problems. If you work at it, you will find that the combination of using it and the speaker-listener technique can make a tremendous difference in your ability to deal with whatever issues you must face as a couple.

# 4

# Handlin' Business
## *Problem Solving*

We hope that what you have learned from the previous chapters helps you talk about issues effectively. In the last chapter, we focused on the need for clear and safe communication when it counts most. We now offer you some problem-solving techniques.

We all want to have a marriage that is free from problems. But to solve a problem, we have to be able to see what it is; we have to understand what we are trying to work on before we can come up with a solution. Understanding, before solving, is crucial for maintaining respect and connection in your relationship.

In this chapter, we present a straightforward approach to problem solving that can help you through those times when you really need a practical, workable solution.

## Three Key Assumptions

There are three research-based assumptions we want to describe before presenting the specific steps that can help you solve problems effectively in your relationship:

1. All couples have problems.
2. Couples who are best at working through their problems work together as a team, not against each other as adversaries.

3. Most couples rush to find quick solutions that do not take into account the real concerns of each partner and therefore do not produce lasting solutions.

Let's talk about each of these points.

## All Couples Have Problems

Have you ever seen a couple who seems happy all the time? They look so in love and don't ever appear to have a difference of opinion. You wonder if they don't have the same life problems as the rest of us. The reality is that they do have problems, of course, but they either hide them well or have found ways to address them. You have probably also known couples who do well for the first few years of marriage, maybe even ten or fifteen years, and then have major problems. This is because the nature of problems that occur in a marriage can change over time.

As we discussed in the first chapters, African American couples have to face unique challenges. We can find common problems happening in African American marriages, but a particular one may sometimes be small and larger at other times. Why does this happen? Our relationships are dynamic, influenced by others and by the changes that occur in our lives as we grow older. Regardless of how long we have been married or how happy we may be with where we are in our relationship, central to most any topic is how communication plays a role in the success a couple enjoys at solving problems.

As an example, during courtship and engagement couples deal with jealousy. This issue reflects a core task that couples take on early in a relationship, establishing trust and boundaries with those outside the relationship. They have to ignore the social icons that picture all African American men as promiscuous and women as untrusting and difficult.

At a later stage in the relationship, most often after getting married, one of the biggest issues that a couple deals with is finance.

Trying to achieve financial stability in a world that does not allow African Americans the same opportunities as others and that places obstacles to financial security can exacerbate the issues a couple faces in trying to agree on how to manage and spend money. As you can imagine (and may have experienced), money is a ripe area for conflict.

The key point to all of this is that although the nature of the problem may differ among couples, and even change as one couple grow older, all marriage partners report problems, reflecting a core set of issues that all couples have to resolve. Granted, some are dealt a more difficult hand in life than others. However, our observation of couples in PREP and in our research dovetail to indicate that couples who handle problems well tend to display a common set of skills and attitudes—*skills that you can learn*.

## Work Together as a Team

When we see what the outside world throws at African Americans, it is easy to see how a couple who can solve conflict and work as a team are a force to be reckoned with. For some, mutual respect and skill combine to produce a powerful sense that they are a team working to find solutions that enhance life and help them address such issues as racism, family problems, the challenge of rearing children, and the like.

Each of us has a clear choice when dealing with a problem. Either you nurture a sense that you are working together against the problem, or you operate as if you are working against each other. This principle holds with all problems, great or small.

Brian and Lisa, a newlywed couple in their mid-twenties, are an example of how teamwork can be a natural part of some couples. In this excerpted conversation, you can see how they work as a team even in hard times. They are talking about how to feed their newborn, Keewan, when Lisa goes back to work at the local hospital, where she is an intensive care nurse. Brian is a professional football player who has just been cut from the team.

LISA: How are we going to feed Keewan when I go back to work?

BRIAN: What do you mean? Can't I just give him a bottle of milk?

LISA: No, I want to breast-feed him.

Brian: My mom asked about that, and I assumed that he would just get a bottle.

LISA: My mom thought breast-feeding wasn't right, but she's old-fashioned, and they say that your baby is healthier if he is breast-fed.

BRIAN: So, how can you breast-feed if you are at work?

LISA: Well, either Keewan nurses on my break or I need to get a pump.

BRIAN: Hmm, Which is easier for you? I could help either way.

LISA: Would you be willing to bring him over to work at lunch time? If he'd nurse well then, that would tide me through the day, and you could give him bottles the rest of the time.

BRIAN: Sure. That sounds cool.

LISA: That would help a lot. I'd also get to see him during the day. Let's give it a try this week.

Notice how Brian and Lisa work together. They listen to each other, and there is a sense of respect and cooperation. This is the way they have learned to approach all kinds of problems: as challenges to be met together.

Contrast the tone of Brian and Lisa's discussion with that of Kristina and Barry. Kristina is a secretary and Barry owns a local barbershop. They have two kids; recently they have begun taking care of their teenage daughter's child so she can complete high school. They find themselves having repeated arguments about housework, which generally go like this.

KRISTINA: *(calmly)* We need to do something about keeping the house looking better. It's such a mess most of the time, it's depressing to be here.

BARRY: *(a bit annoyed)* That's always been your job. You know that I work late, and by the time I get home I'm not going to be in the mood to clean up anything.

KRISTINA: *(hurt and angered)* Yeah, and I work too. There's a lot more to do than you seem to think. You don't go into work till ten, so what's stopping you from helping in the morning?

BARRY: I'd do more around here if you could bring more money in here. You know that baby costs a fortune.

KRISTINA: *(growing angrier)* If your business was doing better, we wouldn't have to worry about money so much. Besides, you need to do more around here; I can't do everything. You agreed to help when she had that baby, but you haven't tried to help at all.

BARRY: Look, I barely have any free time as it is, and now you want me to work all day at home and at work. I didn't agree to kill myself to take care of those kids.

KRISTINA: So I am supposed to? Your life has changed, and you have to get with the program.

BARRY: *(turns away, indicating the conversation is over for him)* You need to take care of your business and let me take care of mine.

This discussion ends with Kristina discouraged and Barry annoyed that she even brought up the problem. There is a definite lack of teamwork. Barry refuses to accept any role in dealing with this problem. He sees her as trying to take something away from him, not as a partner working to make life (and their children's lives) as good as can be. Likewise, Kristina sees Barry as the problem, not as a teammate who is working with her to solve the problem. This discussion has nothing to do with creating a solution to the problem. It leads to a vicious circle that offers no solution to the problem.

All too often, people approach problems as if their partner were an enemy to be conquered. Each has to stand ground or lose a battle. They approach problems as if there will be a winner and a loser, and no one wants to be the loser. The good news here is that you don't have to end up locked into the cycle of one trying to win at the expense of the other. *You can learn how to work as a team.*

You can start by recognizing what role each of you plays on the team. Talk about how comfortable you are with the role or position. Sit down with your spouse. Independently, write down what you see your roles are, and what his or hers are, in your relationship. Come back together and compare notes. Discuss impressions of how your roles are similar and how they differ. Also talk about what you currently do as a team (raising children, handling money, buying presents for relatives, doing the laundry, cooking) and why you think it works well. This can open your eyes to how to make your roles work on other tasks. When you find that each of you is trying to play the same position on the team, discuss how you can assign the task to either one.

## Don't Rush to Solutions

Many well-intended attempts at problem solving fail because the couple do not take the time needed to understand the problem together, which keeps them from working out a solution that both partners can support. If you are deciding which movie to see, not much is at stake in rushing to a solution (except maybe sitting through a boring film). If you are deciding something more important, such as how to deal with a child's teachers or how to divide up household responsibilities, it's critical that you take the time to develop a mutually satisfying solution.

Two major factors propel a couple to rush to solutions: time pressure and conflict avoidance.

### Time Pressure

Most of us are not all that patient. We want it quick; we want it now. Unfortunately, quick fixes seldom last. This reflects the hurried pace of our lives; we usually don't take the time to plan what we're doing in our family relationships.

When it comes to dealing with important issues in the family, a hasty decision is often a poor decision. You must be committed to spending the time to really hash things out if you are going to make good decisions together.

### Conflict Avoidance

The next dialogue is typical of how a couple can rush to a solution that is destined to fail because of the desire to avoid further conflict. Glenn and Barbara have been married thirty-five years, with two children in college, James and Tamara, and one, Theo, a senior in high school. Glenn is in the military and Barbara works as a bookkeeper at a local church. They've always had enough money, but things have gotten much tighter with college bills piling up. An issue for Glenn is that Barbara is devoting so much time to a job that doesn't pay very well. Here is how their attempts to solve the problem usually go.

GLENN: (*testy*) I noticed that the VISA bill is back up to $3,000 again. I just don't know what we're going to do to keep up. I'm doing all I can, with what we have.

BARBARA: (*gives no indication that she is paying attention to Glenn*)

GLENN: (*frustrated*) Did you hear me?

BARBARA: Yes. I didn't think we spent that much this time.

GLENN: (*really annoyed now*) How much did you spend on Theo's school clothes?

BARBARA: (*annoyed, but calm*) Not as much as it could have been, but you know how kids have to have Polo and Nike everything. I told him that anything else he wants he needs to get a job to pay for it.

GLENN: (*settling down a bit*) That's right. Regardless, I can't seem to get us ahead on our bills. We don't have any kind of savings in case something happens. Have you thought about getting another job that pays more?

BARBARA: Why don't we just cancel that card? Then you wouldn't have to worry about it anymore.

GLENN: We could do that, and also plan to put aside an extra $150 a month in our savings account. That would help a lot to get us going in the right direction.

BARBARA: I'll look into getting a raise when the deacon comes back next week. For now, let's try to get rid of the credit card and save more. That sounds good. Let's try it out.

GLENN: OK, let's see what happens.


The one good thing about this discussion is that they have it. But what are the chances of coming to a satisfactory resolution of their money problem? Two months later, nothing has changed, no more is saved, the credit card is still being used, interest is accruing, and they are no closer to working together on the budget.

This example is very much like what couples do all the time: make a quick agreement so that conflict is avoided. Solutions arrived at in this manner rarely last because not all the important information is on the table. In the case of Glenn and Barbara, they do not really address his central concern about her job.

Furthermore, there are no specifics about how their agreement will be implemented. They are not generally into quick fixes, but they do rush to a solution at times because they hate conflict. This conversation is, for Glenn and Barbara, a relatively big fight. Both are eager to get back to being nice to one another whenever they have a disagreement.

Finding a solution can be a relief when you and your spouse are talking about an issue that causes some anxiety. However, if you settle prematurely on a solution, you are likely to pay for the lack of planning with more conflict. See the previous chapter and Chapter Five on ground rules for some ways to avoid this problem.

## How to Handle Problems Well

The approach we take here to solving problems—consistent with the general PREP approach—is structured. In other words, we recommend a specific set of steps that successful problem solvers follow. (Some of the thoughts we present are adapted from ideas in earlier works: *We Can Work It Out: Making Sense of Marital Conflict* by Notarius and Markman; *A Couple's Guide to Communication* by Gottman, Notarius, Gonso, and Markman; and other materials from our Christian PREP program). These steps are very straightforward, but don't be misled by the simplicity of the approach. You must be willing to work together, be creative and flexible, and experiment with change. Under these conditions, you can discover solutions to most of the problems you have to grapple with together.

Here are the steps to handling problems well:

1. Problem discussion
2. Problem solution
   Agenda setting
   Brainstorming
   Agreement and compromise
   Follow-up

As you can see, we present two key steps in handling problems well (problem discussion and problem solution) with four specific substeps to the second step. We describe each part below and then use a detailed example to help you understand them all.

## Problem Discussion

Discussion is critical to handling problems well. In this step, you are laying the foundation for the solution to come. Although you may not agree about how to solve the problem, a good discussion can lead to a clear sense that you're working together and respecting each other.

Whether the problem is large or small, you should not move on to a solution until you both understand and feel understood by the other. This means that you have each expressed your significant feelings and concerns on the topic, and that you each believe the other has seen your point of view clearly. This is the best way to prepare for effective problem solving.

We recommend you use the speaker-listener technique for this step. It is best that you place a premium on validation in this problem-discussion phase. Problem solution proceeds much more smoothly in an atmosphere of mutual respect.

In all the examples so far, the couples experienced great pain and distance because they failed to take the time to discuss the issues before coming to agreement. We have repeatedly seen that when good discussion precedes problem solving, the latter goes quickly and smoothly, even on difficult issues. With all the relevant facts and feelings on the table, the foundation is laid for working as a team.

During problem discussion, it is likely that one or both of you may have a specific complaint that needs to be expressed. If this is the case, it is very important that you each indulge in "constructive griping," presenting your feelings and concerns constructively. One way to do this is to use what Gottman, Notarius, Markman, and Gonso call an "XYZ" statement. An XYZ statement puts your gripe or complaint into this format:

### "When you do X in situation Y, I feel Z."

When you use an XYZ statement, you give your partner usable information: the specific behavior, the context in which it occurs, and how you feel when it happens. This is much preferred to what often happens: a vague description of the problem and some character assassination instead of an *I* statement.

For example, suppose you have a concern about your partner making a mess at the end of the day. Which of these statements do you think gives you a better shot at being heard?

or
### "You are such a slob."

### "When you drop your clothes on the floor (X) as you come in the door at the end of the day (Y), I feel angry (Z)."

Let's say you are angry about a comment your spouse made at a party last Saturday night. Here's a contrast:

### "You are so inconsiderate."

### "When you said that what I did for work wasn't really that hard (X) to John and Susan at the party last Saturday (Y), I felt very embarrassed (Z)."

Unless you are careful, it is all too easy to fall into the nonspecific attack on character. Such statements are guaranteed to cause defensiveness and escalation. The XYZ statement is far more constructive. A specific behavior is identified in a specific context. The "I feel Z" part requires you to take responsibility for your own feelings. Your partner does not "make" you feel anything in particular; you are in charge of how you feel.

Here is an example. Lonnie and Kim always argue about what movies to rent. Lonnie likes action movies (*Posse* and *The Art of War*), while Kim likes dramas (*Soul Food* and *The Best Man*). He usually ends up agreeing to see her movie but resents it. Here is how they use an XYZ statement to communicate their feelings.

LONNIE: When you don't want to ever watch an action movie with me (X) when we rent movies (Y), it makes me mad (Z).
KIM: I like those movies, sometimes. Can we agree to see some of both?
LONNIE: I like how you think!

Keep in mind that no one we know really likes to hear a gripe or criticism, no matter how constructively expressed. But unless you are hiding out in avoidance, there are times when you need to voice your concern, and you have to do it without fostering unneeded conflict. The XYZ format helps you do just that.

Before we turn to problem solution, remember that with problem discussion you are really setting the foundation for productive problem solving as a team. So we repeat: do not move from discussion to solution unless you both agree that the issue or problem in question has been fully discussed.

In many instances, however, you'll find that after an excellent discussion, there's really no problem solving to be done. Just having a good discussion is enough. In fact, in our PREP seminars, we often shock couples by announcing that our experience indicates that approximately 70 percent of issues couples deal with do not really need to be solved, just well discussed. Such a high figure doesn't compute for partners who are raised in a culture oriented to problem solving. "How can that be?" they ask.

It's hard for couples to appreciate this point without experiencing the power of good problem discussion that leaves you with what therapists call an a-ha experience. After such a discussion, there's often nothing left to resolve. This is because we often want something much more fundamental in our relationships than solutions to problems; we want a friend. Nevertheless, we recognize that there are many times when discussion of a problem or issue naturally leads to the next step: working together to find a specific solution. When you need to come up with one, the steps of the problem-solution phase can help you get there.

## Problem Solution

We have found these steps to work well for couples, provided that the task of problem discussion has been done.

### Agenda Setting

The first step in the problem-solution phase is to set the agenda for your work together. The key here is to make very clear what you are trying to solve *at this time*. The discussion may take you through many facets of an issue; now you need to decide what to focus on. The more specific the problem you are tackling now, the better your chance of coming to a workable and satisfying solution. Many problems in marriage seem insurmountable, but they can be cut down to size if you follow these procedures.

Suppose you have had a problem discussion about money, covering a range of issues: credit card problems, checkbooks, budgets, and savings. As you can see, the problem area of money contains several subareas to consider. Take a large problem of this sort apart and focus on manageable pieces, one at a time. It is also wise to pick an easy piece of a problem to work on first. You might initially decide who should balance the checkbook each month, and then deal with budget plans later.

At times, your problem discussion focuses from start to finish on a specific problem. In this case, you don't have to define the agenda for problem solving. For example, you may be working on the problem of where to go for the holidays, to visit your parents or your spouse's. There may be no specific smaller piece of such a problem, so set the agenda to work on the whole of it.

### Brainstorming

As far as we know, the process referred to as brainstorming has been around forever. However, it seems to have been refined and promoted by NASA during the early days of the U.S. space program. They needed a way to bring together many engineers and scientists in looking for solutions to the varied problems of space travel. It worked for NASA, and it came to be frequently used in business settings. We have found that it works well for couples, too. There are several rules regarding brainstorming:

1. Any number of ideas can be suggested. One of you should write them down.

2. Don't evaluate the ideas during brainstorming, verbally or nonverbally (this includes making faces!).

3. Be creative. Suggest what comes to mind.

4. Have fun with it, if you can. This is a time for a sense of humor; all other feelings should be dealt with in problem discussion.

The best thing about this process is that it encourages creativity. If you can edit out your tendency to comment critically on the ideas, you will encourage each other to come up with some great stuff. Wonderful solutions can come from considering the points made during brainstorming. Following these rules helps you resist the tendency to settle prematurely on a solution that isn't the best you can find.

### Agreement and Compromise

In this step, the goal is to come up with a specific solution or combination of solutions that you both agree to try. We emphasize the word *agree* because the solution is not likely to help unless you both agree to try it. We also emphasize *specific* because the more specific you are about the solution, the more likely you will follow through.

Although it is easy to see the value of agreement, some people have trouble with the idea of compromise. We have been criticized for using the term. Obviously, compromise implies giving up something you want in order to reach an agreement. To some, compromise sounds more like lose-lose than win-win. But we mean to emphasize compromise positively.

Marriage is about teamwork. Two individuals may see things differently. They may also make contrasting decisions. But many times the best solution is a compromise in which neither of you gets everything you want. The reason is you are not going to have a great marriage if you get your way all the time.

*Follow-Up*

Many couples make agreements to try a particular solution to a problem. It is just as important to follow up about how the agreement is working out. Following up has two key advantages. First, solutions often need to be tweaked a bit to work in the long run. Second, following up builds accountability. Sometimes we don't get serious about making changes unless we know there is some point of accountability in the near future.

There might need to be a lot of follow-up in the problem-solution phase. Or it might not really be necessary; you reach an agreement, it works out, and nothing more has to be done.

Some couples choose to be less formal about follow-up, but we think this is a risk. Most people are so busy they don't plan the next step, and it just doesn't happen. It is an old but true saying that if you fail to plan, you plan to fail.

## A Detailed Example: Glenn and Barbara

It does not take Barbara and Glenn very long to realize that their problem solving about the credit card, her job, and retirement savings is not working. They decide to try the steps we are suggesting.

To do so, they set aside the time to work through the steps. It may not take much time, depending on the problem, but setting aside time specifically for working on the problem is wise. Let's follow them through the steps.

First, they take on problem discussion, using the speaker-listener technique.

BARBARA (SPEAKER): I can see that we really do have to try something different. We aren't getting anywhere on our savings account.

GLENN (LISTENER): You can see we aren't getting anywhere, and you're also concerned.

BARBARA (SPEAKER): (letting him know he has accurately heard her) Yeah, we need to come up with some plan for saving more and really doing something about the credit cards.

GLENN (LISTENER): You agree we need to save more, and you can see that how we spend on the credit cards may be part of the problem.

BARBARA (SPEAKER): I can also see why you're concerned about my job, when I could be bringing in more money. But working for the church brings in money and serves the Lord. That's important to me.

GLENN (LISTENER): Sounds like you can appreciate my concern, but you also want me to hear that it's really important to you. It's part of how you give thanks to God. [Here, he validates her by listening carefully.]

BARBARA (SPEAKER): Yeah. That's exactly what I'm feeling. Here, you take the floor, I want to know what you're thinking.

[FLOOR SWITCH]

GLENN (SPEAKER): I've been anxious about this for a long time. If we don't save more, we're not going to be able to pay for the next kid in college or maintain our lifestyle in retirement. . . . It's not all that far away.

BARBARA (LISTENER): You're really worried, aren't you?

GLENN (SPEAKER): Yes, I am. I like how we live, and I want to be able to enjoy life and being with you when we decide to retire.

BARBARA (LISTENER): So you're worried we could end up having to keep working when we're old, just to survive.

GLENN (SPEAKER): I'd feel a lot better if we had three times as much saved.

BARBARA (LISTENER): You wish we were much further along in our savings than we are.

GLENN (SPEAKER): [This time, he feels he is really getting her attention.] Yeah, I do. I feel a lot of pressure about it. I really want to work together so we can both be comfortable. [He lets her know he wants to work as a team.]

BARBARA (LISTENER): You want us to work together and plan for our future.

GLENN (SPEAKER): [He suggests some alternatives.] Yes. We'd need to spend less to save more. We'd need to use the credit cards more wisely. I think it would make the biggest difference if you could bring in some income.

BARBARA (LISTENER): You feel that to save more we'd need to spend less with the credit cards. More importantly, you think it's pretty important for me to bring in some money.

GLENN (SPEAKER): Yes. How much money coming in is a bigger problem than how much we are spending.

BARBARA (LISTENER): Even though we could spend less, you think we may need more income. Can I have the floor?

GLENN (SPEAKER): Exactly! Here's the floor.

[FLOOR SWITCH]

BARBARA (SPEAKER): [She responds to Glenn's clarification.] Sometimes I think that you think that I'm the only one who overspends.

GLENN (LISTENER): You think that I think you are mostly at fault for spending too much. Can I have the floor again?

[FLOOR SWITCH]

GLENN (SPEAKER): Actually, I don't think that, but I can see how I could come across that way. [He validates Barbara's experience.] I think I overspend just as often as you do. I just do it in bigger chunks.

BARBARA (LISTENER): Nice to hear that. [She validates his comment. She feels good hearing him taking responsibility.] You can see that we both spend too much, just differently. You buy a few big things we may not need and I buy numerous smaller things.

GLENN (SPEAKER): Exactly. We're both to blame, and we can both do better.

BARBARA (LISTENER): We both need to work together.

[FLOOR SWITCH]

BARBARA (SPEAKER): I agree that we need to deal with our savings more aggressively. My biggest fear is my contribution to the Lord. It's been the most meaningful thing I've done since the kids got older.

GLENN (LISTENER): It's hard to imagine not having that . . . it's so important to you.

BARBARA (SPEAKER): Yes. I can see why more income would make a big difference, but I would hate to lose what I have at the same time.

GLENN (LISTENER): You enjoy it, and you're doing something really useful. I can hear how hard it would be for you to give it up.

BARBARA (SPEAKER): Exactly. Maybe there would be some way to deal with this so that I wouldn't lose all of what I'm doing, but where I could help us save what we need for retirement at the same time.

GLENN (LISTENER): You're wondering if there could be a solution that would meet your needs and our needs at the same time.

BARBARA (SPEAKER): Yes. I'm willing to think about solutions with you.

At this point, they discontinue the speaker-listener technique.

GLENN: OK.
BARBARA: So, are we both feeling understood enough to move on to the problem-solution step?
GLENN: I am, how about you?
BARBARA: (nods)

Here, they agree that they have had a good discussion and are ready to try some problem solving. They consciously turn this corner together to move into problem solving.

## Problem Solution

The next step for them is to avoid trying to accomplish a quick solution.

### Agenda Setting

Here, the important thing is for them to choose a specific piece of the whole issue discussed for solution. This increases their chance of finding a solution that will really work this time.

BARBARA: We should agree on the agenda. We could talk about how to get more into the savings account, but that may not be the place to start. I also think we need a discussion to deal with the issue of how we spend money and the credit cards.

GLENN: You're right. We're going to need to take several different stabs at this entire issue. It seems we could break it all down into the need to bring in more and the need to spend less. I don't want to push, but I'd like to focus on the bring in more part first, if you don't mind.

BARBARA: I can handle that. Let's problem solve on that first, then we can talk later this week about the spending side.

GLENN: So, we're going to brainstorm about how to boost the income.

*Brainstorming*

The key here is to generate ideas freely.

BARBARA: Let's brainstorm. Why don't you write the ideas down—you have a pen handy.

GLENN: You mentioned having Theo get a job. I think that's a great idea.

BARBARA: We can help him get something part-time that won't hurt his grades.

GLENN: OK . . . You're also going to try to ask for a raise from the deacon. We could also meet with a financial planner so we have a better idea what we really need to bring in.

BARBARA: You know, Fred and Letanya are doing something like that. We could talk to them about what it's about.

GLENN: I feel this list is pretty good. Let's talk about what we'll try doing.

*Agreement and Compromise*

Next they sift through the ideas generated in brainstorming. The key is to find an agreement that both can get behind.

GLENN: I like your idea of talking to the deacon. What could it hurt?

BARBARA: I like that too. I also think your idea of seeing a financial planner is good. Otherwise, how do we really know what the target is if I'm going to try to bring in some extra? What about talking to Fred and Letanya about what they're into?

GLENN: I'd like to hold off on that. That could lead them to try to solve our problems. Let's just ask who they talked to, OK? And what about exploring if there are any kinds of part-time jobs we can encourage Theo to apply for?

BARBARA: I'll make a list of some I've seen and give it to you. We can also sit down with Theo and get him to think of places.

GLENN: I like including him in the process so he takes it seriously.

BARBARA: So, I talk to the deacon, you investigate about getting a financial planner, and we both sit down and talk to Theo about part-time jobs.

GLENN: Great. Let's schedule some time next week to talk about how we're doing in moving along for the solution we need.

BARBARA: Agreed.

They set a time to meet and follow up as planned.

*Follow Up*

At the end of the week, Barbara and Glenn meet to discuss what they are finding out and what to do next. To her surprise, the deacon she talked with seems eager to try to work out something. In the meantime, she has gone ahead with looking into various part-time jobs that would meet her needs. Glenn has scheduled a meeting for them with a financial planner for the following week.

In this case, the solution really is a process made up of a series of small steps and agreements. Things are moving on an issue that has been a problem between them for a long time, mostly because it feels good to work together and they are no longer avoiding a tough issue.

Later, they go through the steps again and come to specific agreement about spending less. They decide how much less to spend and agree to record all the credit card purchases in a checkbook register so that they know how they are doing compared to their target. In contrast to their problem solving about income, which is a process lasting several weeks, this specific solution on spending is implemented right away, with not much tweaking needed.

We'd like to tell you that the model always works this well, but there are times when it does not. What do you do then?

## When It's Not That Easy

In our experience with couples, there are a few common dilemmas that often come up in dealing with problems.

First, friction is likely and things can get heated. If things get so heated that you resort to negative behavior, it is time for time out. (More on that in the next chapter.) If you can get back on track by staying with the structure (for instance, with the speaker-listener technique), great. If not, you need a break until you can keep it constructive.

Second, you can get bogged down and frustrated during any segment of the problem-solution phase. If so, it's usually best to cycle back to problem discussion. Simply pick up the floor again and resume your discussion. Getting stuck can mean you have not talked through some key issues, or one or both of you are not feeling validated in the process. It's better to slow things down than to continue to press for a solution that may not work.

Third, the best solution you can reach may not always be the end solution. At times, you should set the agenda just to agree on the next steps needed to get to the best solution. For example, you might brainstorm about the kind of information you need to make your decision.

## When There Is No Solution

There are some problems that do not have a mutually satisfying solution. However, we feel strongly that there are far fewer unsolvable problems than couples sometimes think. Nevertheless, suppose you've worked together for some time using the structure we suggest and no solution is forthcoming. You can either let this lack of a solution damage the rest of your marriage, or you can plan for how to live with the difference. Sometimes a couple allows the rest of a good marriage to be damaged by insisting there must be a resolution on a specific unresolved conflict.

If you have an area that seems unsolvable, you can make an agenda for problem solution to protect the rest of the marriage from the fallout from one problem area. You literally agree to disagree constructively. This kind of solution comes about from both teamwork and tolerance. You can't always have your spouse be just the way you want him or her to be, but you can work as a team to deal with the differences.

Here, we have given you a very specific model that works well to help you preserve and enhance your teamwork in solving the problems that come your way in life. We don't expect most couples to use such a structured approach for minor problems. We do maintain that most couples can benefit from this model in dealing with more important matters, especially those that lead to unproductive conflict. This is one more way to add structure when you need it most, to preserve the best in your relationship. You can solve problems in a variety of ways.

In the next chapter we conclude this opening section of the book, which has focused on handling conflict. Chapter Five builds further on the techniques presented so far to help you prosper in your relationship together. The ground rules we present help you take control of the conflict in your relationship, rather than allowing it to take control of you.

## Exercises

There are three assignments for this chapter. First, we want you to practice making XYZ statements. Second, we invite you and your partner to rate some common problem areas in your relationship. Third, we ask you to practice the problem-solving model presented in this chapter. No amount of good ideas will help you without practice!

### XYZ Statements: Constructive Griping

1. Spend some time thinking about things that your partner has done or regularly does that bother you in some way. On your own piece of paper, list your concerns as you normally might state them. Then, practice putting your concerns into the XYZ format: "When you do X in situation Y, I feel Z."

2. Next, do the same thing except list what your partner does that *pleases* you. You will find that the XYZ format also works great for giving positive, specific feedback ("When you came home the other night with my favorite ice cream, I felt loved"). Try sharing some of the positive thoughts with your spouse.

### Problem Area Assessment

Here is a simple measure of common problem areas in relationships. This is a measure originally developed by Knox in 1971; we have used it for years in our research as a simple but relevant measure of the problem areas in a relationship. As we explain, filling these forms out helps you practice the problem-solving skills we have presented. You and your partner should each fill out your own forms independently.

## Problem Inventory

Consider this list of issues that people in all relationships must face. Please rate how much of a problem each area currently poses in your relationship by writing a number from 0 (not at all a problem) to 100 (a severe problem). For example, if "children" are somewhat of a problem, you might enter 25 next to "children." If children are not a problem in your relationship, you might enter a 0, and if they are a severe problem you might enter 100. If you wish to add other areas not included in our list, please do so in the blank spaces provided. BE SURE TO RATE ALL AREAS.

| | |
|---|---|
| _____ Money | _____ Careers |
| _____ Jealousy | _____ Alcohol and drugs |
| _____ Friends | _____ Children (or potential |
| _____ In-laws (or relatives) | children) |
| _____ Sex | _____ Other |
| _____ Religion | _____ |
| _____ Recreation | _____ |
| _____ Communication | _____ |

## Practice Problem Solving

For practicing this model, it is critical that you follow these instructions carefully. When dealing with real problems in your relationship, the chances of conflict are significant, and we want you to practice in a way that enhances your prospect of solidifying these skills.

1. Set aside time to practice without interruption. Thirty minutes or so should be sufficient to get started with using the sequence on some of the problems you want to solve.

2. Look over your problem inventories together. Construct a list of those areas where you each rate the problem as being less serious than others. These are the problem areas we want you to use to practice the model at the start. We want you to practice with specific problems and look for specific solutions. This boosts your skills and helps you gain confidence in the model.

3. We recommend that you set aside time to practice the problem-discussion, problem-solution sequence several times a week for a couple weeks. If you put in this time, you'll gain skill and confidence in handling problem areas together.

4. Keep the book open to this chapter as you practice, and refer back to the specific steps that are recommended.

Now you are ready for the next chapter, on ground rules. As you'll see, we have some new, powerful principles for you. We also have a good summary of the most important points so far in this book.

# 5

# Ground Rules for Handling Conflict

In the previous chapters, we have seen that problems in an African American marriage can come from many sources, among them the difference between men and women, how you were raised, and the personal choices you make. These differences become problems if you don't manage the conflict that is a part of any couple's life. It takes skill to avoid problematic patterns that can seriously damage a relationship. This is why we now offer six important principles, or what we call ground rules, for protecting your relationship from destructive conflict.

We call them ground rules because they are important fundamentals of engagement that can help you address difficult issues. You have to control difficult issues and not let them control you. These ground rules are important for two reasons. First, they sum up many key points we have made so far. Second, they give you the opportunity to agree on how you want to change the ways in which you communicate and handle conflict together. Agreeing to rules of communication is a significant step in handling conflict and enhancing your appreciation and understanding of your spouse. In our experience, these ground rules are powerful tools for helping a couple stay on track and work as a team.

# Ground Rule One

Rule number one concerns getting perspective on the issue affecting your relationship by stopping the action, discussion, feelings,
and flow to get on a track to good communication.

> **If conflict is escalating, we will call for a time out or
> stop action, and either try it again or agree to talk
> about the issue later at a specified time, in both cases
> using the speaker-listener technique.**

If we could get the attention of every couple and have them all
agree to only one change in their relationships, following this
ground rule is what we would present. This first rule is just that
important! It can really protect and enhance a relationship. Why?
In general, it counteracts the negative escalation process that is so
destructive to a close relationship. This is, of course, a hard thing
to do once tempers and emotions are running high. What is amaz-
ing is how much damaging argument can be avoided and an issue
discussed and solved if escalation can be stopped early.

We suggest you and your partner not only agree to this ground
rule but also describe it with a specific, agreed-upon term, such as
"take a T" or "time out," which helps you interpret positively what
you and your partner are doing. Otherwise, it becomes too easy to
interpret what you are doing as avoidance. In fact, calling for a time
out is one of the most positive things either of you can do for your
relationship. You are recognizing old, negative behaviors and deciding to do something constructive instead.

We want you to approach this as something you are doing
*together* for the good of your relationship. Sure, one of you may call
for time out more often than the other does, but if you both agree
to the rule you are really doing the time outs together. As a team
working toward the goal of a better marriage, it is OK if one takes
the responsibility of calling for more time outs than the other, as
long as both agree that this is teamwork and not one person taking

the responsibility for creating the peace within your marriage. The more this technique is practiced, the more you will have opportunities to balance each other when using time out.

This is critical. You can't stop escalation without both of you working together when the situation warrants it. Anybody can walk away, but as we have explained this just fuels more escalation and delayed hostility. But if either of you calls for a time out, *together* you stop the situation from getting out of hand. Calling time out is in context with the *communication*, not a *person or relationship*. Don't simply say "time out" and leave the room; unilateral action is usually counterproductive. Instead, say something like "This is getting hot; let's stop the action and talk later, OK?" By including your partner in the process, you are making the process mutual and hence deescalating.

Another key to this ground rule is that you agree to continue the argument—but productively—either right now or in the near future, after a cooling-off period. If you are a pursuer, this part of the ground rule addresses your concern that time out might be used by an avoider to stop discussion about an important issue. This ground rule is designed to stop unproductive argument, not to prevent all dialogue on an issue. You still need to discuss important issues; just do it productively. In using the speaker-listener technique when you come back to talking about an issue, you agree to deal effectively with the issue that got out of hand.

The time out itself can give a withdrawer confidence that conflict won't get out of hand. Some withdrawers are even better able to tolerate conflict, knowing they can stop it at any time. Using the speaker-listener technique makes it safer still to deal with the issue that comes up by providing the all-important structure for how you plan to try to solve the issue. This ground rule works without using the speaker-listener technique, but we are convinced that using it is the most effective way to implement it.

If you do decide to talk later, try to set the time right then. Perhaps it's in an hour, or maybe the next day would be a good time to talk. If things are really heated when the time out is called, you may find that you can't even talk then about when you'll come back to the discussion. That's OK. You can set a time after things have calmed down between the two of you.

Here are two dialogues illustrating this ground rule being used correctly by couples who came to our PREP workshops.

Luke and Samantha have been married for twenty years and have two teenage sons. Before learning these techniques, they would have frequent, intense arguments that ended with shouting and threats about the future of the relationship. Both come from homes where open conflict was relatively common, so changing their pattern is not easy. As you will see, they still escalate rather easily, but now they know how to stop it when the argument gets going.

SAMANTHA: (annoyed and showing it) You forgot to get the trash out in time for the garbage man. The cans are already full.

LUKE: (also annoyed, looking up from the paper) It's no big deal. I'll just stuff it all down more.

SAMANTHA: Yeah, right. The trash will be overflowing in the garage by next week.

LUKE: (irritated) What do you want me to do now? I forgot. Just leave it.

SAMANTHA: (very angry now, voice raised) You aren't getting a lot of the things done around here that you are supposed to.

LUKE: Let's call a time out. This isn't getting us anywhere.

SAMANTHA: OK. When can we sit down and talk more about it? How about after you watch "Showtime" tonight?

LUKE: OK. As soon as the show is over.

There is nothing magical here. It's really very simple, but the effect is potentially powerful for their relationship. This couple uses a time out effectively to stop an argument that is not going to be productive. Later, they sit down and talk, using the speaker-listener technique, about Samantha's concern that Luke is not meeting his responsibilities at home. Then, using the problem-solving techniques we presented in the last chapter, they are able to come up with some possible ways to get the chores done.

In the next example, another couple uses this ground rule to save an important evening from potential disaster. Byron and Alexandra have been married for six years and have no children. They want kids but have had trouble getting pregnant. This has added plenty of strain to their marriage. They decide to take a weekend trip to a cottage in the Pocono Mountains, to get away and spend a relaxing, perhaps romantic, couple of days together. They have both been looking forward to this time together for months. This conversation transpires on their first evening away, as they get into bed together:

ALEXANDRA: (*feeling romantic and snuggling up to Byron*) It's so nice to get away. No distractions. This feels good.

BYRON: (*likewise inclined, and beginning to caress her*) Yeah, should have done this months ago. Maybe a relaxed setting can help you get pregnant.

ALEXANDRA: (*bristling at the thought*) 'Help YOU get pregnant'? That sounds like you think it's my fault we're not getting pregnant. Why did you have to bring that up?

BYRON: (*anxious and annoyed at himself for spoiling the moment*) I don't think it's your fault. We've been through that. I just meant. . . .

ALEXANDRA: (*angry*) You just meant to say that there's something wrong with me.

BYRON: Hold on. Stop the action. I'm sorry that I mentioned pregnancy. Do you want to talk this through now, or set a time for later?

ALEXANDRA: *(softening)* If we don't talk about it a little bit, I think the rest of the evening will be a drag.

BYRON: OK, you have the floor. [He picks up the remote control on the nightstand to use it as the floor and hands it to her.]

ALEXANDRA (SPEAKER): I got all tense when you brought up pregnancy, and I felt like you were blaming me for our infertility.

BYRON (LISTENER): So mentioning that subject raised unpleasant feelings, and more so because you felt blamed.

ALEXANDRA (SPEAKER): Yes. That whole thing has been just awful for us, and I was hoping to get away from it for the weekend.

BYRON (LISTENER): It's been really hard on you, and you wanted to just forget about it this weekend.

ALEXANDRA (SPEAKER): And I wanted us to focus on rediscovering how to be a little bit romantic, like it used to be.

BYRON (LISTENER): Just you and me making love without a care.

ALEXANDRA (SPEAKER): *(feeling really listened to and cared for)* Yes. Your turn.

[FLOOR SWITCH]

BYRON (SPEAKER): Boy, do I feel like a butthead. I didn't mean to mess up the moment, though I see how what I said affected you.

ALEXANDRA (LISTENER): You feel bad that you said anything. You didn't mean to screw things up between us tonight.

BYRON (SPEAKER): You got it. And I really don't think it's your fault we're not pregnant. Whatever is not working right in our bodies, I don't think of it as you or me screwing up. When I said what I said about you getting pregnant, I was thinking of *us* getting pregnant, but really, it's you who will actually be pregnant. That's all I meant.

ALEXANDRA (LISTENER): *(with a smile)* You didn't mean to be a butthead.

BYRON (SPEAKER): *(chuckling back)* That's kind of blunt, but yeah, that's what I'm saying. I think we should just avoid that whole topic for the weekend.

ALEXANDRA (LISTENER): You think we should make infertility an off-limits topic this weekend.

BYRON: Yes!

[HE HANDS HER THE FLOOR.]

ALEXANDRA (SPEAKER): I agree. OK, where were we? [Tossing the remote on the floor.]

BYRON: *(big smile)* You were calling me a butthead.

ALEXANDRA: *(playfully)* Oh yeah. Come over here, Butthead.

BYRON: *(moving closer to kiss her)* I'm all yours, Baby.

Notice how effectively they use the time out to stop what could have turned into an awful fight. Alexandra is too hurt to just shelve the issue. She needs to talk right then, and Byron agrees. Doing so helps them defuse the tension and come back together, and it saves their special weekend.

## Ground Rule Two

Talking takes more than words; it also takes style. Couples have to develop styles for talking.

**When we are having trouble communicating, we engage the speaker-listener technique.**

We hope you don't need much convincing on the wisdom of this ground rule. The key is to have a way to communicate safely and clearly when you really need to do it well. With this ground rule, you are agreeing to use more structure when you need it. The example with Byron and Alexandra shows the value of this principle. However, there are times when you don't need to call for a time out but still have to make the transition to a more effective mode of communication.

For example, suppose that you want to talk about a problem such as how the two of you spend money. You know from your history that these talks usually get difficult. You would be wise to follow the second ground rule by raising the issue in this way: "Dear, I'm pretty concerned about money right now. Let's sit down and talk using the floor." Such a statement tells your partner that you are raising an important issue, and that you want to talk it out using added structure. This is the most common application of this ground rule. You can learn to lower the control rods of your reactor before things get too heated.

There are times when things have already escalated and a time out might help but instead you skip right to using the speaker-listener technique. In the next example, Allison and James use this ground rule to get back on track. They also attended one of our workshops and told us later on about this sequence of events. They have been married for twenty-seven years; before working on changing things, they were locked into some unproductive communication and conflict patterns. On this occasion, their new skills really make a big difference.

One evening, they go out to dinner. Even before ordering, they have gotten into an argument about their friends.

ALLISON: (*matter of factly*) That reminds me. My sorority sisters are going to be getting together to discuss some current issues like the lack of blacks on TV this fall. Everyone is bringing their husband, so I told them you would be there.

JAMES: (*very angry*) What! Man, I can't stand those folks—they're so uppity. They don't care about the plight of black folks. They just want to act like they do. You should have told me before you told them I was coming.

ALLISON: (*angry, but speaking in a low, serious tone*) Lower your voice. People are turning to look at us.

JAMES: (*just as loud as before and just as angry*) So what? Let them stare. I'm sick and tired of you making decisions without talking to me first.

ALLISON: Don't raise your voice to me!

JAMES: How 'bout I just don't talk to you at all?

At this point, James gets up and leaves the restaurant to go out to the car. He paces a bit, fuming and muttering about how difficult Allison can be at times. He gets in the car, intending to drive away and leave her at the restaurant. *Wouldn't that serve her right?* he thinks. As he cools off for a moment, he thinks better of that idea.

Cooling off is one of the best but hardest things to do when you are in the middle of an argument. It is hard to step back and try to look at the situation in a way that you think will prevent you from getting caught up in the moment. For many of us, our spouse can push buttons for us (on purpose or accidentally) that require us to really take stock of the moment, take a deep breath, and use some of the techniques we discuss in this book.

James is able to do this. He gets out of the car, walks back into the restaurant, takes his seat across from Allison, picks up a menu and hands it to her, and says, "OK, you have the floor."

This might have been a good moment for a total time out, but instead he decides he wants to talk this one out right then, productively. Allison goes with it.

They told us they proceeded to have an excellent discussion of the issue. As they passed the menu back and forth, others in the restaurant must have thought they were having a terrible time making up their minds on what to order. Their transition to greater structure took them from what could have been a real meltdown to a victory for their relationship. Experiences like this serve to boost your confidence in the ability to work together and keep your relationship strong.

## Ground Rule Three

Separating the forest from the trees is a great way to understand each other.

**When using the speaker-listener technique, we will completely separate problem discussion from problem solution.**

As we stated in the last chapter, it is critical to keep it clear at a given moment whether you are discussing a problem or solving a problem. Too often, couples rush to agree to some solution and it fails. Lots of added problems and hassles come from rushing to agreement without laying the proper foundation of communicating fully with each other about the problem.

Go back to Chapter Three and review the conversation between Sadie and Paul about Malcolm and Sunday school. Notice how they have a great discussion but do not seek a specific solution. They each express their concerns and are ready to proceed to problem solving on this issue. Let's pick it up from where we left off there.

SADIE: I think we're ready for problem solving; what do you think?

PAUL: I agree. I'm feeling like we had a good talk and got a lot out on the table. Now working on some solutions would be great.

With these simple comments, they have made the transition from problem discussion to problem solution. They have learned the value of separating the two. Discussion and solution are different processes, and each works better when you recognize this and act on it.

## Ground Rule Four

Time is your friend, not your foe. Use time to help keep your head on straight about what problem you're dealing with.

**We can bring up issues at any time, but the listener can say "This is not a good time." If the listener does not want to talk then, he or she takes responsibility for setting up a time to talk in the near future.**

This ground rule accomplishes an important thing. It ensures that you do not begin a difficult talk about an issue unless you both agree that the time is right. How often do you start talking about a key issue in your relationship when your partner is just not ready for it? There is no point in having a discussion about anything important unless you're both ready to talk about it.

We emphasize this ground rule in appreciation of a fact of life, namely, that couples generally talk about their most important issues at the worst moment—dinnertime, bedtime, when it's time to get the kids off for school, as soon as you walk in the door after work, when one is preoccupied with an important project or task . . . you get the picture. These are times when your spouse may be a captive audience, but you certainly don't have his or her attention. In fact, these are the most stressful times in the life of the average family and not a good time to talk things out.

This ground rule assumes two things. First, you each are responsible for knowing when you are capable of discussing something with appropriate attention to what your partner has to say. Second, you can each respect the other when he or she says "I can't deal with that right now." There simply is no point in trying to have a discussion if you are not both up to it. You may ask, "Isn't this just a prescription for avoidance?" That is where the second part of the ground rule comes in. The one who is not up to the discussion takes responsibility for making it happen in the *near* future. This is critical. Your partner has a much easier time putting off the conversation if he or she is confident that you really will follow through. We recommend that when you use this ground rule, you agree to set up a better time within twenty-four to forty-eight hours. This may not always be practical, but it works as a good rule of thumb. Here's an example.

Alexus and Ezekial are a couple with two children, a five-year-old girl and a two-year-old boy. As is typical of many couples with young children, they have little time for sleeping, much less talking things out in their marriage. They are often alone only at bedtime, after both kids are finally bathed and asleep.

EZEKIAL: Mary can now recite the story of Harriet Tubman to me at bedtime. She's heard it ten times in a row. I'm glad that she'll know some history as she grows up.

ALEXUS: It's the same thing at nap time. She always wants to hear about Martin Luther King. She's gonna know more black history than both of us do when she's done.

EZEKIAL: Speaking of civil rights, I want to talk to you about what I'm going to say to the EEO officer at work about the comments my boss has been making.

ALEXUS: I know it's important, but I am so tired. That's such a heavy discussion. I want you to have me at my best. Do we have to talk about it right now?

EZEKIAL: I'm pretty beat, too. Well, what would be a good time to talk about this?

ALEXUS: I can come by your office for lunch tomorrow and we can talk about what to say.

EZEKIAL: That sounds like a plan.

It is now Alexus's responsibility to get by his office and make this talk happen. Because their agreement is rather specific, Alexus should be able to show up at lunch for their talk. They may be too tired and busy to ever have a perfect time to talk this out, but there are times that are better than others.

As one variation of this ground rule, you may want to come to an agreement that certain times are never good for bringing up important things. For example, we have worked with many couples who have agreed that neither will bring up anything significant within thirty minutes of bedtime. These couples decided that at bedtime they are just too tired, and that it is important to be relaxing and winding down then.

# Ground Rule Five

Take time to feed the soul of your relationship.

### We will have weekly "couple meetings."

Most couples do not set aside a regular time for dealing with key issues and problems. The importance of doing so has been suggested by so many marriage experts over the years that it is almost a cliché. Nevertheless, we want to give you our view on this sage advice handed down probably for centuries.

The advantages of having a weekly meeting time far outweigh any negatives. First, this is a tangible way to place high priority on your marriage by carving out time for its upkeep. We know you are busy. We all are busy. But if you decide that this is important, you can find the time to make it work out.

Second, following this ground rule assures you that even if there is no other good time to deal with issues and problems in your marriage, at least you have this weekly meeting. You might be surprised at how much you can get done in thirty minutes or so of concentrated attention to an issue. During this meeting, you can talk about the relationship, discuss specific problems, or practice communication skills. This includes using all of the skills and techniques we recommend in the first four chapters of this book.

A third advantage of this ground rule is that having a weekly meeting time takes much of the day-to-day pressure off your relationship. This is especially true if you have gotten tangled in the pursuer-withdrawer pattern. If something happens that brings up a gripe for you, it's much easier to delay bringing it up until another time, if you know there will be another time. If you are a pursuer, you can relax; you will have your chance to raise an issue. Withdrawers are encouraged to bring up concerns they have, at a meeting for doing just this.

You may be thinking that this is a pretty good idea. But to put a good idea into action, you must be consistent in taking the time to make the meetings happen. You may have the urge to skip the weekly meetings during a period when you are getting along really well. We have heard this repeatedly from couples. Don't succumb to this urge.

Consider Roberto and Margaret. They have set aside Wednesday nights at nine as a time for their couple meeting. If they are getting along really well during the week and Wednesday night rolls around, each begins to think, "We don't need to meet tonight. No use stirring things up when we are getting along so well." Then one or the other says, "Hey, dear, let's just skip the meeting tonight, things are going so well."

What Roberto and Margaret have come to realize is that things are going so well partly because they are having their meetings regularly. After they cancel a few, they notice that more conflicts come up during the week. They give up their time to deal with issues and revert to the uncertainty of dealing with things "if and when." But soon enough they decide that if-and-when is not placing the proper importance on their marriage, and they return to the Wednesday meetings.

If you actually do get to a meeting and have little to deal with, fine. Have a short meeting—but have a meeting. Use the meeting to air gripes, discuss an important issue, plan for a key event coming up, or just take stock of how the relationship is going. If there is a specific problem, work through the problem-discussion, problem-solution steps presented in Chapter Four. If there is nothing more pressing, practice some of the skills presented in the program. Take the time, and use it to keep your relationship strong.

## Ground Rule Six

It is as important to preserve the fun as it is to solve problems.

**We will make time for the great things: fun, friendship, and sensuality. We will agree to protect these times from conflict and the need to deal with issues.**

Just as it's important to have time set aside to deal with issues in your relationship, it's critical that you protect key times from conflict over issues. You can't focus on issues all the time and have a really great marriage. You need some time where you are together relaxing—having fun, talking as friends, making love, and so forth—and where conflict and problems are off limits. This is such a key point that we discuss it in the chapters on friendship, fun, and sensuality later in the book.

For now, we emphasize two points embodied in this ground rule. First, make time for these great things. Second, if you're spending time together in one of these ways, don't bring up issues that you have to work on. If an issue does come up, table it for later—perhaps for your couple meeting, to deal with it constructively.

The dialogue earlier in this chapter between Alexandra and Byron makes this point well. They are out to have a relaxing and romantic weekend in the mountains, and this isn't the time to focus on one of their key issues. Using time out and the speaker-listener technique helps them refocus on the real reason they have gotten away. It's better still if you agree to keep such issues off limits during positive times in the first place.

## Conclusion

There is one essential benefit for your relationship embedded in all these ground rules. When used properly, they permit you to agree to control the difficult issues in your marriage rather than allowing them to control you. Instead of having arguments whenever things come up, or at the worst times, you agree to deal with the issues when you both are able to do it well—when you are both under control.

No marriage should impart a growing sense that you are walking in a minefield. You know the feeling. You begin to wonder where the next explosion will come from, and you don't feel in control of where you're going. You no longer feel free to just "be" with your partner. You don't know when you are about to "step in it," but you know immediately when you do. It just doesn't have to be like that. These ground rules go a long way toward getting you back on safe ground. They work. You can do it.

# Exercise

Your exercise for the end of this chapter is very straightforward. Discuss the six ground rules and begin to try them out. You may want to modify one or more of them in some specific manner to make them work better for you. That's fine. The key is to review the rules and give them a chance to work in your relationship. Here they are again. Note changes to any of them.

1. If conflict is escalating, we will call for a time out or stop action, and either try it again or agree to talk about the issue at a specified time later, in both cases using the speaker-listener technique.

2. When we are having trouble communicating, we engage the speaker-listener technique.

3. When using the speaker-listener technique, we will completely separate problem discussion from problem solution.

4. We can bring up issues at any time, but the listener can say "This is not a good time." If the listener does not want to talk then, he or she takes responsibility for setting up a time to talk in the near future.

5. We will have weekly "couple meetings."

6. We will make time for the great things: fun, friendship, and sensuality. We will agree to protect these times from conflict and the need to deal with issues.

At this point, we turn our attention to deep issues and complex processes in relationships. Please continue to practice all of the skills we have presented thus far as we move ahead into the subjects of the next section: hidden issues, commitment, and forgiveness.

# 6

# Timing Is Everything

## *Issues and Events*

In the previous chapters, we have talked about how you can handle the conflict that sometimes occurs in marriage. In this chapter, we offer you some advice on dealing with issues that arise in
your marriage. Some of these issues occur in everyday situations;
others are deeper and often hidden issues that affect a relationship.

## Issues Versus Events

As we pointed out in the Introduction, African American couples
deal with many issues: struggling for financial success, family, racism,
and problems related to the church. Other issues couples commonly
fight about are raising children, recreation, alcohol and drugs, sex,
careers, and housework, just to name a few.

These issues are important, but we find that they're actually not
the things that couples argue about most frequently. Instead, they
argue about the small, day-to-day happenings of life. We call them
*events*. We want to help you separate events from issues, and then
separate out issues that are more apparent (money, racism, family)
from deeper and often hidden ones that affect your relationship.
Arguments about what we identify as issues are started by small
events; they then trigger the issue and usually end up generating bad
feelings for the couple. An example shows you see what we mean.

Clancy and Marie have big-time money issues. Both are first generation out of the 'hood, living in middle-class America. One day, Clancy comes home from work and kisses Marie, who is sitting at the kitchen table working on the bills for the month. He hands her the checkbook and proceeds to change clothes. Marie loses it when she takes a look at the checkbook and sees an entry for $150 made out to a department store. When Clancy walks back into the kitchen, tired after a long day at work, he is looking for some understanding, or at least a "How was your day?" Instead, the conversation goes like this.

MARIE: What did you spend that $150 on?
CLANCY: (*very defensive*) None ya business.
MARIE: (*furious*) I am sitting here trying to keep on track with the bills, and you are off having a good time.

As you can imagine, this argument over money worsens. The timing of Marie working on the bills and seeing that Clancy spent $150 is not good.

Events like this are common to all couples. In this case, Clancy has actually spent the $150 on a new leather coat for Marie's birthday. But that never comes up.

Issues and events work like a shaken bottle of champagne. Each issue is a shake. The issues that are the most trouble give the biggest shakes. The pressure keeps building up as you don't talk about them constructively. Then, in the heat of an event, the cork pops.

Many couples, particularly those in unhappy relationships, only deal with important issues in the context of triggering events. For Clancy and Marie, there is so much negative energy stored up around the issue of money that it's easily triggered. There are issues of middle-class guilt about living in a good neighborhood as compared to where they came from, issues with only having white neighbors, issues about whether they are sharing some of the wealth they have accumulated with others (such as giving a donation to the United Negro College Fund). But they never sit down and talk about money constructively. Instead, they argue all the time when bills come in, or something on the house needs to be fixed, or another money event happens. They never get anywhere on the big issue because they spend their energy just dealing with the crises of events. What about you? Do you set aside time to deal with issues ahead of the time when an event triggers them?

Another couple, Martin and Shanta, have issues about the intrusion of relatives, which they did not discuss in their time together as a couple. One evening, they go to a baseball game; it's the first time they've been out for three or four weeks. On the way, Martin gets a call on his cell phone; it's from his mother. When the phone call ends, Shanta calls Martin out.

> SHANTA: Why does that woman always have to interfere with our relationship? This is our time together.
> MARTIN: (pissed off) Look, that is my mama, and second, what's the problem? We're still going out to have some fun.
> SHANTA: (sounding indignant) Sorry, I forgot you were a mama's boy.
> MARTIN: (angrily) Don't start with me, woman.

Their evening is, of course, destroyed. They never even make it to the ballpark. They spend the night arguing about his mother calling and whether or not she is too involved in their lives.

As in this case, events tend to come up at inopportune times: when you're ready to leave for work, you're coming home from work, you're going to bed, you're out to relax, the kids are around, friends have come over, and so forth. Things come up that disturb you, but it is often at the worst time to deal with the issue.

How do you deal with triggering events?

We suggest that you edit out the desire to argue about the issue *right then*, when an event triggers it. The key to this is saying to yourself, *I don't have to deal with this right now. This isn't the time. We can talk later.* There are simply times when dropping the matter for the moment is the wisest strategy. This is simple wisdom.

In the argument we have just witnessed, Shanta could say, "That phone call from your mother really set me off. Let's sit down and talk about it later." In this way, the event is acknowledged but the issue is left for a time when they can deal with it effectively. Likewise, Martin could say, "Listen, let's take a time out. I can see you're feeling hurt, but let's wait for a better time to talk about the issue. How about tomorrow after dinner?" If they've been practicing the skills we've presented so far, this could save their evening by containing the event so that it doesn't trigger the explosive unresolved issues about his mother and their time together. This is what we mean by separating issues from events; it's a wise thing to do.

When an event does happen, you can also try talking about the issue for a few minutes, agreeing to have a fuller discussion later. You might say, "Hey Boo, let's talk about what just happened for a second and then try to move on and have a nice evening together." You can use the speaker-listener technique if you want to do it really well, so that you both feel heard. Then let it go until later.

One reason people focus on events and let them turn into issue discussions is they don't feel that "later" will happen. So why wait? Jump in now. You wind up in a marital minefield, with the issues being the explosives and the events being the triggers. The effect of being in a minefield is that the two of you become cautious or tense rather than open and relaxed. When what you want most is someone to be your best friend and give you support, but instead you end up mostly feeling anxious around your partner, the effect on your marriage can be devastating.

Practicing the things we've been teaching makes it likely you'll handle events better and plan the time to deal with important issues. This way, you maintain a level of control as to where, when, and how the issues are dealt with.

# Hidden Issues

Most of the time, people can recognize the issues that are triggered by events because they are about the things that most of us deal with every day: money, chores, children, and so on. They almost always have the same old content. With Clancy and Marie, her looking at the checkbook starts the event, and the issue is money. That's not hard to figure out. But you also find yourself getting caught up in a fight around an event that doesn't seem to be attached to any particular issue. Or you find you aren't getting anywhere when talking about particular problems, as if you are spinning your wheels.

These are signs that you aren't getting at the real issue. It's not about money, it's not about careers, it's not about housework, it's not about leaving the toilet seat up. The real issue is deeper and more elusive.

A hidden issue often drives a really frustrating or destructive argument. For example, Shanta and Martin end up arguing about his mother and about his taking calls from her at any time. But the real issue may be that Shanta feels she is not important to him.

When we say these issues are often hidden, we mean they are usually not talked about openly or constructively. Instead, they are the key issues that get lost in the flow of the argument. You may be aware of feeling uncared for, but when certain events come up, that may not be what's talked about. Although Shanta may be aware that she feels Martin doesn't pay enough attention to her, that's not what they ended up talking about. They are missing the forest (the hidden issues) for the trees (the events).

To summarize, events are everyday happenings such as dirty dishes or a bounced check. Issues are the larger topics—family, money, racism—that almost all African American couples must deal with. Hidden issues are the deep, fundamental issues that can come up for you along with any lesser issue or event. In our work with couples, we see several types of hidden issues: power, caring, recognition, commitment, integrity, and acceptance. There are surely others, but these six capture a lot of what goes on in relationships. As you will see, since these issues are deep, they can often have a spiritual significance.

## Hidden Issues of Control and Power

With control issues, the question is status and power. Who decides who does the chores? Are your needs, your desires just as important as your partner's, or is there inequality? Is your input important, or are major decisions made without you? Who's in charge? If you are dealing with issues of this kind, you may be dealing with the hidden issue of control.

Even if there aren't ongoing struggles with control between you, these issues can affect your relationship when various decisions come up—even small ones. For example, what happens if one of you really wants to go get pizza and the other really feels like Chinese food? This is an event without a lot of long-term significance. Nevertheless, if either of you is unyielding in what you want, you can have a lot of conflict over something as simple as carry-out cuisine. You may feel the other is trying to control you, or you need to be in control. A power struggle can result over just about anything.

Whatever the topic or disagreement, control issues are least likely to damage your relationship if there's a good sense of being a team, where each partner's needs and desires are attended to in the decisions they make. That's because such teamwork reflects love and oneness, while control and power issues reflect selfishness. Even if one partner's motives are pure, the other can still react negatively on account of their history. Some people are motivated to be in control because they're actually hypersensitive about being controlled by others. Usually such a person has experienced a controlling and powerful authority figure somewhere in the past, likely a parent. It becomes hard to trust others as an adult, although a marriage that is doing well is probably based on just such mutual trust.

It's no accident that money is rated the number one problem area in study after study. So many decisions in our lives revolve around money. If you have significant power or control issues in your marriage, it's likely you struggle a lot with money, as well as any number of other subjects. Money in and of itself isn't the deep issue, but it precipitates events that trigger the deeper issues.

Whenever you must make a decision together, it's an opportunity for a control issue to be triggered. Working together as a team is the best antidote to the hidden issue of control.

## Hidden Issues of Caring

A second major arena where we see hidden issues emerge involves caring. Here, the main theme is the extent to which you feel loved and cared for. As we'll see, such issues are often felt as concern that important emotional needs aren't being met.

Jason fights with Kayla over putting the soap back in the soap dish. Kayla always leaves the soap on the counter. The soap isn't the real issue fueling their arguments. As it turns out, Jason has always associated putting things away with demonstrating consideration, love, and being taken care of. Since Kayla doesn't do it, he feels she doesn't love him. So he has a hidden caring issue. He is very aware of feeling uncared for, but in their arguments about the soap he doesn't talk about it. Instead, he focuses on what he sees as Kayla's stubbornness and his felt need.

For her part, Kayla is thinking, *What difference does it make if the soap is here or there? He's not my boss, and he doesn't tell me what to do.* She has a control issue about his trying to force her to live a certain way. That really isn't his motive, but she is very sensitive since she was previously married to an abusive and overbearing man. Jason is guilty of being controlling, but not because of the need to be in control of Kayla so much as what feels like a need to be cared for in a certain way. For them, discussing this well brings them closer, and in doing so, soap no longer seems all that important.

JASON (SPEAKER): You know me; I'm not really controlling. My mama raised me by herself and she was really strict. I know that she was strict and had these rules because she loved me. I guess I just thought that the people who cared for me would do certain things.

KAYLA (LISTENER): [She summarizes in her own words.] So for you, the key issue is wanting to know I care, not wanting to control me?

JASON (SPEAKER): [He goes on to validate her as well.] That's right. And I'm sorry, I can see how you'd be feeling controlled without knowing what was really up for me.

[FLOOR SWITCH]

KAYLA (SPEAKER): You're right. You know I fight at the slightest suggestion that someone is trying to control me. You know that comes from having been married to Cedrick.

JASON (LISTENER): So it really did look like I just wanted to control you and, given what you went through with Cedrick, that really set you off.

KAYLA (SPEAKER): Uh-huh. You're my husband, not my master.

JASON (LISTENER): Sounds like you want us to be on the same team.

KAYLA (SPEAKER): That's right, Baby!

As you can see from the tail end of their conversation, by learning to talk about the big concerns each has paved the way for greater connection instead of alienation over soap in the soap dish. This is another example where it would be hard to solve the problem about the event (putting the soap in the soap dish) unless they communicate well enough to get the hidden issues out in the open. But it's hard to talk about the vulnerable stuff if you can't talk safely!

That's the key to being able to constructively talk about a deep issue rather than let it operate as a hidden issue in an argument.

## Hidden Issues of Recognition

The third type of hidden issue involves recognition. Are your activities and accomplishments appreciated by your partner? Caring issues involve concerns about being cared for or loved; recognition issues are more about feeling valued by your partner for who you are and what you do.

One of the couples we talked to was Arlene and Greg. Both graduated with master's degrees in business, and each works for a major company. One evening, they go to their new neighbor's house for a get-together. Greg begins talking to the husbands in the group as they get to know one another. One of the neighbors asks about Greg's work and where his family is from. As he describes his family, he mentions that out of all his family, he is the only one with a master's degree. The conversation changes to other matters, such as houses and kids. Arlene, who has been in earshot of the conversation, grows mad because he hasn't said anything about her—that she is in his family and has a master's degree too.

Greg doesn't acknowledge that Arlene has been successful too. Who knows why he fails to mention her? Perhaps he has some control issues that seep out when he makes such comments. Perhaps he is thinking, *This is the fellas and I am the man of the house; they really want to know about me.* Whatever his hidden issues may be, if any, such events make Arlene feel her contribution to their financial success is trivial. She may slowly pull away from him over time. If they want to prevent further damage to their relationship, they had better talk openly about this key issue.

Such examples are common. For example, many men tell us they don't feel their wives place much value on their work outside of the home to bring in income for the family. Likewise, we hear many women say that they don't feel their husbands appreciate what they do at home for the family, whether or not they work outside the home. In either case, the spouse may try hard for a while to be recognized for what she or he brings to the family, but eventually the spouse burns out if no appreciation is expressed. How long has it been since you told your partner how much you appreciate the things he or she does?

## Hidden Issues of Commitment

The focus of this fourth hidden issue is the long-term security of the relationship ("Are you going to stay with me?"). One couple we worked with, Brenda and Maurice, had huge arguments about raising their children. She would complain bitterly about his contribution to raising their children every time she came home from picking them up from school.

The problem isn't so much related to the children. For Brenda, the hidden issue is commitment. She was married once before; her ex-husband didn't really like kids and left her after four years of marriage. Now, when it's time to care for her kids, she sees Maurice's actions as avoiding contact with them. She associates this with thoughts of him leaving her. Leaving Brenda is the furthest thing from his mind, but since she rarely talks openly about her fear, he isn't really given the opportunity to alleviate her anxiety by affirming his commitment. The issue keeps fueling explosive conflict in these events.

When your commitment to one another is secure, it brings a deeper safety to your relationship than what comes from good communication. This is safety that comes from the lasting promise to be there for one another, to lift one another up in tough times, to cherish each other for a lifetime. Do you worry about your partner's long-term commitment to you and the marriage? Have you talked about this openly, or does this issue find indirect expression in the context of events in your relationship? In Chapters Eight and Nine, we focus in depth on how commitment issues affect relationships.

## Hidden Issues of Integrity

The fifth type of hidden issue deals with integrity. As African Americans, in our daily lives our integrity as human beings is sometimes questioned. It is easy to imagine that if your partner questions your intentions or motives, you can easily be angered or get defensive.

Ruben and Altavist's arguments often end up with each being certain they know what the other means. Most often, they're sure that what the other means is negative. Both are therapists, so you'd think they would know better. They have a serious problem in making negative interpretation. Here's a typical example.

ALTAVIST: Did you call the phone company today?

RUBEN: You didn't ask me to call the phone company, you asked me if I had called the company about the last bill. I told you I hadn't.

ALTAVIST: (*angry at what she sees as his lack of caring about what she needs*) You said you would call about the last bill. Never mind. I know you don't give a—

RUBEN: (*feeling thoroughly insulted*) Hey, that's a bunch of crap. I show you how much I care everyday, so back off.

How Altavist feels and her issue around caring is clear, but these two don't have a constructive, healing talk about it. Ruben's issue, on the other hand, has more to do with integrity. It's not as much in the open, but it's there. He feels insulted at her insinuating that he is an uncaring, inconsiderate husband who never thinks about her needs. He feels judged. Each winds up feeling invalidated.

As we pointed out earlier in this book, it's not wise to argue about what the other really thinks, feels, or intends. Don't tell your partner what's going on inside, unless it's *your* insides! To do otherwise is guaranteed to trigger the issue of integrity. Almost any-one will defend his or her integrity when it's questioned.

## Acceptance: You're Either In or Out

There seems to be one primary issue underlying all the others listed here: the desire for acceptance. Sometimes this is felt more as fear of rejection, but the fundamental issue is the same. At the deepest level, people are motivated to find acceptance and avoid rejection in their relationships. This reflects the deep need we all have to be both respected and connected. Consider again the foundational teaching we looked at in the first chapter.

This fundamental fear of rejection drives many other hidden issues. The fear is real. Marriage involves imperfect people who deeply hurt one another at times. You can see this fear of rejection come up in many ways. For example, some people are afraid that if they act in certain ways, their partner is going to reject them. A low-ered sense of self-worth only makes such fears more intense. Perhaps one partner asks for what he or she wants indirectly rather than directly ("Wouldn't you like to make love tonight?" rather than "I would like to make love with you tonight"). In this manner, many people are indirect about what they ask of their partners. Their real desires are filtered out because of fear of rejection.

There are a number of other ways in which people act out their hidden issues around acceptance and rejection. Consider the exam-ple of Herman and Heidi's problem with his night out with the boys.

Herman and Heidi have been married for seven years, and things have gone well for them all along. They are an interracial couple with two kids, ages three and six. There are few issues they don't handle well. They talk regularly about the more important ones, which keeps things running pretty smoothly. However, there is one problem they've never really handled.

Herman is a member of Omega Psi Phi, and he regularly partic-ipates in a book club with his frat brothers once a week. Wives are allowed but seldom participate. This next argument is typical.

HEIDI: Do you have to go hang out with your frat brothers? The kids are antsy, and I don't feel like dealing with it by myself.

HERMAN: *(a bit defensively)* Come on, girl, you can handle the kids. Anyway, this club keeps me connected to the brothers. You complain about this every time I go.

HEIDI: *(going on the attack)* I just don't think you have to go every week. The kids need you around on Thursdays, too.

HERMAN: Why do we have to have this argument every Thursday? Those are my boys, you know that. You need to deal with this better because I'm not about to give this up.

HEIDI: *(angrier)* Do you even care that your kids want to spend more time with you?

HERMAN: Look, obviously I am not going to win. So. You're always right; you win. I'm a bad father.

HEIDI: Don't patronize me. Don't talk to me like that. That is the way your dad treats your mom, but I'm not taking it.

HERMAN: Heidi, get over it, I'm going, and I'm going to keep going.

What's really going on here? As he gets ready for his weekly night out with the boys, they have a recurring fight. You can see many of the hidden issues being triggered for Herman and Heidi. Deep down, she doesn't feel she is part of his circle of friends. She feels lonely when he leaves, and this is hard to handle since she sees how important it is to him. She wonders if he's happy to be away from her. She feels nearly abandoned, reflecting some commitment issues that are also triggered. Her focus on the kids is a smoke screen for her real concerns.

Herman likes to be in control of his life, so that's another hidden issue triggered here. His remark "Anyway, this club keeps me connected to the brothers" may also reveal a hidden issue of how he might not feel a part of African Americans. Maybe he feels he has to prove that he is "still down" even though he is married to a Caucasian woman. Also, as they argue unproductively, integrity comes up. He feels she's calling into question his devotion as a husband and father. He sees himself as very dedicated to the family; he just wants this time to connect with people he feels close to. He doesn't think that's asking a lot.

Underneath it all, you can see acceptance as the most basic hidden topic driving the issues of power, caring, commitment, and integrity in their argument. Neither believes that the other accepts him or her. It's not that this is such an unresolved issue for them. After all, they really do love each other and have a great relationship. Yet the need for acceptance is so basic for all of us that it can be triggered by just about any event or issue if we let it.

In this argument, Heidi and Herman aren't really talking about the hidden issues in any productive way. The deep issues aren't totally hidden, but they aren't being dealt with directly and constructively, either. Let's discuss how to do this right.

## Recognizing the Signs of Hidden Issues

You can't handle hidden issues unless you can identify them. There are four essential ways to tell when there may be hidden issues affecting your relationship:

### Wheel Spinning

One sign of hidden issues is when you find yourselves talking about some problem over and over again—as though you're spinning your wheels. When an argument starts with you thinking *Here we go again*, you should suspect hidden issues. You never really get anywhere on the problem because you often aren't talking about what really matters (the hidden issue). So you go around and around and get nowhere.

### Trivial Triggers

A second way to identify hidden issues is when trivial issues are blown out of proportion. The argument between Kayla and Jason earlier is a great example. The soap and the soap dish seem like a trivial event, but they trigger horrendous arguments driven by the issues of power and caring.

### Avoidance

A third sign of hidden issues is when one or both of you are avoiding certain topics or a level of intimacy. It could be that some walls have gone up between you. This often means that there are important, unexpressed issues affecting the relationship. Perhaps it seems too risky to talk directly about feeling unloved or insecure. Trouble is, those concerns have a way of coming up anyway.

There are many topics that can be avoided, in reflection of hidden issues in the relationship. For example, we have talked with many couples from a variety of cultural or religious backgrounds who strongly avoid talking about these differences. We think this usually reflects concerns about acceptance ("Will you accept me fully if we really talk about our different backgrounds?"). Avoiding such topics not only allows hidden issues to remain hidden; it puts the relationship at risk since there are important differences that can have great impact on a marriage.

Other common but taboo topics in a marriage are sex, weight, money, and so on. There are many such sensitive topics that people avoid dealing with in their relationships, out of fear of rejection. What issues do you avoid talking about?

### Scorekeeping

A fourth sign of hidden issues in your relationship is when one or both or you start keeping score. We talk more about the dangers of scorekeeping in Chapter Nine. For now, the key is that scorekeeping reflects something wrong between you.

Scorekeeping could mean you are not feeling recognized for what you put into the relationship. It could mean that you are not fully committed, as we explain later. It could mean you are feeling controlled and are keeping track of the times your partner has taken advantage of you. Whatever the issue, it can be a sign that there are important topics not being talked about, but instead just "documented."

## Handling Hidden Issues

What can you do when you realize a hidden issue is affecting your relationship? Start talking about it constructively. This is easier to do if you cultivate an atmosphere of teamwork using the techniques we've presented thus far. We strongly recommend using the speaker-listener technique when you are trying to explore such issues.

Deal with the issue in terms of problem discussion, not problem solution. Be aware of any tendency to jump to solutions. In our opinion, the deeper the issue, the less likely it is that problem solving is the answer. If you haven't been talking about the real issue, how could your problem solution address what's really at stake? What you need first and foremost is to hear each other and understand the feelings and concerns. Such validating discussions have the greatest impact on hidden issues because they work directly against the fear of rejection. There is no more powerful form of acceptance than really listening to the thoughts and feelings of your mate. Safe, open, no-fig-leaf talks have real power to overcome this fear.

## A Detailed Example

We round out this chapter with a detailed example of how the really important issues come out if you communicate clearly and safely.

Cameron and Carla are newlyweds who came to one of our workshops. Both are working long hours to make ends meet. When they do have time together, they frequently run into difficulties with TV, especially because he watches a great deal of sports. She is very upset about this. Many events arise around the TV, but much more important hidden issues are involved.

They could argue forever at the level of the *events* (for example, who should control the TV), but they are making much greater progress in talking about the *issues* with the speaker-listener technique. What follows is one of the first times they have used the technique. You'll see their skills are a little rough around the edges at this point, with some mind reading and less-than-ideal paraphrasing. Yet they are communicating better than they ever have about the real issues.

We haven't told them to focus on hidden issues, but we can see how they come out anyway. We find that this happens regularly when couples are doing a good job with the speaker-listener technique.

CARLA (SPEAKER): You spend more time watching that TV than talking to me. Sometimes you don't come to bed till you're done watching TV, and then you just go to sleep.

CAMERON (LISTENER): So you're saying you think I'd rather watch TV than spend time talking to you?

CARLA (SPEAKER): Yes.

Carla is not feeling accepted or cared for by Cameron. This comes out clearly here, yet in the past when they argued about the TV they never got to what was really going on—at least not in a way that drew them closer together. When he paraphrases that it seems to her that he's more comfortable watching TV than being with her, he really hits home. This is exactly what it seems like to her. She can tell from the quality of his paraphrase that he's really listening to her. This does more to address her hidden issue of wanting to know he cares than all the problem solving in the world could do.

It's not clear whether he agrees that he would rather watch TV than talk to her, but it is clear that he hears her. They go on.

CAMERON (LISTENER): Can I have the floor?

[FLOOR SWITCH]

CAMERON (SPEAKER): Before we were married, I used to watch TV all the time. I was not one to go out clubbing a lot, so I watched a lot of TV.

CARLA (LISTENER): So, what you're saying is that before we got together, watching a lot of TV is just what you used to do.

CAMERON (SPEAKER): Right. And also before we were married, even though we spent time together, you never really had the opportunity to see that I did watch football and game shows all the time.

CARLA (LISTENER): So what you're saying is that I didn't get to see this part of you—watching so much TV—as much as I do now.

CAMERON (SPEAKER): Yeah. I'm not saying that you should have known, but you saw that it was a part of me, whether you want to accept it or not.

CARLA (LISTENER): OK, so what you're saying is that I saw this part of you, so this is something that I should have known was going to come about throughout the relationship. Is that what you're saying?

CAMERON (SPEAKER): I think so; do you?

When Carla complains about Cameron watching so much TV, he feels she is attacking a core part of his identity. So for him, the fundamental hidden issue revolves around acceptance of who he is and recognition of this part of him. He really gets this out in the open in his statement that "you saw that it was a part of me, whether you want to accept it or not."

After enough discussion on these deeper levels, they go on to engage in some effective problem solving about time together and time watching TV. He acknowledges that he is spending time with the TV and not with her, so they started doing more things together during his usual TV-watching time. Without dealing directly with the hidden issues first, we don't believe they could do this.

Our goal in this chapter has been to give you a way to explore and understand some of the most frustrating happenings in a relationship. You can prevent lots of damage by learning to handle *events* and *issues* with the time and skill they require. Using the model presented here, along with all the skills and techniques in the first four chapters of the book, helps you do just that.

For too many couples, the hidden issues never come out. They fester and produce levels of sadness and resentment that eventually destroy the marriage. It just doesn't have to be that way. When you learn to discuss deep issues openly and with emphasis on validating each other, what has been generating the greatest conflict can actually draw you closer together.

## Exercises

We recommend that you first work through these questions individually and then sit down and talk together about your impressions.

1. Think through the list of signs of hidden issues that may be affecting your relationship. Do you notice that one or more of these signs come up a lot in your relationship? Here they are again. What do you notice?

Wheel spinning

Trivial triggers

Avoidance

Scorekeeping

2. Next, we'd like you to consider which hidden issues might operate most often in your relationship. Here's the list again. There may be some other big issue you'd like to add to the list. Consider each issue and to what degree it seems to affect your relationship negatively. Also, how hidden are they for you?

Note if there are certain events that have triggered or keep triggering the issues. Make a list in the right-hand column.

Power and control

Caring

Recognition

Commitment

Integrity

Acceptance

3. Plan some time together to talk about your observations and thoughts. For most couples, there are certain hidden issues that repeatedly come up. Identifying them can help you draw together as you each learn to handle them with care. Also, as you discuss these matters, you have an excellent opportunity to get in some practice with the speaker-listener technique.

Now, we turn to a chapter on expectations to help you further as you consider the issues in your relationship. It also helps you understand what you expect from one another, and where those expectations come from.

# 7

# Unmet Expectations and What to Do About Them

In the last chapter, we explained how hidden issues can fuel con-flict and distance between partners. Now we're ready to build on those concepts by focusing on expectations. In this chapter we help you explore your expectations for your marriage: what they are, where they come from, and if they're reasonable.

At the end of this chapter, there's an important exercise with which you explore and share your expectations for your relation-ship. In fact, this chapter is primarily designed to prepare you for this exercise—it's that important.

Exploring your expectations also helps you understand how issues—hidden or not—are triggered in your relationship. Along with all the skills we've taught so far, exploring your expectations gives you the best shot at preventing the kind of frustrating conflict we discussed in the last chapter. (We also talk about the issue of how your expectations form your commitment in Chapter Eight.)

## How Expectations Affect Relationships

We have expectations for every aspect of our relationships. In the first four chapters, we discussed how an expectation can become a powerful filter, distorting your understanding of what happens in your relationship. Filters lead people to see what they expect to see. There, the focus up to this point has been on how perception can be distorted because of filters.

In this chapter, we focus on your expectations as the way you think things are supposed to be in your relationship. You have specific expectations for such minor things as who refills the orange juice container or who balances the checkbook—the stuff of events. You have expectations about common issues, such as money, housework, family, and sex. You also have expectations for the deeper, often hidden, issues: how power is shared (or not shared), how caring is demonstrated, or what the commitment is in your relationship. Expectations affect everything!

To a large degree, we are disappointed or satisfied in life according to how well what is happening matches what we expected—what we think *should* happen. Therefore, expectation plays a crucial role in determining our level of satisfaction in marriage. As people, when our expectations match what we see we tend to be happy, but if they don't they are a source of frustration and discontent. If we don't expect a lot, what actually happens may easily exceed our expectations. If we expect too much, it's likely that what happens will fall short of what we desire. Thus, the key is to try to form realistic expectations about our spouse and how much we can expect what (and how) he or she thinks, to match what and how *we* think.

Consider Maxwell and Michelle, who have been married for just a couple of years. All things considered, things have gone pretty well for the couple. This is not to say that they don't have issues. One central issue for Michelle is about Maxwell hanging out with the boys. Like many young couples, they have a lot of expectations and issues to resolve about what's OK and what's not.

Maxwell goes out once or twice a week with the boys (longtime friends from high school). They usually go to one of the local bars, play pool, and drink forties. This drives Michelle nuts. Sometimes his going out starts huge arguments between them, like this one.

MICHELLE: (feeling agitated) I don't see why you have to go out again tonight. You've been out a lot lately.

MAXWELL: (obviously irritated, and rolling his eyes) How many times do we have to argue about this? I go out once a week, and that's it. So what's up?

MICHELLE: What is up is you drinking those forties. Those things are nasty and aren't good for you.

MAXWELL: Well, I like them.

MICHELLE: So, you don't think there's anything wrong with drinking those things and coming home drunk?

MAXWELL: (angered, feeling attacked) We don't drink that much, and we're always careful. You need to learn to trust me.

MICHELLE: I just don't think a married man needs to be hanging out at bars getting drunk with his friends. One of these nights you're going to get stopped by the police and be in a world of hurt.

MAXWELL: (turning away and walking toward the door) You ain't my mama. I'm a grown man and I can take care of myself. I'll be back by ten.

Maxwell and Michelle are arguing about an expectation. She didn't expect that he'd still go out with his friends so often after they got married. She associates the guys' going out with drinking too much and putting themselves in danger. Maxwell expects to cut back on the time with his boys, but not to stop seeing them altogether. These nights out mean a lot to him. He sees nothing wrong, except that Michelle worries too much.

In this example, you can't really argue that either expectation is extreme. What's much more important is that their expectations don't match, and this is fueling some conflict. You can easily imagine that hidden issues of caring and control are also at work. She could be worried about his health and the danger of being pulled over by the police. She really cares about his safety and wants to spend more time with him and feel that she is important. He could be feeling she's trying to control him, a feeling he does not respond to warmly.

When expectations are quite unreasonable, studies show that it's likely the relationship is distressed. Do you think Maxwell's or Michelle's expectations are unreasonable? Let's give another example where the answer to the question is obvious.

Stacey and Ron have been married for eleven years. He's an air conditioner repairman and she is a physician's assistant. Sex has become a huge issue over the years. If he had his way, they'd make love every night of the week, and some mornings too. Not only does he have a strong sex drive but he believes there is something wrong with a marriage if a couple doesn't make love at least five times a week.

Since Stacey only seems interested once or twice a week, Ron believes something is wrong with her, and he tells her so. Early in their marriage, she used to want to make love more. He expected they'd keep up that rate. She expected that they would make love less frequently.

Although his expectation about lovemaking is somewhat unreasonable, if Stacey shared it there would be no particular problem. Unless they can negotiate some way out of this problem, there is major conflict in the future.

## Expectations and Hidden Issues

When hidden issues are triggered by events, at times it's because some expectation is not being met. Underlying *power* issues are often related to expectations about how decisions and control are shared or not shared. Underlying *caring* issues are often about expectations as to how one is to be loved. Underlying *recognition* issues are expectations of how your partner should respond to who you are and what you do. Underlying *commitment* issues are expectations for how long the relationship should continue, and most important about safety from abandonment. Underlying *integrity* issues are expectations about being trusted and respected. Under all of them, there are core expectations about being *accepted*.

Hidden issues are frequently triggered by an expectation that is violated. In the last chapter, we described the argument when Altavist told Ruben he doesn't care because he failed to remember to call the telephone company. In doing so, she violates Ruben's expectation to be believed. Conversely, she has strong expectations about being cared for in a certain way that she doesn't feel are being met. The clash of expectations about these most basic issues can ignite conflict. It takes a lot of skill to keep such things from happening.

## Where Expectations Come From

Expectations build up over a lifetime of experiences. These expectations established in the past operate in the present. There are three primary sources for our expectations: family of origin, previous relationships, and the culture we live in.

### Family of Origin

We gain many expectations from the families we grow up in. Our family experiences lay down many patterns—good or bad— that become models for how we think things are supposed to work as adults. Expectations were transmitted both directly by what your parents said and indirectly by what you observed. Either way, you learned expectations in many areas of life. No one comes to marriage with a blank slate.

For example, if you observed your parents avoiding conflict, you may have developed the expectation that couples should seek peace at any price. If there's disagreement and conflict, it may seem to you as though the world is going to end.

If you observed your parents being very affectionate, you may have come to expect that in your marriage. If your parents divorced, you may have some expectation in the back of your mind that marriages don't really last. You get the idea.

Often, two people come from such different families that there is a great mismatch in some key expectations. Makelea and Curtis came from contrasting families. In hers, her father made virtually all the decisions. Curtis was raised by his mother, so she made all of the decisions. His mother left his father because he was abusive. His mother taught him to always treat his wife well and give her a say in everything.

Makelea and Curtis have had some trouble making decisions. She defers to Curtis for many decisions, and he finds this disturbing. He feels the pressure from all the responsibility. Given where he comes from, her letting him make all the decisions means that he is doing something wrong and that his marriage is failing. So he tries to get her to take more responsibility, while she tries to have him take charge. He sees himself as showing respect. She sees him as weak.

Because of their mismatched expectations, they experience many conflicts in the context of decision-making events. Hidden issues are easily triggered. She ends up feeling he doesn't care enough to lead. Although in many ways she is giving him a lot of control, he feels pushed into this role and controlled by her.

They are finally able to talk this through using the speaker-listener technique. Here is part of their breakthrough talk; you can see how they are able to get the issues on the table.

MAKELEA (SPEAKER): The key for me is that I've been expecting you to lead more, to make decisions, because that's what I grew up being used to.

CURTIS (LISTENER): So you've expected this from me because that's what you grew up to expect.

MAKELEA (SPEAKER): Exactly. I never really thought a lot about the expectation, but I can see that I've had it and that it's been affecting us.

CURTIS (LISTENER): So you're saying that while you've had this expectation, you haven't really thought a lot about it before. Yet you can see it's affected us negatively.

MAKELEA (SPEAKER): Yes. That's just what I mean.

[FLOOR SWITCH]

CURTIS (SPEAKER): I can understand better now why you've pushed me to make the decisions. I really want you to hear that it's not that I'm uncomfortable being responsible. But to me, sharing decisions is a way to show you respect.

MAKELEA (LISTENER): So what looked to me like you pushing off responsibilities was really you wanting to share with me in making decisions.

CURTIS (SPEAKER): Yes. That's it. Because of my own background, I've thought that our marriage would be hurt if I just went ahead and took all the control. I thought it meant I wasn't being sensitive to your needs.

MAKELEA (LISTENER): So you have had an expectation that was a lot different from mine, and that led you to worry that we'd have trouble if we didn't share in making decisions.

CURTIS (SPEAKER): And that's really been worrying me.

MAKELEA (LISTENER): It's really worried you because you weren't sure I cared.

CURTIS (SPEAKER): That's right.

They had a much easier time dealing with decisions once they began to talk openly about their expectations—where they came from and the effects on the relationship. Feeling heard, they had a much better shot at negotiating the expectations they wanted to *share* in *their* relationship.

Another couple, Patricia and Isaac, had terrible conflicts about child rearing. Patricia came from a home where her mother and stepfather were extremely harsh in their discipline. Sometimes she would be punished in front of her friends or in a store. She got punished for even small things no matter where she was. She got yelled at for the littlest thing.

Isaac came from a family where the kids could pretty much do whatever they wanted. There were limits, but they were pretty loose. So whenever their five-year-old son Jamie acts up, Isaac responds by raising his voice—but actually doing nothing to set limits on his behavior. Jamie has learned to all but ignore his raised voice. There are no real consequences.

With her background, Patricia expects that someone is about to get hurt when Isaac raises his voice. Her expectation was established in the past but still has real power. She even gets sick to her stomach from the tension if someone is about to get in trouble. It's as if her parents are embarrassing her all over again.

At times, she sees Isaac as being abusive even though he isn't. Her expectations become powerful filters, distorting her perception of what is really going on. Actually, Isaac, like his parents, is quite lenient. Sure, he loses his temper and yells from time to time, but he doesn't follow it with violence.

As a consequence of their expectations, neither Isaac nor Patricia provide consistent discipline for Jamie. The boy suffers for their lack of consistency. His teacher reports that he is one of the most difficult kids in the school. Jamie doesn't understand why the teacher is so insistent on him observing the class rules. What kind of expectations do you think he'll have when he grows up? What kind of implications do you think this has for a young African American male going through school? In this example, you can see how many expectations get handed down from generation to generation.

If we had the space, we could give literally thousands more examples. Suffice it to say, you and your partner have many expectations based on your families of origin. Understanding this basic fact is the first step in dealing effectively with those expectations and preventing increased conflict.

*Previous Relationships*

You have also developed expectations from all the other relationships in your life—most important, from previous dating relationships or an earlier marriage. You have expectations about how to kiss, what is romantic, how to communicate about problems, how recreational time should be spent, who should take the first move to make up after a fight, and so on.

Suppose, for example, that you found in previous dating relationships that when you begin to open up about painful childhood events, you get dumped. Logically, you might have developed the expectation that such a topic is off limits with certain people. On a deeper level, you may expect that people can't be trusted with knowing the deepest parts of who you are. If so, you'll pull back and withhold a level of intimacy in your present relationship.

Studies show that people who have come to expect that others can't be trusted have difficulty in relationships. If you look at such a person's entire life, it usually makes sense why there is such an expectation. Yet it can lead to trouble if the mistrust is so intense that the person can't even allow someone he or she really loves—such as a partner—to get close. This would be all the greater reason to learn how to make it safer for verbal intimacy in the relationship.

Many expectations are about such minor things that it's hard to imagine they could become so important. But they can. It all depends on what meanings and issues are attached to the expectations.

For example, Phillip's past girlfriend drilled it into him that she didn't want him opening doors for her. He thought, "Cool." Now, with his wife Janet, he finds quite the opposite. She likes men to hold doors, and she gets upset with him when he forgets. He has to work hard to unlearn the expectation he once learned so well.

Door-opening events happen pretty often in life. For Phillip and Janet, this triggers conflicts because she interprets his trouble remembering as a sign that he doesn't care about what is important to her. This is another example of negative interpretation causing more damage than the actual event. His devotion challenged, he gets angry at her. To her, his anger just confirms what she already believes: "I knew he didn't care."

Are you aware of how many expectations you have for your partner that are really based in experiences with others? It's worth thinking about this, since your partner isn't the same person as those you've known, dated, or been married to in the past. It may not be realistic or fair to hold the same expectations for your partner that you had with someone else in the past.

### Cultural Influences

A variety of factors from American culture influence our expectations. Television, movies, religious teachings, and what we read all have powerful effects on expectation.

What expectations do you have about marriage, for example, from watching thousands of hours of TV in America? For most of us, this is not a hypothetical question. Shows like "Moesha," "The Jeffersons," "Amen," the Wayan brothers, "The Cosby Show," and the BET network in general all send powerful messages about what is expected, acceptable, hip, and even what is black and what is not. Not to mention the daytime soaps and talk shows. What expectations do people learn from talk shows like those starring Jerry Springer or Jenny Jones, where people air their dirty laundry with real or made-up shows on the order of "I've been cheating with your best friend"?

## What to Do About Expectations

Expectations can lead either to massive disappointment and frustration or to deep connection between the two of you. There are three keys to handling expectations well:

1. Being *aware* of what you expect

2. Being *reasonable* in what you expect

3. Being *clear* about what you expect

*Being Aware of What You Expect*

Whether you are aware of them or not, unmet expectations can lead to great disappointment and frustration in your relationship. You don't have to be fully aware of the expectation to see it affect your relationship.

Clifford Sager, a pioneer in this field, noticed how people bring a host of expectations to marriage that are never made clear. These expectations form a contract for the marriage. The problem is, people are not told so clearly what's in the contract when they get married. Sager went further, to suggest that many expectations are virtually unconscious, which makes them hard to be aware of. We don't mean to say that all expectations are deeply unconscious. But many do become such a part of us that they function automatically. Like driving a car, much of what you do in a marriage is automatic; you don't even have to think about it.

At the end of this chapter, you have the opportunity to increase your awareness of your own expectations. One great clue to expectations is disappointment. If you're disappointed in your relationship, some expectation hasn't been met. It's a good habit to stop a minute when you sense disappointment and ask yourself what you expect. Doing this can help you become aware of important expectations that otherwise may be unconsciously effecting your relationship.

Chris is very disappointed that his wife, Kelly, doesn't want to go to Bible study with him on Saturday mornings. On Friday night, he always asks her if she is going to Bible study in the morning, and more often than not she says, "That's OK, go ahead without me and say a prayer for me." She'd rather try to get a few extra winks on Saturday. Chris feels that he lives a blessed life, and worshipping the Lord is an important part of his thanksgiving for all he has.

Kelly does her Bible study on her own and doesn't feel the need to worship with a group to keep up with reading her Bible.

Chris's sadness is a clue that there is some important expectation at work. In thinking about it, he realizes that he expected they would share this very important interest of his. If she doesn't, what does it mean? If nothing else, he feels torn between spending time with her and time worshipping.

Although Kelly loves him dearly, the expectation or hope that she will go to Bible study is really about connecting at a deep spiritual level. Once he is aware of his expectation and the reasons for his sadness, he can express what Bible study with her means to him. She has had no idea and is glad to come more often once she knows it means so much to him.

After becoming aware of an expectation, the next step is to consider if your expectation is really reasonable.

### Being Reasonable in What You Expect

As we noted earlier, many key expectations people have simply are not reasonable or realistic. Some unreasonable expectations are quite specific. For example, is it reasonable to expect that your partner will never seriously disagree with you? Of course not. Yet you'd be surprised just how many people expect it.

Another example of the unreasonable is to expect that once you're married, your partner will forsake all contact with old friends. Some people actually expect things like this, nonetheless.

Acting on unreasonable expectations is likely to lead to conflict. A specific example of this is Valarie and Randy. Both have high-pressure jobs in accounting, so it is critical that they learn how to handle conflict and free time well.

In counseling, they have made tremendous progress with all the techniques we presented in the early chapters of this book. They are handling what was significant conflict better than ever. Unfortunately, their progress is held back by Randy's expectation that, since they now possess these techniques, they won't have any more negative events. It's just not a reasonable expectation.

Meanwhile, Valarie feels really unappreciated for all the efforts she has made to change the relationship. Randy's unreasonable expectation colors everything so that minor conflicts are seen as evidence that they haven't made any progress at all. Not only does he expect they will no longer have conflict but this has become a perceptual filter leading him to miss all the great changes that actually are occurring.

We hope couples who consistently apply our principles will have fewer and less-intense negative events. But events will always happen, and sometimes issues will erupt in them. There's a difference between not having any issues and handling issues well. Randy's expectation leads him to discount virtually all the striking changes that are occurring in his marriage. His expectation of no conflict is unreasonable and actually generated a lot of conflict until we pushed him to take a hard look at it. To overcome it, he has had to become aware of the unrealistic expectation and challenge it within himself. It isn't an expectation for them to meet so much as it is one for Randy to change—and he has.

### Being Clear About What You Expect

A specific expectation may be perfectly reasonable but never clearly expressed. It's critical to express expectations, but not simply to be aware of them or evaluate their reasonableness. We all tend to assume that our model of the ideal marriage (made up of the sum total of our expectations) is the same as our partner's. Why should we have to tell our partner what we expect? In effect, we assume he or she knows what we expect.

This is actually a form of unreasonable expectation. You are assuming that your partner should know what you want, so you don't bother to make it clear enough.

For example, how many people make the assumption that their partner should know just what is most pleasing sexually? We see this over and over again. One or both partners are angry that the other is failing to meet a desire or expectation. But more often than not, they've never expressed their expectations. That's expecting your partner to be good at mind reading.

Worse, if key expectations are not read by one partner, it's easy for hidden issues to be triggered. The one with the unmet expectation can feel that the partner doesn't care because he or she hasn't figured out the expectation. We deal with the sexual problems that this causes in Chapter Thirteen.

Martha and Ray have regular eruptions of conflict whenever they go to his mother's house. Martha maintains an expectation that whenever they visit his family they will stay in a hotel nearby. Her issue is that she doesn't like being left alone in conversation with his mother, whom she perceives as prying into the secrets of their marriage. In contrast, Ray is thinking that he should give Martha as much opportunity as possible to get to know his mother. He often senses that Martha is distant after visiting, but he doesn't understand why.

Martha's expectation for Ray to stay with her at his mother's house is perfectly reasonable. Yet until she tells him that's what she wants, he is left to his own assumptions. He thinks she will like it when he goes to run errands for his mother, leaving Martha with his mother. Once she expresses her real expectation, he can act on it to help her have a better time. Unless you make your expectations clear, you'll have trouble working as a team. You can't work from any kind of shared perspective if you don't share your perspective. You need to be aware of your expectations, willing to evaluate them, and ready to discuss them. Otherwise, expectations have the power to trigger all the big issues in your relationship. Without dealing with them openly, you also miss an opportunity to define a mutual vision for how you want your marriage to be.

The exercise we are about to present is highly important. It takes time to do it well. It also takes considerable follow-up. We hope you can find the time and motivation to do the work. If you do, you will improve your understanding of mutual expectations. Combining this knowledge with the skills you are learning can have a major impact on the strength of your relationship, now and into the future.

## Exercise

1. Use this exercise to explore expectations of your relationship. Spend some time thinking carefully about each area. Then write your thoughts down so you can share them with your partner. Each of you should use a separate pad of paper. Each point below is meant to stimulate your *own* thinking. There may be numerous other areas where you have expectations. Please consider everything you can think of that seems significant to you. You won't get much out of this exercise unless you are able and willing to really put some time into it. Many couples have found such an exercise extremely beneficial for their relationship.

The goal is to consider expectations for how you want the relationship to be or think it should be, not how it is and not how you guess it will be. Write down what you expect, whether or not you think the expectation is realistic. The expectation matters and will affect your relationship whether or not it's realistic. Consider each question in light of what you expect and want for the future.

It's essential that you write down what you really think, not what sounds like the "correct" or least embarrassing answer.

It can be valuable to consider what you observed and learned in each area in your family growing up. This is probably where many of your beliefs about what you want or don't want come from.

What do you want regarding . . . (or how do you think things should be regarding . . .)

A. The longevity of this relationship? "Till death do us part?"

B. Sexual fidelity?

C. Love? Do you expect to love each other always? Do you expect this to change over time?

D. Your sexual relationship? Frequency? Practices? Taboos?

E. Romance? What is romantic for you?

F. Children (or more children)?

G. Children from previous marriage? If you or your partner have children from a previous marriage, where do you want them to live? How do you expect that you should share in disciplining them?

H. Work, career, and provision of income? Who will work in the future? Whose career or job is more important? If there are or will be children, will either partner reduce work time out of the home to take care of the children?

I. The degree of emotional dependency on the other? Do you want to be taken care of, and if so, how? How much do you expect to rely on each other to get through the tough times?

J. Basic approach to life? As a team? As two independent individuals?

K. Loyalty? What does that mean to you?

L. Communication about problems in the relationship? Do you want to talk them out, and if so, how?

M. Power and control? Who do you expect will have more power, and in what kind of decision? For example, who will control the money? Who will discipline the kids? What happens when you disagree in a key area? Who has the power now, and how do you feel about that?

N. Household tasks? Who do you expect will do what? How much household work will each of you do in the future? If you live together now, how does the current breakdown here match up with what you ideally expect?

O. Religious beliefs and observances? How, what, when, where? If you have no kids yet but plan to, what then?

P. Time together? How much time do you want to spend together (as opposed to spent with friends, at work, with family, and so on)?

Q. Sharing feelings? How much of what you are each feeling do you expect should be shared?

R. Friendship with your partner? What is a friend? What would it mean to maintain or have a friendship with your partner?

S. The little things in life? Where do you squeeze the toothpaste? Is the toilet seat left up or down? Who sends greeting cards? Really think about the little things that have irritated you or could irritate you (or that have been going really well). What do you want or expect in each area?

T. Forgiveness? How important is forgiveness in your relationship? How should forgiveness affect your relationship?

U. With your mind primed from all of the work above, consider again the hidden issues we described in the last chapter (power, caring, recognition, commitment, integrity, and acceptance). Do you now see any other ways that they influence or are influenced by expectations? What do you expect in these areas (if you haven't already gotten it from this exercise)?

V. List all the other expectations for how you want things to be that are important, that you are aware of, or that are not listed here already.

2. Now, go back to each area and rate the expectation on a scale of 1 to 10 for how reasonable you think the expectation really is. Use this scale:

**10 "Completely reasonable. I really think it is okay to expect this in this type of relationship."**

**1 "Completely unreasonable. I can honestly say that while I expect or want this, it just is not a reasonable expectation in this type of relationship."**

For example, suppose you grew up in a family where problems were not discussed and you are aware that you honestly expect or prefer to avoid such discussions. You might now rate that expectation as not very reasonable.

Next, place a big check mark by each expectation in the full list that you feel you have never clearly discussed with your partner.

3. After you and your partner have finished the entire exercise so far, begin to plan time and spend time together discussing these expectations. *Please don't do this all at once.* You should plan on a number of discussions, each covering only one or two expectations. Discuss the degree to which you each feel that the expectation being discussed has been shared clearly in the past.

4. Talk out the degree to which you both feel the expectations are reasonable or unreasonable, and discuss what you want to agree to do about these.

5. Talk about what your overall, long-term vision is for the relationship. What expectations do you share about your future together?

From the standpoint of giving you a lot to think about, we expect that this is one of the hardest chapters in this book. In addition to going carefully through the exercises, you might want to read over the chapter once or twice more. Really think through what your key expectations are and how they affect your relationship.

In the next chapter, we move on to the concept of commitment. This is a topic of great importance for relationships, one in which people have quite a few expectations.

# 8

# Stickin' Together
## Commitment

On the underground railroad, we had to stick together to make it to the north. What an example of teamwork that was. Why don't African Americans do that today?

Perhaps more than any other type of relationship, marriage is founded on mutual commitment between partners. Most African American couples consider commitment the backbone of their marriage. Put another way, commitment is the glue that holds it all together. Therefore, one of the most important things to consider in fighting for your marriage is your level of commitment to marriage in general, and to your partner in particular. It is important for you to think about the ways of being committed, and what they mean to how your marriage is likely to do over time.

## Two Kinds of Commitment?

In our research and study, we have identified two broad attitudes toward commitment in an African American marriage: feeling trapped (or what we call the "ball and chain" attitude toward staying together) or feeling dedicated and devoted to working together forever (which we call the "full commitment" kind of marriage). Let's take a look at some examples of how this works in typical African American marriages.

## Ball and Chain

Freddy and Letanya (who are the friends mentioned by Barbara and Glenn in Chapter Four) have been married seven years. They met at a National Black Leadership Conference when they were both in their third year of college, Fred at Morehouse and Letanya at North Carolina A & T. During their senior year, dating long distance, Letanya got pregnant. Her mother put constant pressure on her to keep the baby. Freddy and Letanya decided to marry after they graduated and before their baby, Freddy Jr., was born. Letanya's mother was happy and helped with the cost of prenatal care.

Since that time, the couple have had another child, Sonia. So their married lives have always involved raising children. In addition, Letanya's mother is constantly telling the couple how to raise Freddy Jr. ("Don't let him sleep on his back; don't feed him carrots because babies can't digest them. . . ."). Many of her mother's suggestions are old wives' tales and not at all in agreement with what she has read in books. The lack of agreement between her mother's ways and what she is learning causes her stress. Between Letanya's mother and raising two children, they don't have much time alone. When they are alone, it is hard for them to know what to do as a couple. It has become increasingly apparent that they have little in common, and they don't know how to redefine their relationship.

Soon after Sonia turned three, Letanya goes back to work full-time. Having majored in communications, she has found an opportunity to get in on the fast track to a management position with a local TV station. The station wants to hire an African American to show their commitment to diversity. However, they are overly cautious about putting the "right person" of color on the air to represent them. Letanya knows this means proving her worth and dedication to the higher ups, which translates into long hours and an irregular schedule. Her mother makes herself available to help out (and put more of her two cents in about how the children are being raised).

At the same time, Freddy wants to take some time off from his job, leave the kids with his parents, and take a week-long vacation. But Letanya isn't interested. She is afraid she will miss out on the break she is looking for to move up and get regular hours so she can be with her family more. Freddy thinks, *If we could just get away, the two of us, we could get things straight.*

The more Letanya gets involved in her work, the more she looks back on her marriage and isn't very happy or satisfied. She has even thought about divorce a couple of times. Freddy also feels unhappy in the marriage, but he hasn't thought much about divorce because he knows how much his church frowns on it. He hopes for more in the relationship and doesn't understand why she wants to spend so much time at her job and away from him. He doesn't understand why the kids have to spend so much time with her mother. He also feels tired of trying to do things, like getting away for a week. He has gotten tired and is beginning to feel that it is no longer worth investing much energy in the marriage because he does not see anything coming back from her. The tension between them continues to escalate.

Letanya feels that she has put more into the marriage than Freddy but has seen little in return for her time and effort. As a black woman trying to get a start in the communications industry, she is under a lot of pressure. She also feels pressure to raise her kids on her own. She resents that he doesn't seem to appreciate all she's done for him in providing support, making a home, trying to increase their income, and taking care of the kids. She wonders why he cannot be more supportive now that she's finally getting a chance to concentrate on her career. Both have come to a place of scorekeeping, with neither faring well on the other's scorecard.

As Letanya thinks about divorce, she grapples with difficult questions. First, she wonders how their children will respond to divorce. Will she have to rely even more on her mother? How can she better balance her career and family, given how difficult it is already? Will she be able to provide for them everything they have now? Will she be able to give Freddy Jr. what he will need to be a good black man? Will Freddy let her go or put up a fight of some sort?

As Letanya considers these questions, she decides the costs of getting a divorce may be greater than she wants to bear, at least for now. She's not happy in the marriage, but she doesn't feel she has the financial base to leave. She may well stay, but she does not feel like investing much with Freddy at this point. She feels trapped; Freddy is her ball and chain.

## Full Commitment

Karin and D'Andre were married twelve years ago. They have two boys, eleven and nine. They have few regrets about marrying one another but have been through some really stressful times. Having children turned out to be much more difficult than either imagined. Both children had health problems: their older son, Sammy, had difficulty with his eyesight, and Shawn has attention deficit disorder and requires a lot of their time. D'Andre became a store manager for a national retail store and Karin stayed at home with the kids. During their first few years of marriage, D'Andre's job didn't pay benefits, so even though he now makes good money they are in a lot of debt from health care for the kids when they were younger.

Despite these challenges, Karin and D'Andre enjoy each other's support as they face life together. Almost everyone has occasional moments of regret about marrying, but these times are rare for this couple. Partly for their boys and partly because of their faith, they resist thinking about divorce, even during rough times. More important, they regularly do things that affirm their mutual dedication. They talk about what they want to do in the future, such as taking the boys on a vacation to the Blacks in Wax Museum in Baltimore. They change their schedules to accommodate each other's needs— a kind of sacrifice. Each has resisted the temptation to dwell on what-ifs when they have money troubles, or frustration with D'Andre's job, or with dealing with the children's needs.

They genuinely respect and like each other, do things for each other, and talk about their struggles with living in an all-white neighborhood. They have developed their trust for one another over years of hard work and struggle. They claim that being able to communicate their feelings in a secure relationship is one of the keys that have helped them. They also talk about their dreams and aspirations for their marriage and for life. Most of all, they keep a clear emphasis on *we* as they go through life. Simply put, they feel like a team.

As we can see from these stories, Freddy and Letanya and D'Andre and Karin have very different marriages. Freddy and Letanya are pretty miserable, and D'Andre and Karin are enjoying life. Both marriages reflect commitment of a sort, and both are likely to continue for the time being. But these marriages do show contrast in commitment. It's not just the level of happiness that differentiates them. D'Andre and Karin have a much fuller kind of commitment than Letanya and Fred have right now. To understand the difference, we need to better understand what commitment is all about.

## Dedication or Constraint?

Ask yourself what comes to mind when you think about commitment. There are two common responses. The commitment of *personal dedication* refers to the desire to maintain or improve the quality of the relationship for the mutual benefit of both partners. Personal dedication is characterized by a desire not only to continue in the relationship but also to improve it; sacrifice for it; invest in it; link personal goals to it; and seek the partner's welfare, not just one's own.

In contrast, *constraint commitment* refers to forces that keep individuals in a relationship whether or not they're dedicated. Constraint commitment may arise from external or internal pressures. Constraints help keep a couple together by making ending the relationship economically, socially, personally, or psychologically costly.

If dedication is low, constraints can keep people in a relationship they might otherwise want to leave.

Letanya and Freddy have a commitment characterized by constraint. She in particular is feeling pressure to continue the marriage, but with very little dedication to him. She feels compelled to stay for a host of reasons: their kids, money pressure, family opinions, and so on. She knows that as a black single mother, she will not find such opportunity to advance and make a career because people will think she is unreliable and will always have to take care of her kids ahead of her job. Freddy also has high constraint commitment and little dedication, though he's less dissatisfied with their day-to-day life.

Like those two, Karin and D'Andre have a good deal of constraint commitment, but they also have a strong sense of *dedication* to each other. Constraints are a normal part of marriage, and they accumulate with time and the developmental changes that most marriages go through. For example, when a couple goes from engagement to marriage, the constraints increase. Likewise, in going from married without children to married with children, there is a substantial increase in constraint. The point is that any marriage generates a significant amount of constraint over time. Happy, dedicated couples are just as likely as less happy couples to have considerable constraints, but happier couples just don't think a lot about the constraints (and when they do they often draw comfort from them).

Constraints are a matter of fact in marriage—and mostly function positively to provide a rootedness together—but it is dedication that hovers around the all-important day-to-day decisions we make in our marriages. Dedication is the aspect of commitment that you make regular choices about, and those choices have a lot to do with how good your marriage will be in the years to come.

Enough about constraints. Let's focus on what constitutes the strongest glue holding a relationship together.

# The Commitment of Personal Dedication

The most common feature of dedication in a strong relationship is *wanting the relationship to continue* into the future: wanting and expecting your relationship to last, so that you can grow old together. It's a core part of dedication. This long-term expectation for the relationship to continue plays a critical role in the day-to-day quality of a marriage. One man in his early thirties said, "I know what else is out there on the dating scene. It is hard to hook up with someone who is professional because either they're working or I am. I wanted a strong black woman in my life, and I waited, searched, and found one I can't think of living without." This is the motivating factor for him to work on resolving issues and keeping his marriage alive. Through this motivation he has a force to drive doing his part to develop a full commitment with his spouse.

But we have learned that there are other important features of dedication in a strong African American relationship.

## The Priority of the Relationship

Priority is the importance you give your relationship relative to everything else. If people are dedicated to their partner, they are likely to make decisions for the relationship when it competes with other things for time and attention. By contrast, if dedication is weak, the relationship is likely to take a back seat to things like work, hobbies, and kids. To some degree, this can reflect as much a problem with overinvolvement elsewhere as with lack of dedication.

Unfortunately, as people get busier and busier, too many partners end up doing what I (SMS) call, in my book *The Heart of Commitment*, "no-ing" each other rather than knowing each other ("No, I don't have time to talk, page me later"; "No, I can't take Friday off to make it to the doctor appointment; I have that project that has to be done"; "No, I promised Tyrone I'd come over Saturday and watch the game"). To protect your relationship at this crucial time of transition, you have to be good at saying no to some of the other things in your life that seem important but that really don't matter nearly as much in the long run as your happiness together.

Unfortunately, Freddy and Letanya have allowed their marriage to become a low priority, and they're suffering for it. Their marriage isn't so much bad as it is neglected. It's possible to turn things around. By contrast, Karin and D'Andre are truly important to each other. There are times when D'Andre feels Karin is overly focused on Shawn and his ADD, but he doesn't seriously doubt he matters to his wife. Likewise, Karin sometimes thinks D'Andre is too involved with work but recognizes his dedication to her.

*We-ness*

"We-ness" refers to the degree to which one views the relationship as a team rather than two separate individuals focusing mostly on what's best for themselves. The *we* transcends the *I* in thinking about the relationship. It's crucial to have a sense of an identity together if the relationship is to be satisfying and growing. Without this sense of being a team, conflict is likely, since problems are seen as me against you instead of us against the problem. Our research clearly shows that couples who are thriving in their marriages have a strong sense of *us*. In African American marriages, this *us* takes on a grand meaning of us against the world. Each partner feels he or she has the other's support in dealing with family issues or racist provocation.

We aren't suggesting that you should merge your identity and lose your individual sense of self. Most couples do best with a clear sense of two individuals coming together to form a team. Dedicated couples experience this sense of being a team. Instead of selfishly grappling to get their own way, they feel the team's goals are at least as important as their individual goals. What a difference this makes in how they view life together. One couple in a focus group reported that the best part of their marriage was their "shared struggles and accomplishments and having survived life stresses as a couple."

## Satisfaction with Sacrifice

The next aspect of commitment is the degree to which two people feel a sense of satisfaction in doing things that are largely or solely for the partner's benefit. The point is not to find pleasure in being a martyr, but to find joy in an honest choice to give of yourself for your partner. Research indicates that people who are doing the very best in their marriages are those who feel best about giving to one another—and they are also those who report that they would give up the most for their marriage and their partner. In these marriages, partners get pleasure from giving to one another. A relationship is generally strong if both partners are willing to make sacrifices. In the absence of this willingness to sacrifice, what do spouses have? A relationship in which at least one is in it mostly for what he or she can get, with little focus on what the person can give. That's not a recipe for happiness or growth.

Letanya and Freddy have stopped giving to each other. He doesn't think he'll get anything back if he gives more, and she already feels she's given more than her share. Neither feels like sacrificing anything at this point. They've lost the sense of *us* and of a clear, long-term future that promotes giving to one another without resentment.

## Alternative Monitoring

Alternative monitoring refers to how much you keep an eye out for another possible partner. The more you are attracted to or attuned to a potential partner, the less personal dedication you show to your current partner. Do you find yourself frequently or *seriously* thinking about being with people other than your spouse? We must emphasize *seriously*, because almost everyone is attracted to someone else from time to time.

Dedication is in jeopardy if your attraction to others becomes strong (especially if you have a particular person in mind). There is some research evidence that highly dedicated people actually mentally devalue attractive potential partners in the process of protecting their commitment to their spouse. This is something you have a choice about. D'Andre has been tempted a couple of times by people at work, especially a woman named TeTe. Aware of the attraction, D'Andre considers it a threat to his marriage and makes himself focus more on TeTe's negative aspects than dwelling on her positives. Though tempted to look, he focuses on why the grass *isn't* greener on the other side of the fence. If you're planning on keeping your marriage strong, keep your focus on tending to your own lawn.

## How Does Commitment Develop?
## How Does Dedication Die?

Dedication is believed to develop mostly out of the initial attraction and satisfaction in a relationship. Think back to how you got involved with your partner. Because you liked being together, you became dedicated to staying together.

As your dedication to one another became apparent, you may have noticed you were relaxed about the relationship. In most relationships, there's an awkward period during which the desire to be together is great but the commitment is unclear. This produces anxiety about whether or not the two will stay together and how much they are willing to risk (physically, emotionally, financially, and so on) in the relationship. As mutual dedication grows clear, it seems increasingly safe to invest in the relationship.

Here is where the interplay between dedication and constraint becomes really interesting. Because of your dedication, you make decisions that increase constraint. For example, as dedication grows, you decide to go from a dating relationship to an engaged relationship. As dedication grows further, you decide to get married, buy furniture, buy a home, have children, and so on. Each of these steps, taken as a reflection of the current level of dedication, adds to the constraint. Essentially, today's dedication becomes tomorrow's constraint. It's normal for the level of constraint to grow in marriage, but it's more a decision of your will as to whether or not dedication withers or grows.

Greater dedication usually leads to greater satisfaction, and dedication grows out of satisfaction in the first place. When truly dedicated, people are likely to behave in ways that protect their marriage and please the partner. The effect on satisfaction is strongly positive. It's comforting to see that your mate really cares about you and protects your relationship from the alternatives available.

If most couples have a high level of dedication early on, such as when they are engaged or early in their marriage, then what happens to mess up dedication over time? For one thing, if conflict isn't handled well, satisfaction with the marriage steadily declines. Because satisfaction fuels dedication, dedication begins to erode. With dedication in jeopardy, giving to one another erodes further, and satisfaction takes a big dive.

The secret to satisfying commitment is to maintain not just constraint but also dedication at a high level. Although constraint commitment can add a positive, stabilizing dimension to your marriage, it can't give you a great relationship. Dedication is the side of commitment that is associated with a great relationship. Dedicated couples report more satisfaction with their relationship, less conflict about the problems they have, and a greater level of self-disclosure. Dedication can seem like an overwhelming issue that involves years of work and sacrifice. It is much easier, though, to think about dedication as a day-to-day thing that you have a lot of control over. Being dedicated is part of the package of responsibility, constraint, and choice you accept if you want to have a solid marriage.

Now that we have a better understanding of commitment, let's focus on how to apply some of this information to maintaining a healthy and long-lasting marriage by considering the special topics of selfishness and the importance of the long view.

## Overcoming Selfishness

American culture encourages devotion to self. In contrast, notions of sacrifice, teamwork, placing a high priority on our partner, and a dedicated relationship are part of many African cultures. The more we attempt to achieve economic success, the more we are separated from those African ideas. As we have become integrated into American culture and become who we are today, African Americans, we have relied more on the ideas of "rugged individualism." The problem is that we have so few opportunities that are afforded us, we end up like "crabs in a basket" if we don't help others succeed. In fact, American society seems to glorify self and vilify whatever gets in the way. As African Americans, we are often hurt, not helped, by chasing that part of the American Dream.

Dedication to one's partner and perhaps less to oneself is fundamental to a healthy relationship. Selfishness is fundamentally destructive to a marriage. It may sell as a means to economic prosperity in this country, but it doesn't bring about a lifelong happy marriage. For the African American couple, dedication involves sharing the American Dream, which can be thought to embody economic prosperity and freedom to enjoy the fruits of one's labor. The African American couple working as a team dedicated to shared achievement has always prospered.

Dedication is more about being team-centered or other-centered than self-centered. To be team-centered is to be sensitive to your partner, take your partner's perspective, seek to build your partner up, and protect your partner (in an appropriate way) because you are a team. It means making your partner's health and happiness a priority. It means doing what you know is good for your relationship—such as listening to your partner—even if you don't particularly want to. It means protecting your commitment from alternative attractions. This doesn't mean that you don't take care of business. Quite the contrary. It means balancing your life by doing your part in the relationship while keeping your eye on the prize of financial security for your family. It's a tough balancing act that takes time and practice.

Just as the long-term view is important, these acts of giving to one another are particularly crucial when you are in a major transition, such as having a first child or entering the empty nest. Your life is in upheaval of a sort now, and it's going to be for some time to come as you adjust to this new stage of marriage. If this is the first born or last child to leave, the change in who you are as a couple is really profound. It's the best possible time to demonstrate your commitment to one another by solid teamwork and active giving of yourself to the other.

Selfish attitudes and behavior can and will kill a relationship. Such attitudes aren't compatible with dedication. Dedication reflects we-ness, and at times sacrifice. You just can't have a great marriage if each partner is primarily focused on what's best for self. In a culture that reinforces self, it's hard to ask oneself, *What can I do to make this better?* It's a lot easier to ask, *What can my partner do to make me happier?*

We are *not* advocating martyrdom. In the way the term is commonly used, a martyr does things for you not out of concern for what is best for you, but because the martyr wants to put you in debt. This is not dedication. It's usually insecurity and selfishness masquerading as doing good.

The key is to think about not only what you do for your partner but also why you do it. Do you do things with the attitude that "You'd better appreciate what I'm doing"? Do you often feel your partner owes you? There's nothing wrong with doing positive things and wanting to be appreciated. But there is something wrong with believing you are owed, as if your positive behavior is building up a debt for your partner. The kind of deeply intimate, caring, and lasting marriage most people seek is built and maintained on dedication to one another, expressed in the kind of constructive behavior we advocate throughout this book. Too many people are self-centered too much of the time; they'll never truly experience the kind of relationship they deeply desire.

## The Importance of a Long-Term View

At the heart of it, if people are fully committed they have a long-term outlook on the relationship. This is crucial for one simple reason: *no relationship is consistently satisfying.* What carries a couple through hard times is the long-term view that commitment brings. There's an expectation that the relationship will make it through thick and thin.

We're not saying every couple should devote Herculean effort to saving the marriage they find themselves in, since some marriages are abusive or destructive. However, for the great number of couples who genuinely love each other and want to make their marriage work, a long-term perspective is essential for encouraging each partner to take risks, disclose about self, and trust that the other will be there when it really counts. In the absence of a long-term view, people tend to focus on the immediate payoff. This is only natural. If the long run is uncertain, we concentrate on what we are getting in the present.

As opposed to feeling *accepted*—a core issue for everyone—there is pressure to perform when commitment is unclear. The message is, "You'd better produce, or I'll look for someone who can." Most of us resent feeling we could be abandoned by someone from whom we expect to find security and acceptance. Any major transition in life can raise issues that we thought were long settled. So much can change at once. Joint understanding of the commitment can become unsettled, and if not dealt with it fuels doubtful commitment, an underlying issue (hidden or not) affecting the quality of your marriage. A great marriage is simply not possible if the commitment becomes unsettled. A quote from M. Scott Peck's *The Road Less Traveled* embodies what we mean here: "Couples can not resolve in any healthy way the universal issues of marriage—dependency and independence, dominance and submission, freedom and fidelity, for example—without the security of knowing that the act of struggling over these issues will not destroy the relationship" (1985, p. 141).

People generally do not invest in a relationship with an uncertain future and reward. For example, Freddy and Letanya are held together mostly by constraint. There isn't the sense of a future together that comes from both dedication and constraint, and they are suffering greatly for it. A couple who have a strong expectation of a future rooted in balanced commitment talk about plans for life together. They have maintained their commitment, especially dedication. They do things for one another, show respect, and protect their marriage in terms of priorities and alternatives.

The long-term view allows each partner to give the other some slack, leading to greater acceptance of weaknesses and failings over time. Whereas Freddy and Letanya experience anxiety or resentment around the core issue of acceptance, D'Andre and Karin feel the warmth of a secure commitment—each conveying the powerful message "I'll be here for you." This is the essence of what commitment is about. It's not only believing you will be there for one another in the future; it's that you can count on one another through the ups and downs of life.

## Renewing Your Commitment

In recent years, it has become popular for couples to reaffirm their love and commitment at some later point in life. Often, such ceremonies are performed in a religious service, much like so many wedding services that begin marriages. For some couples, an event of this kind means declaring before others the reality of a commitment that has not wavered. For others, it means reclaiming what has weakened through a decision to renew personal dedication.

You may or may not like this idea, as it is commonly done. You may not be religious, or you may simply be a private person who does not care to engage in a public event. However, any couple in which both partners are willing can plan some way of reaffirming the love and commitment that they started with, whether they've been married thirty years or two.

You could go away to some place special, perhaps a place with historical meaning—such as where you took your honeymoon, or back to homecoming at the black college where you first met, or maybe even to Africa. You could plan some ongoing activity that has great symbolic value to the two of you in affirming your union. Dancing lessons? Commitment to some public service as a team, such as Big Brothers Big Sisters of America? We don't know what would be most meaningful to you, but if the two of you like the idea a little thought will lead you to a plan that has great meaning for you both.

When you break it down, commitment is about knowing you will be there for each other in the future and that you can count on one another in the present. There's no better time of life than now to do all you can to affirm your commitment to one another.

## Exercises

Here are several exercises to help you get the most out of this chapter. You have the opportunity to examine your constraint and dedication commitment, consider your priorities, and think about rededicating your devotion to one another.

1. *Assessing constraint commitment.* Jot down your answer to each item using this scale to indicate how true the statement seems to you.

**1 = strongly disagree, 4 = neither agree nor disagree,
7 = strongly agree**

The steps I would need to take to end        1  2  3  4  5  6  7
this relationship require a great deal of
time and effort.

A marriage is a sacred bond between          1  2  3  4  5  6  7
two people, which should not be broken.

I would have trouble finding a suitable      1  2  3  4  5  6  7
partner if this relationship ended.

My friends or family really want this        1  2  3  4  5  6  7
relationship to work.

I would lose valuable possessions if I left  1  2  3  4  5  6  7
my partner.

I stay in this relationship partly because   1  2  3  4  5  6  7
my partner would be emotionally
devastated if I left.

I couldn't make it financially if we broke   1  2  3  4  5  6  7
up or divorced.

My lifestyle would be worse in many          1  2  3  4  5  6  7
ways if I left my partner.

I feel trapped in this relationship.         1  2  3  4  5  6  7

It is important to finish what you have      1  2  3  4  5  6  7
started, no matter what.

Your answers to these few questions can tell you a lot. What constraints are you aware of? How powerful are they? What kind of constraint seems most powerful?

Most important, do you feel trapped or stuck? Just about everyone does from time to time, which is normal. Having a good deal of constraint but not feeling trapped is normal for a healthy couple. The best relationships are those in which both partners are dedicated to each other and feel comfortable with the stability implied by constraint.

2. *Assessing dedicated commitment.* These next items help you gauge your level of dedication. Use the same rating scale you used to examine constraint commitment.

**1 = strongly disagree, 4 = neither agree nor disagree, 7 = strongly agree**

Jot your responses on a separate piece of paper.

| | |
|---|---|
| My relationship with my partner is more important to me than almost anything else in my life. | 1  2  3  4  5  6  7 |
| I want this relationship to stay strong no matter what rough times we may encounter. | 1  2  3  4  5  6  7 |
| It makes me feel good to sacrifice for my partner. | 1  2  3  4  5  6  7 |
| I like to think of myself and my partner in terms of *us* and *we* more than *me, him,* or *her.* | 1  2  3  4  5  6  7 |
| I am not seriously attracted to anyone other than my partner. | 1  2  3  4  5  6  7 |
| My relationship with my partner is clearly part of my future life plans. | 1  2  3  4  5  6  7 |
| When push comes to shove, my relationship with my partner comes first. | 1  2  3  4  5  6  7 |
| I tend to think about how things affect us as a couple more than how they affect me as an individual. | 1  2  3  4  5  6  7 |
| I don't often find myself thinking about what it would be like to be in a relationship with someone else. | 1  2  3  4  5  6  7 |
| I want to grow old with my partner. | 1  2  3  4  5  6  7 |

We can give you an idea of what your score means on these dedication items. To calculate your score, simply add up your ratings for each item. In our research—with a sample of people who were mostly happy and dedicated in their relationships (including people married for more than thirty years)—the average person scored about 58 on the items in this scale. If you scored at or above 58, we'd bet you're pretty highly dedicated. However, your dedication may be quite low if you scored below 45. Whatever your score, think about what it may mean for the future of your marriage.

3. *Considering priorities.* An important way to look at dedication is to consider your priorities. How do you actually live your life? What does this say about your commitment?

Take a piece of paper you can divide into three columns. In the first column, list what you consider your top five priorities in life, with number one being the most important. Possible priority areas might be work and career, your partner, adult children, religion, house and home, sports, future goals, education, possessions, hobbies, pets, friends, relatives, coworkers, television, car. Feel free to list whatever is important to you. Be as specific as you can.

Next, in the second column, list what you think *your partner* would say are *your* top five priorities. For example, if you think your partner would say "work" is your top priority, list that as item one.

In the third column, list what *you* believe are *your partner's* top five priorities.

When both of you have completed your lists, compare them. Don't be defensive. Consider how the answers each of you have given affect your relationship as a couple. If you see a need to make your relationship a higher priority, talk together about specific steps you can take to make this happen. You might find it helpful to use the problem-solving process you learned in Chapter Seven. The next chapters in this book are about enhancing your relationship. They provide additional suggestions of how to make your relationship a high priority.

4. *Rededication of your devotion.* The idea we raised near the end of this chapter, about a rededication celebration, may not be for everyone. We want to encourage the two of you to consider whether or not there is some idea there that is right for the two of you. If you are open to the basic idea, don't try to come to a decision about how to enact it too quickly. Plan some time for brainstorming. Come up with all the ideas you can, and see what jumps out at you. You may find several ideas have real meaning and appeal. You could even plan to do a number of them!

# 9

# Core Belief Systems
## Religious, Spiritual, and Otherwise

We've discussed how to enhance your relationship with a focus on friendship, fun, and physical intimacy. Now we're going to look at how spiritual or religious dimensions tend to influence and enhance the overall quality of the relationship for many couples.

Let us start off by saying that we see a difference between spiritual and religious dimensions of your marriage. Our thinking is that the religious dimension of your marriage has to do with the activities that you do, such as going to church, tithing, church bake sales, Bible study, and even ministering to others. We see spirituality as the personal relationship, the belief, the prayer that you engage in to develop your relationship with God.

As African Americans, we owe much of our existence to the strength we have found in the church. Although we know how important the church is for many African American couples, the challenge here is to try to capture how religion and spirituality play out not in church but in the relationship issues for a couple.

If you aren't at all religious or spiritually inclined, you may think that we aren't saying anything relevant to you and your marriage. Or if you're very committed to a particular faith, you might see this chapter as watered down, or too secular. Either way, we now invite you to explore the kind of impact these dimensions can have on a relationship. We want to point the way for you and your partner to have intimacy-enhancing discussion on these core issues.

African Americans are known for participating in Baptist churches, but of course we also attend Presbyterian, American Methodist Episcopal (AME), Catholic, and Lutheran churches in large numbers. One of the other major religions for African Americans, which became particularly popular starting in the 1960s and 1970s, is Islam. Since the time of slavery in this country, the church, in its many forms, has been a source of strength for the African American family. Even today as we struggle with economic inequality, racism, and the ravages of drugs and violence in many of our communities, one of our saving graces is the church. It gives us guidance, direction, and a sense of moral grounding in a world that is often quite short on morality. For the African American family, it is truly the guiding institution for establishing how we raise our children, how we treat our spouses, and the importance of our mothers and fathers no matter what age we are.

Our religion gives us many core beliefs about life, its meaning, and how one should live. We must keep clear that as we talk about church there are two parts to it: the traditions that we follow for our particular religion, and the deeper spiritual relationship.

Most of the research we describe here is based on religious beliefs and practices rather than spirituality. This is because you can't conduct research on things you can't measure, and although it's not hard to measure religious activity or even core beliefs, it's extremely difficult to measure spirituality. We're not saying spirituality isn't important; it's just that most of the research is on religious *behavior*.

## Research on Religious Involvement

The impact of religion on marriage has been studied for years. Most of this research has been conducted with those involved in traditional religious systems, particularly along the Judeo-Christian spectrum. You may not be in of one of those traditions, but there are implications from these studies that can benefit any couple. This is because many religions codify core beliefs, values, and practices as promoting stability and health in relationships. Our goal here is to *decode* these findings and highlight key implications for all couples, religious or not.

## Who Gets Married?

Religious people are more likely to get married in the first place. Bernard Spilka is a colleague of ours at the University of Denver and an expert in the scientific study of religion. He attributes the lower rate of marriage among the nonreligious to two factors. First, religious involvement brings people together. Even Ann Landers seems to regularly suggest that singles go to church or synagogue to meet people.

Second, Spilka points out that people who are less religious are, in general, less conforming; they don't tend to see themselves fitting in to a variety of traditional structures in society. Therefore, they may be less interested in institutions such as marriage.

## Religion and Marital Quality

Many studies show that religious involvement is, on average, beneficial to most couples in marriage. For example, couples who are more religious tend to be a bit more satisfied in their marriage. They're also less likely to divorce. In one of our studies, married subjects who rated themselves high on religious behavior showed a somewhat higher level of satisfaction, a lower level of conflict about common issues, and a higher level of commitment than those who rated themselves low.

Those who are religious were also likely to say that divorce is wrong, especially those who are conservative. They were likely to report being satisfied in sacrificing for one another and having a strong sense of couple identity. These findings make sense, given the values that are emphasized in traditional religious groups.

It's not that more religious couples have substantially better marriages. The effects we're talking about are consistent and statistically significant, but the difference is also often rather small. One major study found that greater religious involvement only led to fewer thoughts and plans about divorce, but not greater happiness. But many studies do show the positive effects. It would be most accurate to say that something about the factors associated with religious involvement gives couples an edge in keeping a marriage strong.

Given that the relationship between religious involvement and marital success is weak but consistent, various researchers have sought to better understand what kind of religious involvement matters most when it comes to maintaining a happy and healthy marriage. A number of major studies suggest that the protective benefits of religious involvement are strongest for those partners who actively practice their faith together. Of course, this is hard to do if they have differing faiths or other core beliefs. Let's look at that situation next.

Annette Mahoney, Kenny Pargament, and their colleagues at Bowling Green State University conducted one of the most impressive studies ever done on religious life and marriage. As in other studies, they found that such factors as being religious and having similar faith backgrounds benefit couples. But far more important, they discovered that what matters most is what couples do together in their religious practice.

Couples who actively practiced their faith together and who tended to view marriage as having a special spiritual meaning tended to be happier, have less conflict, work more as a team, and engage in less of what we have called danger signs. What this all means is that there seems to be something particularly protective of marriage in the partners' viewing their marriage in light of their faith and in actively practicing their faith together. Among many possible benefits that these couples receive, it's likely that these dynamics contribute to a powerful sense of being on the same page in life.

If you and your partner are not religious, you may have experienced something like this if you share other core beliefs in life. This is even more likely if they are beliefs you act on or that contribute to a mutual worldview. Take the chance presented to you in working through this book to explore what each of you believes and what it all means for how you live your life.

## Interfaith Marriage

Because of profound changes in society, people are now far more likely to marry out of their faith than they used to be in the past. Interfaith marriages are less of an issue because many Protestant religions have similar worship traditions and beliefs. This is definitely not to say that they are all the same. As we African Americans try to achieve economic success, we have frequently had to move away from our families, home towns, and many times from our connections with a religious community. This can make it hard to maintain regular worshipping; intermarriage and divorce become more likely.

Many of us are told that if you want to find a good girl or guy, you need to go to church. People who grow up with religious education are likely to marry within their faith. Finding someone who matches your faith probably becomes a higher priority the more you are strongly grounded in it.

Whatever the reasons for interfaith marriage, research consistently shows that such couples are likely to divorce. No nationally representative studies have looked at this, but various studies suggest there is an increased risk for an interfaith marriage. It seems likely that these effects would be related to the degree of commitment one has to one's faith. When people of different backgrounds marry but maintain little allegiance to those backgrounds, we would assume the risks for divorce are lower.

Many interfaith marriages start out just fine, with couples thinking they can beat the odds; love will conquer all. Although love can conquer a lot—especially if translated into loving and respectful behavior—the more there is to conquer, the greater the risk of failure. But as for any couple, it's going to be most critical how the interfaith couple handles these differences in their relationship.

There are two key reasons such early optimism may give way to problems later. First, people tend to grow religious or spiritually inclined as they age—perhaps because death is closer. Also, the challenges of life can change one's perspective on religious or spiritual issues. So what looks unimportant early in life can become more of an issue with age.

Second, when a couple starts thinking about children, they face a host of decisions about how the child is to be raised regarding religious and spiritual beliefs. This is when past religious upbringing can become critical, even if they don't see themselves as "a believer." Here are some of the key decisions and questions that come up:

- Do you have a boy circumcised by religious ceremony, or by the doctor, or not at all?

- Is the baby to be baptized? Does baptism happen later, at the age of accountability and personal belief, or shortly after birth?

- What do you do about religious holidays? Christmas, Rosh Hashanah, Passover, Easter, Ramadan, and so on?

- What about religious schooling? Parochial or public school? Sunday school?

- What about confirmation, dedication, and so on?

Kindra and Mohamed met when in college at North Carolina A & T. They fell madly in love and hoped to get married when they graduated in the spring. During the fall of their last semester, they had a chance to meet one another's parents.

Kindra was the daughter of an Episcopal minister and Mohamed was raised in the Islamic faith. After they returned to school, the phone was ringing off the hook from their respective parents asking how they could think that a marriage would work with someone who didn't share their beliefs and religious traditions. Kindra and Mohamed had not discussed what difficulties the differing faiths might pose. Being young and in love, they thought that they could simply work around any difficulty. Love would conquer all.

They decided to get married. To appease each family, they had two ceremonies, Episcopalian and Islamic. This seemed to comfort each family's woes and gain some positive belief that their children's marriage might work. Overcoming this trial strengthened the resolve to make their marriage work.

They settled down in Kindra's hometown, Atlanta. She went to work as an engineer and Mohamed as a coach for the high school football team. They were happy in their work and in their life together.

But with time, things changed. Two years into their marriage, just before Christmas, Mohamed was to celebrate Ramadan. During this period, Mohamed had to fast from sun up to sun down, with nothing to eat or drink. Kindra's thoughts turned to Christmas and the yearly Christmas party at her job, at which there was always an announcement of who the employee of the year was. That year Kindra was to be awarded this great honor.

Mohamed was very proud of his wife but a bit uncomfortable about the party. He knew Kindra's coworkers had never accepted him because of his Islamic beliefs, so the party represented a great conflict for him. He knew that others would be looking at him because he would neither be able to drink a toast to his wife or enjoy holiday snacks because of the time of day the party would be held. Kindra was very upset when she and Mohamed sat down to discuss their predicament.

This situation led the couple to discuss their future, particularly how their religious differences might be an issue with raising children. The discussion grew particularly heated as they talked about children and the holidays. He was very set on the idea that his children would be Islamic. She was not so set on the children being raised Episcopalian but had great concern about their being raised Islamic. Till now, the two had just spent the holidays on their own and followed their own ways of worship. But she knew her parents had a deep sense of family and that it was heightened around the holidays. Her family was very devoted to Christmas and celebration of that holiday (with any prospective grandchildren). These differences in core beliefs lead to several heated arguments; they found themselves voicing diametrically opposed views about life, living, and happiness.

Two months after Christmas, the two agreed to separate, thinking they needed time apart to get their heads straight. As with most couples who separate, what they were unable to do when together they were equally unable to do when separated. This led to divorce, and the couple never reconciled.

Of course, a great many interfaith marriages don't come to this, but you can readily understand the kind of pressure that such couples can undergo. We know of other couples who have made interfaith marriages work well. The key difference is how they handle conflict, religious or otherwise. Of course, this is a core theme of the PREP approach.

Another interesting example of interfaith marriage is the case of James and Mary. James and Mary started off as high school sweethearts, married at twenty-six, and have now been married for six years. One of the issues for their marriage is that Mary was raised Catholic and James in a traditional southern Baptist family. Their families have always supported their marriage; he would attend his services and she would attend hers.

This arrangement has worked well for the first six years of their marriage, but they have come to a point where they feel they want to have children. Each parent is active in his or her church and naturally wants to have the children raised with the religious training and doctrine of that faith. Their parents have for the first time seen difficulty with the marriage; each set of parents are strongly pulling for their grandchild(ren) to be raised the way they raised James and Mary.

After the initial conflict starts, James and Mary take time away from family and friends to find a way to solve their differences. They come up with a plan to try to integrate both of their religious traditions. They decide that they will raise their children with both religious practices, and once they are twelve or thirteen they will be able to decide for themselves which religion is for them. The parents are not in agreement but willing to abide by this decision. This is all academic, of course, because they have yet to have their first child.

As they come to this first-step agreement, they now have to discuss how many children to have. Mary wants six; James, one. He only wants one child so that they can continue to work on their careers and not feel overwhelmed with the needs of lots of kids. He also thinks he wants to be able to spend enough time with his child to raise him or her right; he believes having too many kids won't allow that. Mary wants six because she was taught to think that the more, the merrier. She also doesn't want their child to be lonely for friends; brothers and sisters can fill the need.

The couple come to a compromise and agree on having three. This is a number they both feel they can live with and not end up overwhelmed or deprived.

As James and Mary's marriage demonstrates, couples can make mixed-faith marriages work. It just takes more work than other couples might have to do. But even this depends a lot on how committed each partner is to a belief system. If one partner or both in an interfaith marriage are not strongly committed—and if they don't commit later as a result of changes in life—such differences in background will have much more potential to produce friction and conflict.

To summarize, the findings about the religious influence on marriage indicate that couples who are religiously inclined and from same-faith backgrounds appear to have an edge in maintaining a satisfying marriage and avoiding divorce. We next offer an analysis of why this might be, in hopes of stimulating you to consider how to strengthen your own relationship.

Since this is a secular book, we focus our understanding on pretty down-to-earth explanations, though we recognize that you might also consider a more spiritual explanation for such effects. In our attempt to decode the meaning of these studies for all couples, we focus on two key factors: the value of social support for your relationship and the effect of having a shared worldview. Let's look at these in detail.

## Who's Got Your Back? Social Support

No matter what else, religious and spiritual beliefs bring groups of similarly minded people together. There's a clear benefit for most people in being part of a social group—religious or not—so long as they have a clear sense that they belong or fit into the group. In fact, research by our colleague Ken Pargament has found that church and synagogue members who fit well into their religious community have a higher level of mental health than those who don't.

Studies have consistently shown that people who are isolated are at great risk for such emotional difficulties as depression and suicide and those accompanying health problems and poverty. Many studies in the field of stress management demonstrate how vulnerable people are if they have significant stressors but no social support system to help. It's just not healthy for most humans to be isolated. To paraphrase John Donne, no person is an island!

Religious involvement brings ready-made social structure. A religion specifies a code of behavior and rituals, many of which cause natural points of connection between those involved. For example, most religious and spiritual groups meet regularly for numerous kinds of activity. Spiritual activities include worship, prayer, reading, study, discussion groups, and so forth. Social activities are coffee hour, ice cream socials, picnics, group outings, get-together dinners, softball leagues, and about anything else you can think of. Service activities are also common: food drives, visiting shut-ins, ministry of service to disadvantaged groups, community outreach, volunteer work, support groups, and so on. Social links to a community are important for couples, no matter how you obtain them.

William and Connie are a couple who met in the same church where they got married. They were involved for years in the denomination before they decided to tie the knot. They invited the entire church to the wedding, as well as friends and family. The turnout was large, and the outpouring of support very clear. They didn't get married in front of just friends but before a whole community who knew them, supported them, and would be regularly involved in their lives.

As you can imagine, this couple has a tremendous support system. They are involved in weekly meetings, church on Sunday, and other activities based in their religious community. Their relationship is supported and encouraged in the social network and by teachings that place great value on marriage and commitment, especially dedication.

Of course, there are other ways people meet and spend time with one another in our culture: neighborhood get-togethers, political groups, interest groups, sports, clubs, and so forth. Our key point is that it's important for every couple to have a strong support system for their relationship. Are you socially connected to a group that supports and somehow helps your relationship? If not, do you want to be? These are important questions for you and your partner to address directly.

A number of couples we've met have not been interested in becoming part of a religious group, but they have seen the need for a support system for their marriage. One such couple, John and Marsha, got involved with an organization called ACME, the

Association for Couples in Marriage Enrichment. ACME is a national support network offering programs where couples can meet regularly for friendship, encouragement, and support directed at keeping marriages vibrant and growing.

For John and Marsha, ACME has been just what they wanted. The focus is on support for marriage. Since neither of them is religious, this involvement has been a great way to meet their need for support and connection. The friends they've made and the group activities in ACME have helped them through some tough spots in their marriage. Such social support is critical for a relationship.

Now we turn to other key implications of the research we've described. When you consider the spiritual or religious realm, you are dealing with core beliefs about worldview—in other words, how you make sense of all of life. Everyone has some explanation for the big questions, no matter how complex or simple, how religious or not. Hence everyone has some core belief system. If you as a couple share such a belief system, you have a shared worldview.

## Shared Worldview

University of Denver communication expert Fran Dickson's studies show that couples who have stayed together for fifty years have a shared *relationship vision* that includes personal dreams and goals for the future. When there's a shared belief system—including mutual understanding about the meanings of life, death, and marriage—it's likely to be easier to develop a relationship vision. In turn, having a relationship vision supports the long-term view of commitment.

In most religions, there's a common understanding and language system for thinking and talking about core beliefs. So another explanation for the benefit of religious involvement is that these couples have a belief system that facilitates developing and maintaining the shared worldview. A quartet of experts in the study of religion, Hood, Spilka, Hunsberger, and Gorsuch, put it this way in their book *The Psychology of Religion*: "Since it is fairly likely that the religious feelings of spouses tend to be similar, among the more religious, who probably come from religious homes, there may be a supportive complex of perceptions leading to increased marital satisfaction" (p. 105).

That is, a shared worldview.

## Three Aspects of Worldview

One important factor for all couples is to consider the impact of worldview on the marriage. Do you share a core belief system? How are the similarities and differences in views being handled? Think about these questions as we look at three specific areas where your worldview can affect your marriage: core relationship values, moral judgments, and expectations. Then we'll take a look at how a couple might handle these issues.

### Core Relationship Values

Let's focus on four key values that are emphasized in many belief systems, values with an obvious positive implication for a relationship such as marriage: commitment, respect, intimacy, and forgiveness.

When you and your partner have similar core belief systems, it's likely you also have a similar understanding of these values and how you can give life to them in your marriage. Regardless of core beliefs, we see the need for all couples to have some way to reinforce such values.

*Commitment* in various aspects is greatly emphasized in many belief systems, both in terms of dedication and constraint. Although there are great differences among belief systems about the morality of divorce, there is wide agreement across beliefs about the value of commitment. A long-term relationship needs a sustained sense of commitment. It's so important that we have taken two chapters to present it.

*Respect* is a core value emphasized in most religious or spiritual groups. Various religions hold to specific beliefs that others may reject, but the value and worth of others is still emphasized in most systems. Respect is a core need of all people; as a couple, your value system needs a strong emphasis on respecting each other.

In the PREP approach, even if you have significant disagreements and differences you can show respect for one another in how you communicate. This is validation. You show interest in and respect for your partner even as the two of you see things quite differently. You can't have a good relationship without basic respect.

*Intimacy* is prized in most religious and spiritual systems. It may be variously understood, but it's usually emphasized and encouraged, especially in marriage. All of the traditional religious systems in Western cultures seem to place high value on the importance of marriage and the relationship between the two partners.

One way to think about everything we're saying in this book is that a couple must have clear ways to maintain and enhance intimacy. Furthermore, poorly handled conflict can do great damage to all that is intimate. All couples seeking long-term, satisfying marriages need to value intimacy and the importance of preserving and protecting it.

*Forgiveness* is a core theme for relational health. Long-term, healthy relationships need an element of forgiveness. Otherwise, emotional debt can be allowed to build in a way that destroys the potential for intimacy and teamwork. This is why we devote all of Chapter Ten to dealing with that topic alone. A marriage needs forgiveness to stay healthy over the long run.

The PREP approach is quite specific and skill-oriented. We hope you can see how the four core values discussed here are reflected in the skills and attitudes we encourage. Religious belief systems have been emphasizing these values for thousands of years in ethics, codes of conduct, and standards for dealing with others. In doing so, these belief systems reflect the importance of commitment, respect, intimacy, and forgiveness.

Whatever your religious or spiritual background, our understanding of marital success and failure leads us to emphasize these same values. In essence, the PREP approach teaches ways of thinking and acting that enable a couple to put these values into action; they are relevant for every couple. In a sense, as you practice and put into effect the kinds of strategy and structure we advocate, you are building positive relationship rituals for the future health of your marriage.

In contrast to these four relationship values, people vary a great deal in other aspects of worldview that are based on individual core belief systems—specifically, moral judgment and expectation. Depending on how they are handled, such differences can have a positive or a negative impact on a marriage.

### Moral Judgments

How two partners view what is and isn't moral can have a bearing on their ability to develop a shared worldview. Consider this list of moral issues:

- Sanctity of life versus choice and freedom:
  Is abortion OK?

- Personal responsibility versus community responsibility: Why do people do wrong?

- Capital punishment

- Responsibility toward your fellow humans, animals, and the environment

- Sexual behavior: what is appropriate? Why? On what do you base your judgment?

- Drug or alcohol use: What's OK with you? Why?

These are just a sampling of the questions people grapple with in life. Many partners derive a good deal of similarity on moral views from a shared religious belief system. Likewise, for a nonreligious or less religious couple, a similar philosophy of life would enhance the shared worldview in this regard.

But what is the impact on a couple when moral views such as these aren't shared? This is the kind of question that sparks great controversy and conflict in our culture. In marriage, such issues can be discussed in ways that really enhance intimacy, or they can lead to conflict. Being able to talk comfortably together about such matters—the ones you disagree about—leads to greater understanding of who you are individually. In fact, these are topics of the kind many friends talk about because it can be fun and interesting. Being able to handle such differences well has much to do with being able to communicate, enjoy each other as friends, and with keeping differences from triggering hidden issues of acceptance and rejection.

One of the couples we spoke to had opposing viewpoints on several such moral issues. Frances was raised Catholic and is conservative in her views. Her husband, Craig, was raised Baptist and is much more liberal in his thinking. There are many moral issues on which they greatly disagree. Nevertheless, they can have talks that maintain their friendship rather than damage it. For example, in discussing contraception, this is how they communicate.

FRANCES: I can't believe they're advertising condoms on TV. I can remember when you would never see such a thing. Oh, the good old days.

CRAIG: Yeah, those were the good old days all right. Now there's AIDS, and our folks are more likely to get it than anybody else.

FRANCES: I know, but that brings up the topic of premarital sex. If they weren't doing it in the first place, it wouldn't be a problem. We have so many teenage mothers, I don't get why they would put themselves at risk of getting pregnant.

CRAIG: I agree. Abstinence is the best prevention for AIDS and pregnancy. But, you know how it is when you're young, and you see music videos filled with half-naked girls and dudes. It's hard to resist.

FRANCES: I agree there's a lot of sex and promiscuity on TV. Do you think it will ever change?

CRAIG: I don't think so. But I see your point about condoms making people think that they're safe. I guess I'm glad that some people try to protect themselves, since not everyone believes in abstinence.

FRANCES: You're right. Remember when we were dating? It was hard to resist—because you're so fine! (*they laugh*) But I'm glad that we didn't do it. That's one reason why I married you. I thought you respected me and my views.

CRAIG: Yeah, your strong conviction was attractive to me too. I knew a lot of church-goin' girls in college that said they weren't having sex but would always be the ones you would see creeping around the dorms in the early morning hours.

FRANCES: I know. There were a lot of guys who would try to play games with your head. I was tempted, but I never did anything about it. It was hard and I felt like I was the only one.

CRAIG: That's why people take risks with premarital sex. They think they are the only one not doing it.

FRANCES: I still don't like seeing condom ads on TV. But I see your point.

CRAIG: Well, I can see how frustrating it is for you that more people don't agree it's wrong.

And on they go. The key to maintaining your friendship in such conversations is to keep the focus off rushing to agreement or the need to solve moral dilemmas, and concentrate instead on learning more about how your partner thinks. After all, to what degree does your marriage depend day-to-day on you sharing the same viewpoint on such matters? These differences only threaten your marriage if they trigger deeper issues of acceptance and rejection.

As you listen to Frances and Craig having such talks, you don't hear any defensiveness or attacking. Even when they criticize the position the other holds, they don't demean the other person for how he or she thinks. This keeps an air of respect in their talk, so much so that they actually enjoy these talks (most of the time).

Let's come back to how such differences are handled after discussing the last factor related to worldview.

*Expectations*

Another area in which your worldview can significantly affect your marriage is in shaping your expectations, regarding child rearing and discipline, intimacy, dealing with in-laws, marital roles, and so on. In contrast to the moral viewpoints, this aspect of your worldview has significant implications for your marriage on a daily basis.

The potential for difference in expectation to spark conflict is so great that we devoted Chapter Seven to encouraging you to make such expectations clear, no matter where they come from. If two people share a perspective on key relationship expectations, they are going to have an easier time negotiating life. Shared expectations lead to shared rituals and routines that guide a couple smoothly through the transitions and trials of life.

In religious systems, such viewpoints tend to be clear and codified in the beliefs and rituals, which might make it easier to have a shared worldview in terms of everyday expectations. This could explain, in part, the research findings showing that religious couples and those with similar-belief backgrounds have a somewhat easier time in marriage than nonreligious couples and those with dissimilar belief backgrounds. Sharing a structured belief system brings clarity about many expectations—those that, as a consequence, don't have to be worked out or negotiated. Presumably, a couple who isn't religiously involved can derive this same benefit if they share some philosophical view that makes it easier to maintain a shared view on expectations.

Whatever your backgrounds and beliefs, you and your spouse shouldn't take these factors for granted in your relationship. Key similarities and differences in your viewpoints must be identified and talked about in a way that helps you work together as a team. Let's look at three couples before we finally recommend some exercises for you to do.

### Couples of Type One: Shared View

For many couples, similarity in core beliefs leads to low likelihood of conflict for the various reasons we have outlined. There is simply less to work out in all sorts of areas. However, all couples still must clarify key expectations for how they will handle marital and family matters. It's best for such differences to be discussed early on, with decisions made that form the default settings for your relationship. This means there is basic agreement about how various things are handled—the default—so that you aren't constantly adjusting to differences in worldview in the context of events.

### Couples of Type Two: Views Not Shared But Respected

With the second type of couple, there's a significant difference of opinion on core beliefs but they handle the difference with respect. It doesn't produce alienation and may, in fact, be a source of intimacy if they are able to enjoy the exchange of perspectives— as do Craig and Frances.

For a couple to accomplish this, the partners need at least two things: the skills required to maintain respect in light of the differences, and enough personal security about the core beliefs to not be overly threatened by absence of agreement. For these couples, views and expectations aren't shared in the sense of being similar, but they can be shared in the sense of open expression that doesn't trigger hidden issues of acceptance and rejection.

### Couples of Type Three: Views Not Shared and Conflict

Other partners don't share the same perspective but find that conflict is easily sparked and generally not handled well. Such a couple isn't able to talk freely about difference in viewpoint and maintain mutual respect at the same time. Either they argue unpleasantly about the differences or they avoid talking about them. It's easy to trigger hidden issues of basic acceptance. The difference in core beliefs becomes a barrier, with the partners being unable to share openly about their perspectives on the deepest issues of life.

Mohamed and Kindra fall into this category. Although they shared many core beliefs, the idea of having children brought up significant difference in expectations rooted in their core belief systems. Had either or both of them not become so interested in the beliefs and practices of their religions, there probably would not have been much conflict. But key life transitions have a habit of putting us in touch with our core beliefs—transitions such as marriage, birth, and death. Most religions specify key rituals around such events.

We suggest that having a shared worldview is most beneficial to your relationship if you are going through a major life transition. At such a time, similarity in core beliefs guides you through with less stress and disruption. Transition is also the time when having social support is most critical. Without the shared view, the next best thing you can do is to be clear about your expectations and agree how you will proceed as a couple. Anticipate the key transitions of life so that you can talk together about how you will handle things.

In summary, you and your partner may have differing perspectives, even if you were raised similarly. When you think about religious and spiritual differences, a lot is at stake. Likewise for any core belief system, such as a philosophy of life. Everyone believes something, and it's not likely that there's a couple where both partners line up perfectly on these dimensions.

The point here is that you need to grapple with the effect on your relationship. The exercises for this chapter are designed to help you do just that: grapple. We want you to explore your beliefs on religious or spiritual dimensions and talk them over together.

Exploring and sharing clearly what you believe and expect about some of these key questions of life can be an enriching, if not eye-opening, experience in your relationship. Talking about these issues with respect can be an intimate experience. Try it and see what we mean.

## Exercises

There are three exercises for this chapter. We follow the key themes used to explain the research findings regarding the impact of religion and spiritual values on relationship. First, we ask you to take stock of your social support system. Second, we ask you to consider what your core values are, where they come from, and how they affect your marriage. Third, we want you to explore your core belief systems and the expectations specifically related to them. You and your partner each need a separate pad of paper to do these exercises.

1. We'd like you to consider what your core values are in life. What values are central for you? Where did they come from? Spend some time thinking about this individually. Jot down some notes. Then share with each other what you've been thinking about.

You may have some additional ideas after you work on the next exercise. In addition to other ideas that come up for you, specifically discuss together your views of the core relationship values mentioned in this chapter: commitment, respect, intimacy, and forgiveness. What is your view of these values?

2. Talk together about your social support system. Do you have a strong support system—people to rely on, to encourage you, to hold you accountable at times? Are you involved in a community that supports and nurtures your growth in your marriage? Do you want

to be? What could you do as a couple to build up more support if you see the need to do that?

3. Now, we want you to explore on your own, and share with your partner, issues relevant to your core belief system. For many people, religious faith or spiritual orientation reflects or determines core philosophical, moral, and cultural beliefs and practices. If that's the case for you, it makes the most sense to answer these questions in that light. If not, these questions may seem less related to religion and more having to do with philosophy.

Either way, it is important for partners to understand one another's core belief system, whether based in spiritual or religious beliefs or another philosophy of life. This exercise helps you accomplish this goal. It's very much like what you did in the chapter on expectations, only focused on the area of core belief systems.

These questions are designed to get you thinking about a broad range of issues related to your beliefs. There may be other important questions that we've left out, so feel free to answer questions we don't ask as well as those we do. We would like you to write down an answer to each question as it applies to you. This helps you think clearly about the issues and also helps you when the time comes to talk with your partner about them.

As you think about and answer each question, it can be especially valuable to note what you were taught as a child versus what you believe or expect now as an adult.

1. What is your core belief system or worldview? What do you believe in?

2. How did you come to believe in this viewpoint?

3. What is the meaning or purpose of life in your core belief system?

4. What was your belief growing up? How was this core belief practiced in your family of origin? your religious practice? any other source?

5. Do you make a distinction between spiritual and religious beliefs? What is your view on these matters?

6. What is the meaning of marriage in your belief system?

7. What vows will you say, or what vows did you say? How do they tie into your belief system?

8. What is your belief about divorce? How does this fit your belief system?

9. How do you practice, or expect to practice, your belief in your relationship? (This could mean religious involvement, spiritual practice, or otherwise, depending on your belief system.) How do you want to practice your belief?

10. What do you think the day-to-day impact of your belief system should be on your relationship?

11. Are there specific views on sexuality in your belief system? What are they? How do they affect the two of you?

12. If you have children (or if you plan to have children), how are they raised (or how will they be raised) with respect to your belief system?

13. Do you give, or expect to give, financial support to a religious institution or other effort related to your belief system? How much? How will this be determined? Do you both agree?

14. Do you see potential areas of conflict regarding your belief systems? What are they?

15. What do you believe about forgiveness in general? How does forgiveness apply in a relationship such as the one with your partner?

16. In your belief system, what is your responsibility to other humans?

17. How do you observe (or expect to observe) religious holidays?

18. What is the basis for respecting others in your beliefs?

19. Are there any other questions you can think of to answer in this regard?

After you and your partner have finished the entire exercise, begin to plan and spend time together discussing these expectations. You should plan on a number of discussions. Discuss the degree to which you each feel the expectation being discussed has been shared clearly in the past. Use the speaker-listener technique if you would like some additional structure to deal with these difficult issues.

Regarding any expectations that came up, talk out the degree to which you both feel they are reasonable or unreasonable, and discuss what you want to agree to do about them.

Now we move on to presenting some key ideas for getting the most out of what you have been learning in this book.

# 10

# Forgiving, Forgetting, and Intimacy

We have discussed in previous chapters how the African American marriage can be a safe haven from the slings and arrows that the world hurls at you. Although in its best form a successful marriage can become a safe haven, it can also be the source of hurt feelings from time to time under the best of circumstances. There are many sources of major and minor hurts: put-downs, avoidance, negative interpretation, abusive comments, forgetting something important, making decisions without regard for the partner's needs, extramarital affairs, self-centeredness, addiction, impoliteness, and so on.

Unless you have fully unrealistic expectations, you know that both of you will have to accept sins of omission and commission over the course of your marriage. Minor infractions are normal, and it's important to expect them to happen. It's far more valuable to learn how to move on at these times than it is to expect them not to happen at all. For some couples, major sins happen as well. When that's the case, some effort is needed to put the events in the past. The more significant the issue or event that causes harm, the more likely you'll need some of the specific steps we recommend in this chapter.

Let's look at two couples in need of making forgiveness happen. Both examples demonstrate the need for forgiveness. But the infractions are quite different. One is minor and one is major, and the implications differ significantly.

## "Oops, I Forgot": Toni and Larry's Story

Toni and Larry are both high school teachers. They met during a summer training conference held at the school where they work. Toni had been married before and was raising four kids as a single mom. Both Toni and Larry shared Christian beliefs, and a deep devotion to teaching.

Toni's former marriage was not healthy, but she did a remarkable job of raising four good kids. She and Larry were not without their issues from the past, but together they have handled the myriad stresses of a large family with limited resources and children going through demanding development. Even though Larry has no biological link to the kids, over the ten years of their marriage they have become his own and he claims them with pride. Sometimes the kids even act like him more than like their mother. Toni and Larry have their ups and downs, but they handle the problems that come up with respect and skill.

Larry's devotion to young people also shows in his teaching; he was recently recognized as his school's Teacher of the Year. Although he doesn't care so much about the public recognition, he is happy for the award, and happier still to receive a bonus in his next paycheck for his work and dedication to teaching excellence.

Larry asks Toni to attend the luncheon, and she says of course she'd be glad to come. He is proud to be honored and wants Toni to share the moment with him. Larry tells the principal and his fellow teachers that Toni will be coming. A place is kept for her at the front table, right beside Larry.

Toni has to take their youngest child to the doctor that day. The girl needs a shot and she wants to do something special to make her daughter better. She is distracted with getting her daughter a treat on the way home from the doctor and completely forgets about the big luncheon. While she is out picking up some ice cream, he is at the award luncheon feeling embarrassed. He is also a little bit worried, since it is unlike Toni to miss an important event. Here are his peers honoring him, and his wife fails to show up, without explanation. So he makes the best of the embarrassment, telling his coworkers that she must have gotten hung up at the doctor's office with one of the kids.

As soon as Larry walks in the door that evening, Toni remembers what she has forgotten.

TONI: *(distressed)* Oh no! Larry, I just remembered.

LARRY: *(cutting her off)* Where were you? I've never been so embarrassed. I can't believe you just blew this off.

TONI: I didn't blow it off; I just started hanging out with Noelle after her doctor's appointment.

LARRY: So where were you? I tried calling.

TONI: We went to Chucky Cheese to have lunch, and I completely spaced out your ceremony. I feel terrible.

LARRY: So do I. I didn't know what to tell people, so I made something up about you maybe being at the doctor's office with one of the kids.

TONI: That's the truth, really. I'm very sorry. Can you forgive me?

Should he? Of course. What does it mean for him to forgive in this context?

Now consider a very different example in which the same question has a much more complicated answer.

## Maybe the Grass Is Greener: Jody and Marcell's Story

Jody and Marcell have been married for three years. They were high school sweethearts and got married two years after high school. Marcell was going to a local college and due to graduate with a degree in sociology. Jody was a singer; she grew up in the church singing gospel songs and when she graduated she found an agent and worked hard to make a name for herself in the pop music business. Both spent a lot of time away from home. Marcell spent his days and many nights at school in the library; Jody's work took her on the road, often for a week or more at a time, working as a backup singer for a well-known R & B performer. They had no children but dreamed of having some once Marcell finished school and Jody was in a place in her career where she could take a break.

The first two years of their marriage were fine, but the third year was filled with hard times. Jody was traveling more and more. Marcell insisted that she get a cell phone so he could call and stay in touch with her. She got the phone, but many evenings he could never reach her. She would say that she was in a recording session or that she had just left the phone turned off in her purse. But Marcell grew ever more suspicious.

He began to feel as if he did not know Jody anymore; he suspected she was having an affair. He was at college, where there were attractive ladies everywhere. So wasn't it possible Jody was meeting someone she was attracted to in some bar somewhere?

Marcell gets sick and tired of wondering and being suspicious, so one night he tells her he's going to the library; she says she has a gig at a local bar. Instead of going to the library, he follows her in a friend's car—right up to an apartment complex, noting the door where she goes in. He sits, and sits, for an hour. Then he goes up to check the name on the mailbox. It says Terence something-or-other.

As he stands outside, he grows angry and hurt. *Why should I wait to see if she's up there?* he thinks. He knows she is. So he proceeds to climb the steps and knock on the door. After several minutes, he hears a voice from behind the door.

TERENCE: Can I help you, Brother?

MARCELL: (*cool outside and destroyed on the inside*) Ya. Tell Jody I'm out here in the car and I'd like to talk to her.

TERENCE: (*assuredly*) Jody? Yo, Man, you got the wrong house.

MARCELL: (*keeping cool*) Hey, my beef is not with you. That's my wife you have in there, did you know that? She's married to me. Or didn't you care?

TERENCE: Look man, I told you there ain't nobody here named Jody!

MARCELL: (*yelling out as Terence closes the door*) Yo, tell her don't bother coming home! Peace out.

Jody shows up at 1:00 A.M.—which is when she said she would. She denies the whole incident. Marcell never backs down and tells Jody she has to leave. "Cheating is bad enough," he says, "but you don't even have the guts to admit you were out doin' wrong."

Jody leaves the next day and goes to stay with a friend. She becomes depressed; as the days pass she starts drinking. Marcell still loves her, but his anger and hurt grow the longer they are apart. *I thought we had something,* he thinks over and over; *I thought I could trust her. I can't believe she would cheat on me!*

Jody talks with her friends about what to do. Some of them even call Marcell and ask him if it's really over. His family knows how much Jody means to him and they suggest he try to work it out. He isn't sure if he wants her back. He is so torn up inside that he considers dropping out of school. This goes on for a month, until one day Jody comes home and waits in the kitchen for Marcell to arrive from school.

JODY: (*desperately*) Hey, Marcell how are you?

MARCELL: (*cool outside, raging inside*) I'm cool, but you shouldn't worry about that anymore.

JODY: Why, Baby?

MARCELL: (*icily, controlling his rage*) You lost that right when I caught you over at that man's house. You couldn't even admit what you had done.

JODY: (*tears welling up*) OK, OK. I'll tell you the truth. I've been having an affair. I met this man at a club one night. I didn't plan for anything to happen; it just did.

MARCELL: It seemed to work out awfully well for something you didn't plan. How long has this been goin' on?

JODY: Only for about a month.

MARCELL: (*voice raised, anger coming out*) *Only* a month. Am I supposed to feel better because you have only been screwing some guy for a month and not a year?

JODY: No. Look, Baby, I love you. It just seems like you don't ever have time for me. There's been so much distance between us.

MARCELL: (*enraged*) So what? What, you're a little lonely so you go find someone to replace me. You make me sick. (turning away, heading into the next room) So tell me, why are you here?

JODY: I want you. I need you to forgive me. I need you back in my life. Please, let me try again. You can believe in me.

MARCELL: I don't think I can. I don't know what to do.


At this point, he has some big decisions to make. Should he forgive her? Can he forgive her? He has already decided that he might never trust her again, not completely. She clearly wants to come back, but how would he ever know she won't do it again the next time they can't spend a lot of time together?

What do you think? Should he forgive? What does it mean to forgive her?

## What Is Forgiveness?

Forgiveness is a decision to give up your perceived or actual right to get even with, or hold in debt, someone who has wronged you. The dictionary says it means to give up resentment or the desire to punish, to give up all claim to punish; it also says the word can mean to cancel or remit a debt. The picture of forgiveness is a canceled debt.

*Forgive* is a verb. It's active; it's something you must decide to do. When one of you fails to forgive, you can't function as a team so long as one of you is kept one down by being indebted to the other.

Because of this, lack of forgiveness is the ultimate in scorekeeping, with the message being "You are way behind on my scorecard, and I don't know if you can catch up." In this context, resentment builds, conflict increases, and ultimately hopelessness sets in. The real message is "Maybe you can't do enough to make this up." People often walk away from debts they see no hope of paying off.

As we have seen, infractions can be small or large, with the accompanying sense of debt being small or large as well. Toni has a much smaller debt to Larry than Jody has to Marcell. Either way, the opposite of forgiveness is expressed in statements such as:

"I'm going to make you pay for what you did."

"You're never going to live this down."

"You owe me. I'm going to get even with you."

"I'll hold this against you for the rest of your life."

"I'll get you for this."

These statements sound harsh but are quite meaningful for understanding what it means not to really forgive the other person for a mistake. When you fail to forgive, you act out statements like this.

Now let's talk about some of the most important issues in forgiveness raised by couples we have seen in our work. These issues usually have more to do with what forgiveness is not than what it is.

## What Forgiveness Is Not

Maxine, a fifty-five-year-old in her second marriage, was brought up to believe that to forgive means to forget. She asked us, "It seems so hard to forgive and forget; how can you really do this?"

In defining forgiveness, we have said nothing about forgetting. You hear the phrase "forgive and forget" so often that the two are equated, when in reality they have nothing to do with one another. This is one of the greatest myths about forgiveness. Can you remember a painful wrong someone caused in your life, one for which you feel you have forgiven the person? We bet you can. We can, too. This underscores the point; it's not forgotten.

Just because you have forgiven—and given up a desire to pay the person back—doesn't mean you have forgotten the event ever happened. Fortunately, when people say "forgive and forget," they usually mean to put the infraction in the past. There's value in that, although forgiveness should not be measured in this way. But if putting it in the past simply means you've given up holding it over your partner's head, that's right on.

One misconception related to the forgetting myth is the belief that if a person still feels pain about what happened, he or she has not really forgiven. In fact, you can still feel pain about being hurt in some way, yet forgive fully the one who harmed you.

Marcell may come to a point of completely forgiving Jody, as we define it here. He may work through and eliminate his rage and desire to hurt her back. However, in the best of circumstances, what happened will leave him with a wound and grief that remains for many years.

In the case of Toni and Larry, how she hurt him is far less severe, with fewer lasting consequences. As it turns out, he does forgive her. He doesn't dwell on it and he need not grieve about it. However, when he is reminded of it, such as at company events, he remembers. He feels a twinge of the humiliation that he felt on that day. This doesn't mean he's holding it over her or trying to get even. He has forgiven. He just has a painful memory along the road of their marriage.

George, a newlywed in his mid-twenties, asked us about responsibility. He is afraid that forgiving means ignoring responsibility. He asks, "But in forgiving, aren't you saying that the one who did wrong is not responsible for what was done?"

This is the second big misunderstanding about forgiveness. When you forgive, you are saying nothing about the responsibility of the one who did wrong. The person is responsible for the wrong done, period. Forgiving someone does not absolve him or her of responsibility for the actions. It does take the relationship out of the mode of one punishing the other, but it shouldn't diminish the responsibility for the wrong done.

In this light, it's important to distinguish between punishment and consequences. You can be forgiven from the standpoint of your partner not seeking to hurt or punish you, but you can still accept and act on the consequences of your behavior.

Let's summarize so far. If your partner has done you wrong, it's up to you to forgive or not. Your partner can't do this for you. It's your choice. If you've wronged your partner in some sense, it's your job to take responsibility for your actions and, if needed, take steps to see that it doesn't happen again. This assumes the infraction is clear and you are both humble and mature enough to take responsibility. The key is that if you want your relationship to move forward, you must have a plan for forgiving. Even if you don't want to forgive—perhaps because of your own sense of justice—you may still need to do so for the good of your marriage.

Toni and Larry follow this model in the ideal sense. She takes complete responsibility for missing the luncheon—apologizing and asking him to forgive her. He readily forgives her, having no intention of holding it against her. Their relationship is actually strengthened by the way they handle this event. He gains respect for Toni in her total acceptance of responsibility. She gains respect for Larry in his loving and clear desire to forgive and move on.

Before we proceed to specific steps you can take to keep forgiveness going, we want to discuss a crucial distinction: between forgiveness and restoration in a relationship. What do you do if one partner can't or won't take responsibility? How can you move forward then?

## You've Been Wronged But Your Partner Won't Take Responsibility

Forgiveness and restoration usually go hand in hand in a relationship, as with Larry and Toni. Intimacy and openness in their relationship are quickly restored; no barriers are placed in the way. Each handles his or her responsibility without complication. When this happens, restoration naturally follows. What we mean by restoration is that your relationship is repaired for intimacy and connection.

But what do you do if you've been wronged in some way and your partner takes no responsibility? Do you allow the relationship to continue as it was? For one thing, you must be open to examining the possibility that your partner really didn't intend to do anything wrong, even though you were hurt by what happened. There can be a sincere difference in interpreting what happened and why.

Ray and Aretha have been married twenty-one years, with things generally going well. Although they don't handle conflict all that well, they are churchgoing folk who believe in marriage; their dedication to being married remains strong.

One day, he is cleaning out the garage so he can keep his new riding lawn mower inside and put all sorts of boxes out in a shed in the back yard. He thinks he's doing a great job, too; the garage hasn't looked this good in years and he has a space for his new pride and joy.

Aretha was at work at the time. As she is coming home from work, it begins to rain. When she gets home, Ray shows her how clean the garage is. She is pleased but asks where all the old boxes went. He tells her he put them in the old shed in the back yard. A few days later, she goes to look for some important papers that are in one of the boxes Ray has moved. She finds the box—soaking wet, her papers ruined. It is, of course, an accident. He thought they were things that they wouldn't need to put their hands on, so he was storing them away but didn't know the roof on the shed would leak.

Aretha is enraged. She accuses Ray of being "stupid, insensitive, macho, and domineering." She feels he doesn't care; his throwing out her stuff is just another sign of his need to control everything—or so she sees it.

What happened is unfortunate. Aretha has every right to be upset; those papers mean a lot to her. But it really is just a mistake. With the control issue triggered, Aretha is being unfair in accusing Ray of intentionally hurting her. This is quite a negative interpretation, since in fact he is trying to do something he knows she would like to have done.

When harmed in this way, it's OK to expect an apology, not because your partner intends to hurt you but because a mistake *has* hurt you. Ray can apologize to Aretha. But she has a long wait ahead if she needs to hear him say "You're right, I threw out your things because I'm a control freak and I think I can do whatever I want with anything in our house. I'll work on it." Not likely.

Whether or not you and your partner agree on the nature of the infraction or mistake, you can still move ahead and forgive. It may be hard, but if you don't, you and the relationship will suffer added damage. Indeed, there's good reason to believe that by hanging on to resentment and bitterness you put yourself at risk for such psychological and physical problems as depression, ulcers, high blood pressure, and rage. That's no way to live.

Now, for the really difficult case. Suppose it's very clear to you that your partner has done something quite wrong and isn't going to take any responsibility, as in Jody and Marcell's situation. Virtually no one is going to deny that she has done something wrong. She must accept responsibility for her behavior if the marriage is to have any chance of moving forward. Sure, they are both responsible for making time to keep their communication going. They've made other things a priority, and neither is more to blame than the other for that. However, in response it was her decision to have the affair. She's responsible for that action, he isn't.

When Jody shows up in the kitchen asking for forgiveness, the worst thing Marcell could do is to go on as if everything has returned to normal. It has not. You can't sweep things like this under the carpet. He could decide there and then to forgive her. But this is a separate decision from whether or not he should allow a full restoration of the relationship. Here's what we mean.

When she shows up back at the house, he doesn't know what level of responsibility she is taking for the affair. *What if she really blames me for it?* he might wonder; *What if she thinks it's my fault for not being more affectionate?* If he thinks she feels justified or is not serious about changing, why should he allow restoration of the relationship? It really is a great risk to take her back. Still, he can forgive. Either way, it'll take time.

Here is what actually happened to these two people. For the week following their talk, they have some nasty talks on the phone. With so much tension in the air, it's easy to escalate. Yet she persistently states her desire to rebuild the marriage. She wants to come back.

Marcell asks her to come to the house one night for a talk. He meets her and pours out his anguish, pain, and anger. She listens. She focuses on how her behavior has affected him—not on her motives and weaknesses. She takes responsibility, to the point of a sincere apology. She doesn't try to blame him for the affair. Now he thinks there is a chance they can get through this. Their talk concludes this way:

JODY: I've spent a lot of time alone thinking about what I've done. I made a really bad decision that hurt you deeply. I shouldn't have been with Terence.

MARCELL: I appreciate the apology. I needed to hear it. I love you with all my heart, Girl, but I can't just act like nothing happened. . . . I need to know that you're not going to play me again.

JODY: What do you want me to do?

MARCELL: I don't know. I guess that I need you to show me that I can trust you and believe in you. When you said you were wrong in what you did, it did a lot for me.

JODY: Marcell, I really do know how wrong I was. It's also clear to me that I want our marriage to work not just for today but forever. I'll do whatever is necessary to make it up to you.

MARCELL: I believe that you are sorry.

JODY: Marcell, I want to come home and make it up to you.

MARCELL: OK, Baby.

JODY: I also want us to get some help.

MARCELL: Like counseling? I've never been down for that, but I am willing to try. Because I can't go through something like this again.

JODY: I know. I don't want to either. That's why I want us to go see someone to make what we have better.

MARCELL: Just because you're coming home doesn't mean I'm over this. I'm very, very angry with you right now.

JODY: I know, and I won't pressure you to act like nothing happened.

MARCELL: OK.

As you can see, he really opens up and she validates his pain and anger. She doesn't get defensive. If she did, she might end the marriage. She gains hope from this talk.

He knows he can forgive; he's a forgiving person. He knows it will take some time, and she knows they need help. The future looks uncertain. There's a lot to work through if they're going to restore the relationship.

She does the best she can under the circumstances. The next day, she begins calling around to find the best counselor available. She wants a professional who knows what they need to do to move forward. This shows him that she is serious about repairing their marriage—some evidence of long-unseen dedication.

The relationship cannot be restored until they get to work. It takes time, but they do it. He remembers—he's not going to be able to forget—but the ache in his heart gets weaker all the time. They are able to move forward through forgiveness and on to restoration of their relationship.

## What About Regaining Trust?

We're often asked how to regain trust when something has damaged it. The question is not so relevant for minor matters of forgiveness; there is no loss of trust in Toni and Larry's incident. But for Jody and Marcell, there's a great loss of trust.

Whatever the incident, suppose forgiveness proceeds smoothly and you both want restoration. How do you regain trust? It's not easy. There are two key points we make about rebuilding trust: it takes time, and it demands responsibility.

### Trust Builds Slowly over Time

As we said in the last chapter, trust builds as you gain confidence in someone being there for you. Even though research shows that people vary in their general trust for others, deep trust only comes from seeing that your partner is there for you over time.

Marcell can only regain his trust in Jody slowly. The best thing that can happen is for a considerable amount of time to go by without another serious breach of trust. This takes commitment and a new way of living together. They can't afford to let the same kind of distance build up again. If she has another affair, it will probably be impossible for him to trust her again.

*Trust Demands Responsibility*

The best chance for rebuilding trust comes if each partner takes appropriate responsibility. The greatest thing Jody can do to regain Marcell's trust is to take full responsibility for her actions. If he sees her doing all she can do to bring about serious change without his prodding and demanding, his trust will grow. Seeing her effort, he gains confidence that things can get better—not perfect, but really better. As we said in the last chapter, it's easier to trust if you can clearly see your partner's dedication to you.

He can also help rebuild her trust. For one thing, she must see that he doesn't plan to hold the affair over her head forever. Can he really forgive? If he reminds her about it, especially during an argument, she won't be able to trust that he really wants her to draw closer and move ahead.

## Making Forgiveness and Restoration Happen

So far, we've focused on the meaning of forgiveness and what is required for it to come about. In keeping with our approach, we want to give you a specific and structured approach for making forgiveness happen. In suggesting specific steps, we don't mean to imply that forgiveness is easy or accomplished by simply saying "I'm sorry" enough times. But we do want you to be able to move forward with some specific steps to get you through the toughest times.

The steps we outline here are much like the process suggested in Chapter Four on problem solving. These steps can work well to guide you in approaching forgiveness if you have a specific event or recurring issue to deal with.

Each step has some key pointers. We use the example with Aretha and Ray to highlight the points and summarize many of the points made in this chapter, as well as provide a road map for handling forgiveness.

## Step One: Scheduling

Schedule a meeting for discussing the specific issue related to forgiveness.

If an issue is important enough to you as a couple that you want to focus on it in this way, then do it right. Set aside the time without distraction. Prepare yourselves to deal openly, honestly, and with respect. As we said in Chapter Five on ground rules, setting aside a specific time for dealing with issues makes it likely that you'll actually follow through and do it well.

After the initial rush of anger, Aretha and Ray agree to work through the incident with the box of papers. They set aside time on an evening when the kids are at a school function.

## Step Two: Agenda

Set the agenda to work on the issue in question.

Identify the problem or harmful event. You must both agree that you are ready to discuss it in this format at this time. If not, wait for a better time.

When Aretha and Ray meet, the agenda is pretty clear: how to forgive and move on from what happened with her box of mementos. They agree this is the focus of their meeting, and they agree they are ready to handle it.

## Step Three: Exploration

Fully explore the pain and concerns related to this issue for both of you.

The goal in this step is to have an open, validating talk about what has happened that harmed one or both of you. You shouldn't try this unless you as an individual are motivated to hear and show respect for your partner's viewpoint. The foundation for forgiveness is best laid through such a talk or series of talks. Validating discussions go a long way toward dealing with the painful issues so as to bring you closer together. This is a great place to use the speaker-listener technique. If there's ever a time to have a safe and clear talk, this is it.

Using the speaker-listener technique, Aretha and Ray talk it out for about thirty minutes. He really listens to her anguish about losing the things that mean a lot to her. She edits out her prior belief that he has somehow done it on purpose. She has calmed down and can see that blaming him in this way doesn't make a lot of sense. She listens to how badly he feels for her, for her loss. She also validates his statements that he specifically tried not to throw out her things. They feel closer than they have in quite a while.

## Step Four: Asking for Forgiveness

The offender asks for forgiveness.

If you have offended your partner in some way, an outward appeal for forgiveness is not only appropriate but healing. An apology is a powerful addition to a request for forgiveness. A sincere apology validates your partner's pain. To say "I'm sorry. I was wrong. Please forgive me" is one of the most healing things that can happen between two people.

Apologizing and asking for forgiveness is a big part of taking responsibility for how you have hurt your partner. This doesn't mean that you sit around and beat yourself up for what you did. You have to forgive yourself, too!

But what if you don't think you have done anything wrong? You can still ask that your partner forgive you. Remember, forgiveness is a separate issue from why the infraction or mistake occurred. Even if you don't agree you've done anything wrong, your partner can choose to forgive. This is harder, but it's doable.

Listen carefully to the pain and concern of your partner. Even if you feel you have done no wrong, you may find something in what is said that can, within the relationship, lead to a change on your part for the better.

## Step Five: Agreeing to Forgive

The offended agrees to forgive.

Ideally, the one needing to forgive clearly and openly acknowledges the desire to forgive. This may be unnecessary for a minor infraction, but for anything of significance this step is important. It makes it real and memorable; it increases accountability between both of you to find the healing you are seeking.

There are several specific implications of this step. In forgiving, you are attempting to commit the event to the past. You are agreeing that you will not bring it up in future arguments or conflict.

You both recognize that this commitment to forgive does not mean that the offended will feel no pain or effects from what happened. But you're moving on. You're working to restore the relationship and repair the damage.

## Step Six: Commitment to Change

If applicable, the offender makes a positive commitment to change the recurrent pattern or attitude that gives offense.

Again, this step depends on your agreement that there is a specific problem with how one of you has behaved. It also assumes that what happened is part of a pattern, not just a one-time event. For Toni and Larry and for Aretha and Ray, this step is not so relevant. For Jody and Marcell, it is critical.

If you have hurt your partner, it also helps to make amends. This is not the same as committing to make important changes. When you make amends, you make a peace offering of a sort—not because you owe your partner, but because you want to demonstrate your desire to get back on track. It's a gesture of good will. One way to make amends is to carry out unexpected positive acts. This shows your investment and ongoing desire to keep building your relationship.

In Aretha and Ray's case, he schedules a dinner for just the two of them at her favorite restaurant. He goes out of his way to show her that she is special to him. She has already forgiven, but this gesture takes them further along the path of healing. Besides, it's fun. Their friendship is strengthened.

## Step Seven: Taking Your Time

Expect it to take time.

These steps are potent for getting you on track as a couple. They begin a process; they don't sum it up. The steps can move the process along, but you may each be working on your side of the equation for some time to come. A relationship can be healed even when a painful event has come between you. It's your choice.

------

We hope you are encouraged by the possibility for forgiveness and reconciliation in your relationship. If you've been together for only a short time, this may seem like an academic discussion more than a set of ideas that are crucial for your relationship. If you've been together for some time, you understand the need for forgiveness. Hopefully, it happens naturally in your relationship. If so, keep at it. Do the work of prevention. The rewards are great.

If you need to initiate forgiveness but barriers of resentment have built up, get after tearing them down. You can do it. These seven steps help you get started.

## Exercises

There are two parts to the assignment, one to do individually and one together.

1. Individually. First, spend some time in reflection about areas where you may harbor resentment, bitterness, and unforgiveness in your relationship. Write these things down. How old are these feelings? Are there patterns of behavior that continue to offend you? Do you hold things against your partner? Do you bring up past events in arguments? Are you willing to push yourself to forgive?

Second, spend some time reflecting on times when you may have really hurt your partner. Have you taken responsibility? Did you apologize? Have you taken steps to change any recurrent patterns that give offense? Just as you may be holding onto some grudges, you may be standing in the way of reconciliation on some issues if you've never taken responsibility for your end.

2. Together.  As with everything else we have presented, practice is important to really put positive patterns in place. Therefore, we recommend you plan to sit down at least a couple of times and work through some issues using the model presented in this chapter. To start, pick a less significant event or issue, just to get the feel of things. This helps you build confidence and teamwork.

If you have identified significant hurts that have not been fully dealt with, take the time to sit down and tackle one of these meatier issues too. It's risky, but if you do it well the resulting growth in your relationship and capacity for intimacy will be well worth it. It's your choice.

We have been dealing with many deep and often misunderstood concepts. Acting on what we've presented takes a lot of reflection and skill. If you do the work, we believe you will find it worth the effort.

In the remaining chapters, we turn to the sublime. The direction shifts to how you can enhance all the most wonderful aspects of marriage: fun, friendship, spirituality, and sensuality. We have literally saved the best for last. If you've been working on what we've presented thus far, you're now ready to experience the wonders of your marriage.

# 11

# Preserving and Protecting Friendship

If you talk to older couples and ask them how it is that they're still together, the most common answer is "Because we're friends." Many say that their spouse is their best friend. Their friendship sustains them when the rest of the world is cold and hard. Friendship within a marriage can fulfill your needs for acceptance and security.

The latest statistics on the AIDS epidemic suggest that African Americans, as a group, seem to be at greatest risk for getting the disease. If there is anything positive that can be drawn from the horrible disease of AIDS, it is that it has forced many people to slow down in their relationships and focus on knowing the person before engaging in physical intimacy. In looking for a lasting relationship, what underlies our assessment of what we like or don't like about someone of the opposite sex is a mate who will be our best friend for life. The divorce rate suggests that the person that many African Americans marry is probably not their best friend.

To be best friends with your spouse is definitely an excellent goal. The question is how it happens, what it means to be a best friend, and how we sustain being best friends in a marriage. Friendship needs to be nurtured in ways that many married couples fail to realize until their friendship is gone. Here, we want to help you preserve and deepen your friendship in your marriage for many years to come or for a lifetime.

## What Is a Friend?

How would you answer the question of what a friend is? People reply to us that a friend is someone who has your back, is there for you to talk with, can see your side of how the world is, and is a companion in life. In short, friends are people we chill with, open up to, and count on. We talk and do fun things with friends. Our friends also serve as people on our side as we look at and have to deal with a racist world. There is a great deal of research backing this point up. The more friends people have (especially at least one really good one), the better they do in almost every conceivable way in life, particularly in terms of physical and mental health.

Being supportive and encouraging most of the time does not rule out an occasional loving challenge. When you and another are good friends, tight friends, you trust him or her not to "player hate" on you when good things happen. Your friend is also the person who stands by you and gives you a reality check when you need it, even if it's not what you want to hear.

One of the most powerful aspects of friendship is deep intimacy. Intimacy can take many forms. In part, it means being able to share what's in your heart. This may mean your blessings, hopes, frustrations, fears, and crosses. It is critical in a marriage to learn to hear your partner's heart in a way that leaves him or her comfortable sharing it. Sharing at this level means different things to different people. In fact, we're all different, so this is one of those areas where there can be a really unique blending of who you each are in the mystery of oneness. Whether you are quiet or outspoken, a key to great friendship in your marriage is to learn to share, and listen carefully for, what's on each other's hearts.

# Barriers to Friendship in Marriage

So if friendship is one of our main goals in marriage, why aren't more married couples good friends, or even best friends? Sometimes we allow barriers to spring up and prevent our being friends with our spouse. Here are some common ones.

## There's No Time

We all lead busy lives. What with work, the needs of the children, keeping a house, and all the rest of our daily responsibilities, who's got time for friendship? The friendship that is the very core of your relationship may take a back seat to all these competing interests.

Eve and Henry, a dual career couple, have been together for about five years. They have a three-year-old daughter, China. Although they are happy with their marriage and life together, they know something is changing about their connectedness.

HENRY: Remember when we used to listen to this song?

EVE: (*doing a little dance*) Oh, yeah. Those were the days. We used to go and take the boom box and a basket of food to the park and talk till it got dark.

HENRY: Mmm, I loved those times. I could really hear you, and I felt like you really heard me. Why don't we do that any more? Is it that with China we just don't have time any more?

EVE: We don't make time! We bring work home or deal with caring for my parents. We let our other responsibilities keep us from ever going back to the park.

HENRY: It seems like we're letting something slip away.

All too often, couples fail to take the time just to talk as friends. The other needs and cares of life crowd out this time to relax and talk. It may be a matter of priorities. When a couple dates before marriage, they usually spend lots of time together. Life might be less busy at that point in the relationship, but it's also a higher priority to find the time to be together. Still, that's not the only reason friendship weakens over time.

## We've Lost That Friendship Feeling

Many people have told us that they were friends with their spouse to begin with, but not anymore; now they're "married." It's as if once you're married, you can't be friends anymore. You can be one or the other, but not both. Well, that's a mistaken belief.

The strongest marriages we've seen have maintained a solid friendship over the years. Take Laura and Jerome, who've been happily married for forty-two years. We asked them what the secret is, and they said commitment and friendship. They started out with a great friendship and they never let it go. They said they have had many fights over the years, but they never went to sleep mad. They always tried to work out their problems even if they didn't always understand why there was a problem in the first place. They always tried to take the other person's perspective and keep a deep respect for one another as friends who can freely share thoughts and feelings about all sorts of things, in an atmosphere that was always nonjudgmental. This kept their bond strong and alive. So don't buy into the expectation that because you're married you can't also be and stay friends. You can indeed!

## We Don't Talk Like Friends Anymore

If you've been married for some time, think for a moment about a friendship you enjoy with someone other than your spouse. How often do you have to talk with that person about problems between the two of you? Not often, we'd bet. Friends aren't people with whom we argue a lot. In fact, one of the nicest things about a friendship is that you don't usually have to work out a lot of issues. Instead, you're able to focus on mutual interests in a way that's fun for both of you.

Friends talk about sports, spiritual matters, politics, perceptions of the world, philosophy of life, humorous anecdotes in the families, fun things they've done or will do, dreams of the future, and thoughts about what each person is going through at this point in life. In contrast, what do couples talk about most after they've been together for years? Some of the common subjects are problems with the kids, concerns about who can take care of Mama, problems with too many bills and not enough money, problems with getting the car fixed, concerns about who's got time to get some project around the house done, problems with figuring out who is going to see the kids' teacher for a conference, problems with the neighbor's dog, concerns about each other's health . . . and the list goes on and on.

If couples aren't careful, most of their talks end up being about problems and concerns—not about joy and fun. Problems and concerns are part of married life, and they must be dealt with, but too many couples let these issues crowd out the other, more relaxed talks they once shared and enjoyed. Since problems and concerns can easily become events that trigger issues, there's much more potential for conflict in talking with a spouse than a friend. This brings us to the next barrier.

## We Have Conflicts That Erode Our Friendship

One of the key reasons couples have trouble staying friends is that conflicts arise during friendship-building activities and discussions. When this happens consistently, there is no base for developing and fostering the friendship dimension of the relationship. For example, when you're angry with your partner about something that's happened, you're not going to feel much like being friends right then. Or worse, when you do have the time to be friends, a conflict comes up that takes you right out of the relaxed mode of being together and into a battle mode. We believe that this is the chief reason some couples talk less and less like friends over the years. They may think that they're avoiding having issues damage their friendship.

To keep conflict from arising, some couples talk less and less about the very things they *need* to talk about as issues arise. We addressed this very point in Chapter Six, on issues and events.

One couple, Siesha and Trace, are having real trouble protecting and preserving friendship in their relationship. They have been married for eleven years and have three kids; Trace's cousin Tee Tee, who is terminally ill, is living with them. There is always something to do, and they are rarely able to get away just to be together. They finally get someone to watch the kids and the cousin so they can spend a long weekend away in the Bahamas, away from the city and their worries. This is their first chance to be away alone in years.

As they are dressing for dinner, they launch into a conversation that causes a conflict on their first free weekend in ages.

SIESHA: *(very relaxed)* I love this room. It's like a second honeymoon.

TRACE: *(equally relaxed)* Yeah. This is great. I can't believe how cheap this room was.

SIESHA: Me either. Now, if we only had some money to gamble with, we would be straight.

TRACE: *(tensing up a bit)* I told you we couldn't blow all our little stash on this weekend. We still have to pay for Cousin Tee Tee's trip to that clinic.

SIESHA: *(sensing his tension, and now her own)* Yeah, I know, more of the same. Why are we footing the bill for your cousin? Why aren't your brothers helping out with the cost? We're taking care of him; the least they could do is try to help pay for some of his treatment.

TRACE: *(growing angry)* You know that you can't depend on my brothers like that. And Tee Tee practically raised me. I can't deny him anything that he needs.

SIESHA: *(getting pissed off, too)* You are always letting your brothers get off easy and not making them take any responsibility. Then I have to suffer for it.

TRACE: *(turning away)* Hey, I have to suffer too. But that's the way my family is; you got to love them, but you don't have to like what they do. Anyway, your family is not the pinnacle of responsibility either. No one wants to put your mama in a home because they don't want to pay for it.

SIESHA: *(looking right at Trace, with growing contempt)* We let my mama do as she pleases, and she doesn't want to go to no home. Get that through your thick skull.

TRACE: *(angry and unbuttoning his shirt)* I am not in the mood to go eat. I will just order something up here. You can do whatever you want.

Notice what happens here. They are relaxed, spending some time together, being friends. But their talk turns into a conflict about issues. As Siesha raises the issue of the high cost of caring for cousin Tee Tee, they get into an argument in which a number of issues are triggered by family responsibility, their opposing styles in dealing with siblings, and money. Perhaps some hidden issues are triggered as well. What has been a great talk as friends until now turns into a nasty argument as spouses.

When couples aren't doing a good job of keeping issues from erupting into their more relaxed time together, it becomes hard to keep such positive times going in the relationship. The worst thing that can happen is that time spent in talking as friends becomes something to avoid. As we said earlier in the book, the growing perception is that talking leads to fighting—including talking as friends. So the baby gets thrown out with the bath water. This is one of the chief reasons some couples lose touch with friendship over time. But as we'll see, you *can* prevent this from happening.

## We Are Victims of Reckless Words

One of the major barriers to friendship in marriage is that things shared in a tender and intimate moment are used later as weapons in a fight. When this happens, it's incredibly destructive to friendship.

Turner and Martha have been married for two years and have just had their first child. Both are feeling overwhelmed by the demands of Martha's career and their new baby, so she's begun to have regular talks with a counselor at church. After one particularly emotional but productive session, she shares with Turner that she is feeling vulnerable and not very confident about her parenting ability.

Later in the same week, they get into a fight over who should get up to be with the baby in the middle of the night. As the fight escalates, Martha accuses Turner of faking sleep so she'll have to get up all the time. He goes on the defensive and blurts out something like "Why are you on my case about taking care of that child? You are the one who has to see a counselor to feel better about being a mom. Maybe if you work more with him you can feel better about what you do and stop blaming me." This infuriates Martha and she leaves the room, fuming and swearing she'll never tell him anything personal again.

Unfortunately, events like this happen all too often in relationships. Through positive, intimate experiences as friends, we learn things that can be used as powerful weapons later when we feel more like enemies. But who's going to keep sharing personal and vulnerable information if it might be used later in a fight?

## Protecting Friendship in Your Marriage

We've found some core principles that help us protect and enhance friendship. If you have a good friendship going, these principles can prevent your friendship from weakening over time. If you've lost something in terms of being friends, these ideas can help you regain what you've been missing.

## Make the Time

It's great to be friends no matter what you're doing, but we think you can benefit by setting time apart specifically for talking as friends. For this to happen, you must make the time. Otherwise, all the busy stuff of life will keep you occupied with problems and concerns.

We mentioned how Laura and Jerome have preserved and deepened their friendship during their forty years of marriage. One of the things they do to keep friendship alive is plan time to be alone together. They take long walks together and talk as they walk. They go out to dinner. They take weekend vacations from time to time. They make the time, and it's been paying off for more than forty years.

If couples are really serious in telling us that they want to make friendship important, they need to plan time to be together as friends. You need to make it a priority in this aspect of your intimacy. This is one of the key investments you can make in your relationship. The problem we all face is that there is much less *quality time* when there is little *quantity time*. You need to put some boundaries around all the other things you do in life to carve out time for friendship. But that's not all you need to do to protect friendship.

## Protecting Your Friendship from Conflict and Issues

In the first portion of this book, we focused on skills and techniques for handling conflict well, such as using the speaker-listener technique, good problem solving skills, and ground rules. In the middle chapters, we added to this theme by presenting the issues-and-events model as well as concepts on forgiveness. These strategies are powerful tools for dealing with conflict. You didn't get together to have a lifelong mate with whom you could handle conflicts, but you do have to handle conflict well if you want to protect the more wonderful aspects of intimacy in your marriage. This requires setting time aside to deal with issues as issues, taking time out when conflict intrudes on the time you set aside for friendship, and forgiving one another for problems in the past so that the trust that friendship thrives on is nurtured.

Never use information shared in a moment of intimacy as a weapon in a fight. Nothing adds fuel to the fire like betraying a trust in this way. If you do, apologize and make every effort not to do it again. As we said earlier, this is incredibly destructive and creates huge barriers to future intimacy. If you find yourself so mad that you're even tempted to do this, you probably aren't handling issues well enough in your relationship. You may need to work harder—and together—on all of the principles and techniques we emphasized in the early chapters of this book. It takes a lot of skill and practice to get to the point where you can handle conflict with respect and skill. Acting on all the material earlier in this book makes it much more likely that you'll have a great friendship that can grow deeper over time.

You might be surprised how simple yet powerful it can be for the two of you to agree that some of the time is friend time and therefore off limits for conflict and issues. For example, you could decide that whenever you take a walk in your neighborhood, it's automatically friend time. Or, you can go out to dinner and specifically agree that "This is friend time, tonight, OK?" You are working together to define the times you are off duty in your marriage. Even better, you can agree that unless you have both agreed to deal with an issue at a particular time, the understanding is that you are still in friend mode. Think about how you can act out this principle in your relationship. The key is to realize together that you are not at the mercy of your issues. You can keep issues in their place and thereby preserve space for the promise of deepening friendship in your marriage.

## How to Talk Like Friends

Now let's move on to discuss how you can talk like good friends. We want to highlight some points about how friends talk to help you protect and enhance your relationship.

*Listen Like a Friend*

Good friends listen with little defensiveness. You don't have to worry so much about feelings getting hurt or worry that your friend will be offended. This is because a friend cares about what you think and feel, and relationship issues are rarely at stake. Our friend and colleague, Bill Coffin, once noted, "A friend is someone who's glad to see you and doesn't have any immediate plans for your improvement." When you're talking as friends, you are not trying to change one another. You can both relax and just enjoy the conversation. Even when we let our hair down and talk about something really serious, we don't want a friend to tell us what to do; we just want the person to listen. It feels good to know someone cares. Friends often provide that kind of support, and you can do this for each other in your relationship.

*Friends Aren't Focused on Solving Problems*

Most of the time, when you're with a friend you don't have to solve a problem. There may be a limited amount of time, but there's no pressure to get something done. As we said in Chapter Four, if you feel pressed to solve a problem, it's easy to cut off discussion that can bring you closer together. This is why it's so important not to talk about relationship issues when you're together as friends. With relationship issues, there's too much temptation to solve something and give advice.

---

Like so many other things you've learned in this book, friendship is a skill. It is also a natural outcome of a solid marriage. Make it a priority to take care of the friendship dimension of your marriage. To keep your friendship strong and alive, you may have to work on it. We can't think of anything of greater importance for the long-term health of your marriage than to stay friends.

In this chapter, we've tried to outline some of the things that really make friendships work, especially in how you communicate. As we move to the next chapter, we change the focus to fun. This is another key area of intimacy and friendship in marriage that's often taken for granted. We'll go into that topic after suggesting some friendship exercises for you.

# Exercises

Plan some time for these exercises. Have fun, relax, and enjoy your friendship.

1.  Plan quiet, uninterrupted time. Take turns picking topics of interest for each of you. Ban relationship conflict issues and problem solutions. Then consider some of these topics:

>   A.  Some aspect of your family of origin that you've been thinking about
>
>   B.  Personal goals, dreams, or aspirations
>
>   C.  A recent book or movie (pretend you're a professional critic, if you like)
>
>   D.  Current events: sports, politics, and so forth

2.  Take turns pretending to be your favorite TV interviewers, and interview your partner about his or her life story. This can be a lot of fun, and it's really in the spirit of listening as friends. The best interviewers on TV are really good at listening and drawing their guests out of themselves. Try to draw one another out in your sharing together as friends.

3.  Talk together about how you can build time for friendship into your weekly routine. If you both believe friendship time should be a priority, how do you want to demonstrate it?

Now let's move on to the importance of preserving and enhancing your ability to have fun. As with friendship, most people want to have fun with their partners. We hope you do too, because we have some specific ideas about how you can preserve enjoyment in your relationship.

# 12

# Marriage and Fun

## *They Go Together!*

Fun plays a vital role in the health of a relationship. In the early versions of PREP, fun was a very small part of our program. However, as a result of some studies we and our colleagues conducted, we learned that we weren't paying enough attention to the role of fun in marriage. It always seemed like common sense that fun was important, but this research highlighted that fun is as important an issue as those discussed regarding commitment (Chapter Eight) or solving problems (Chapter Two).

## Research on Fun

In a nationwide random phone survey conducted in 1996, we (SMS and HJM) found that fun was an important marital dimension in understanding how the couples were doing across the board. Couples responded to more than fifty questions on all aspects of their relationship: satisfaction, commitment, communication, sex, and just about anything else you can think of (including "When was the last time you went out on a date?").

Among all these variables, we were surprised to find that the amount of fun these partners had together emerged as a key factor in understanding their overall marital happiness. The message: a good relationship stays great when you're preserving both the quantity and the quality of your fun times together. (Later on we share the surprising answers we received to our question on dating one's spouse in marriage.)

## Barriers to Fun

Most couples have a lot of fun early in their relationship. But for too many, fun fizzles out as time goes on. Here are some of the most common explanations we hear from couples.

### We're Too Busy

Couples often stop making time for fun in their busy lives. Early in a relationship, people tend to put a high priority on going out to the movies, window shopping, walking hand in hand, going bowling, and so forth.

That's the way it was for Kathy, twenty-eight, and Alan, thirty. When they were dating, they would go out every night. They didn't have a lot of money, but they always had a lot of fun. They would also take long walks in the sand and talk about their future together. After they got married, they went out only on weekends. A few years later, they had their first child and began to spend much less time having fun and much more time centered on their child having fun. Sure, their daughter, Jovan, was a blessing, but it was rare for Kathy and Alan to actually go out and have fun as they used to.

They have noticed over time that life isn't as much fun as it used to be. They are happy together and their eight-year-old marriage is solid, but they've let something slip away. It's really pretty simple. Life is more fun when you *do* fun. The rest of life crowds out fun if you don't make time for it to happen. We encourage you to find the time to keep up the fun and playfulness that can make your relationship delightful.

Eric and Coren are a good example of a couple who have preserved time for fun in their marriage. They've been married for twenty years and haven't let fun slip away. Every Friday night, for most of those years, they've gone out on a date to have fun together. That's just one way they've preserved fun in their relationship. They've made use of baby-sitters and haven't let things come between them and this time together. It's a priority in their marriage.

They also vary what they do for fun: dinner and a movie one week, swimming together another, dance lessons at times, walking in the park and watching the sun set, and so forth. They've tried lots of things, and they've made the time. Their marriage has benefited. Their fun experiences have built a positive storehouse of pleasant times and memories together. You can't overestimate the value of that.

To give you a research-based idea on how busy the typical couple is today, we asked people in our poll how long it's been since they were on a date. We divided couples into groups according to the stage of the relationship, as to whether it was the husband or wife who responded. In general, couples had dates every five weeks. Although this may seem like a short time between dates for some, for us it reflects that couples are not having a lot of fun!

There were two other major results. First, the couples having the least fun were those in the midrange of marital duration (five to fifteen years), at which point they were busy raising children and investing in their careers. The most fun-loving couples were the engaged couples (no surprise) and those married more than thirty-two years. Hey, there is light at the end of the tunnel of love!

Our most intriguing finding is that men report going out on dates substantially more than women. Why is this the case? Do men and women have different definitions or standards for what a date is? Our workshop participants (at least the women) generally agree that men may be likely to feel that sitting home watching TV together is a date, while for women a date tends to require thought and effort. The key for your relationship is to use this finding to stimulate some conversation (of course, not *during* a date) about what a date means to each of you.

### Play Is for Kids

Many preschool experts say that playing is the work that children need to do. Through play, they gain developmentally relevant social, emotional, and cognitive abilities. We believe that the developmental importance of play doesn't stop after childhood but continues throughout life. Fun and play allow a release of oneself from all the pressures and hassles of being an adult.

The relaxed togetherness of playful times is important in developing an initial bond between two people. This is because when we're engaged in fun through play, we're often relaxed and ourselves. It's under these conditions that people fall in love—when one sees in the other the relaxed self in the context of fun times together. It's not too often that you hear someone say, "I really fell in love with him when I saw how much he loved to work."

We mentioned how Kathy and Alan used to go to the ocean more often earlier in their relationship. During the time there, they'd splash in the water, make sand castles together, rub suntan lotion on one another, and bury each other; they played together like kids. During these times, they'd frequently look at one another and smile in the delight of the moment. There's no putting a price tag on the value of time that builds such a basic bond.

Kathy and Alan still experience that kind of bond when playing with Jovan, but they could use a lot more relaxed and playful time together. As we said above, the couples in really super marriages create this time to play together, which keeps refreshing the bond. So be a kid from time to time.

## Conflict

Mishandled conflict can erode friendship and is a real killer of fun times together. In fact, we make the same point in the next chapter, on sensuality. Poorly handled conflict can ruin the most enjoyable aspects of any relationship.

Elon and Carl are a middle-aged couple who have been making the time for fun. That isn't the problem. All too often they are out to have a fun time and then some event triggers an issue that kills the playfulness of the moment.

On one particular night, they arrange for a sitter for the kids and go out to take a class in line dancing. They are thinking, *This will lead to going dancing more often and have another way of having fun.* A great idea. As the instructor makes a point to the class about how to follow the rhythm of the group, Elon whispers to Carl, "Follow!" Carl whispers back, "I've been trying to tell *you* that for years." Elon is instantly offended. She feels attacked and moves away from Carl, folding her hands across her chest in disgust.

This event triggers some hot issues for Elon and Carl. For years, Carl has felt that Elon doesn't follow his lead as the man of the house—which hits an issue of respect. He is bothered that it seems as though she doesn't respect their interaction on decisions at home, and now even out in public. Elon has been feeling that Carl is too traditional about their relationship and that there is no king of the castle but rather sharing in decision making. At the instant mentioned, she thinks to herself, *Can't he even lay off when we're out to have fun?* On this evening, they don't recover well. Elon suggests they leave the class early and go home. They do—in silence.

There are times for every couple when a conflict erupts during fun time. But if it begins to happen a lot, fun times won't be so much fun anymore. The whole idea with fun is that you're doing something together that is relaxing and that brings out positive emotions you can share together. Poorly handled conflict disrupts these times. The sense that conflict could erupt at any moment isn't compatible with relaxed playfulness. We set ourselves up to fail at fun if we allow a grievance or anger to carry over into our special fun time.

Now that we've spent some time discussing what prevents fun from being a regular part of some relationships over time, let's see some ideas for keeping fun a significant part of your relationship.

# A Primer for Having Fun in Marriage

You may be thinking that you know how to have fun and don't need strategies and skills. If so, that's great. But we think we have some pointers for any couple that can keep them on track. Here are some suggestions as to how to accomplish it.

## Making the Time

It's hard to have fun together without setting aside time for it to happen. Sure, you could have a moment of fun just about anywhere, anytime, if the mood strikes you both. Even a quick joke together or seeing something funny on TV can be fun. But to get the full benefit, we suggest you make this a priority so that you can get into the flow of fun together. You have to be serious about setting time for not being so serious.

Most people are so busy and harried by life that it takes some time just to switch gears into the fun mode. That's why, for many couples, the first day or two of a vacation can be more stressful than fun. You're making a transition. The same holds true for shorter periods of fun time. It often takes time just to wind down to get relaxed. But once you are relaxed and playing together in some way, the opportunities to draw closer together in the bond of the positive emotion really take hold.

To make the time for fun together, you might actually have to pull out a schedule and arrange it. This may not sound all that spontaneous, but for most couples there's so much else going on that it takes a deliberate act to make the time happen. Also, you may need to arrange for a baby-sitter for the kids. If you don't have a sitter you trust, it may be time to look hard and find one. If you have kids, there's nothing that helps you relax more when you're out to have fun than knowing your little ones are with someone you trust.

Lastly, if you're making the time for fun, try to arrange for time with no possibility of distraction. If your job requires you to wear a beeper, do you have to wear it when you've carved out time to play with your spouse? It's not very relaxing to know you could get beeped at any moment. Make the time and shut out the distractions of the rest of your life. It's worth it. It might even give you something to look forward to.

## Protecting Fun from Conflict

As we said for friendship, the material on handling conflict presented in Chapters Two through Four is critical if you are going to preserve the fun in your relationship. As a couple, you need to control the times and conditions under which you deal with the difficult and conflictual issues in your relationship. When you've blocked out time to have fun, don't do conflict. Block out a separate time to handle the tricky issues.

Many couples finally buy into the wisdom of date night or some such idea to get away to enjoy each other. However, in our experience many couples try to do too much with the time they've set aside. They try to have fun together *and* resolve difficult issues "while we have this time together."

For example, one night Frank and Karen went out to an ice skating show. As they were seated and waiting for the show to start, Frank said, "We haven't had time to talk out that budget problem. Let's see what we can get done right now." Big mistake. Their budget was a serious conflict area between them, and it deserved far more focused time to deal with than they were going to have waiting for an ice show to start. As you can imagine, they didn't get anywhere in the time they had on the budget and only succeeded in getting on edge with each other when they were out to have fun.

Although it's understandable and expected that conflict is sometimes going to come up during fun time, we can't see why couples set aside the time and then deliberately spend some of it to deal with issues. Dealing with issues isn't compatible with what brings the greatest benefit to your relationship in having fun time together: being relaxed and upbeat with one another.

Deal with the important issues in your relationship in meetings arranged for that purpose—not during time for fun. When issues get triggered during time you set aside for fun, table them. Call a time out. Come back to it later. It's not hard to do once you try it a few times. In our experience, there's no more powerful change a couple can make quickly in their relationship than to agree to keep conflict out of time set aside to have fun.

## So What Can We Do for Fun?

OK, you've appointed the time for fun and you've agreed to put conflict aside to protect the time. Now what? For many couples, this is a difficult question. For others, like those in the super marriages we described, there are plenty of ideas. Some of you have gotten rusty at coming up with fun things to do together.

In many ways, coming up with fun things to do is a skill just like all the others we're emphasizing in this book. You have to practice such skills if they're going to work for you. If you're rusty at fun or want to keep your fun skills sharp, here are some of our ideas that might help.

### Brainstorming About Fun Activities

Of course, a couple may do many activities for fun. What do you do? Sit down together and think about the most enjoyable, interesting, and fun things you've ever done, or things you would like to do together. Make a list to which you both contribute, putting down all ideas no matter how foolish or outrageous they may seem. Part of the fun is brainstorming about fun—throwing out the wackiest ideas you can. Avoid getting into a rut.

### Ideas We've Heard from Couples

To help you get started, we'd like to mention some of the great ideas we've heard from couples over the years. Maybe one of these ideas will cause a cascade of others to form in your own mind.

Couples have suggested such activities as exercising, yoga, or massage together. These are all activities that not only build oneness but are important for your physical health. Stress destroys the body and causes many of the major health problems that African Americans experience—hypertension, stroke, and diabetes, to name just a few. By engaging in these stress-relieving activities together, you help your relationship and help to make sure that you will have fun together for a long time.

Fun doesn't have to be something that's elaborate or costs money. These are things couples can do almost anywhere if they find them fun. In contrast, skiing is a wonderfully fun activity but it can be very expensive. But if you have the time and the money, it can be great to spend the day together. There is an African American ski group called the National Brotherhood of Skiers that meets every year.

Many couples enjoy going to the movies. This is not a very original idea, and you've probably already thought of it, but how long has it been? Or if you go regularly, how long has it been since you made out in the back row of the theater? If you've never kissed your way through a movie, give it a try.

Cards or dominos are always fun. Tunk, Michigan Rummy, Hearts, Crazy Eights, Twenty-One, and Spades are card games that we've all played. What about trying some strip poker? These are good games if it doesn't get too competitive. Talking trash can be part of the fun in these games (though for some folks too much of that can spoil the fun).

You can bake cookies together, and make a big mess. You can go to the gym together, or read the same book. You can go walking or go to the park and have a picnic. How about renting a classic seventies movie like *Shaft* or *Superfly* and cuddling on the sofa with a bowl of popcorn? Have you ever shared a soda with two straws? Have you ever tried cooking a meal together and then feeding it to each other?

Even things that seem like work can be fun if that's your attitude. According to one husband, "My wife and I found out that something really fun was to do yard work together. It's fun to be together sprucing up our home, and at the end of the day it's rewarding to see what we accomplished. We're both city folks living in the country, but in the summer time we try planting different flowers. We work hand in hand in planting every bulb. There's something about creating that gives us both great pleasure and pride. These things are fun for us because it's us doing them together."

Over the years, we've noticed that when we have couples brainstorm about fun things to do, sex usually isn't mentioned until other things come up. Couples tend to forget that sexual intimacy is one of the most fun things they can do together. Several variations, to suit your personal preferences of course, should be on your list. How about setting aside an evening without the kids to make love?

We want you to be at the place where any fun time you have together is something to be eagerly anticipated. Be creative.

### To Get Going

Try this to get the creative juices going. Make a personal fun deck by taking a deck of index cards, and write down on each card one of the items from your brainstorming. We suggest maybe twenty-five to thirty ideas to start with; they can cover a whole range of topics. Once you've made the deck, set aside particular times to choose activities and do them. Don't let anything stop you.

Since you're going to have more fun if you are both up for the activities you choose, here's one way to make sure this happens using your fun deck. Each of you can pick three cards from the deck describing things you'd find fun to do that day. Trade cards. Then you each choose one card from the three your partner picked and you take responsibility for making that one activity happen. This way, you're each picking something you know your partner will like, but since you get to choose among the three, you're likely to like it too. Don't worry about which one your partner wants you to pick. If you don't get to it today, you'll have another chance tomorrow.

If you follow the key points in this chapter, you'll be qualified for a degree in relationship fun. You can do it. Early in a relationship, it comes easily. It's not hard if you make the time, protect the time, and make fun happen.

Sensuality and sexuality can be fun, too. All too often, however, the sensual and sexual area also falls victim to the barriers against fun discussed earlier. Some professionals believe that sexual chemistry inevitably decreases over the years. Yet many couples are able to sustain and even improve their sex lives over time. We don't believe that couples fall out of attraction. Rather, the biggest reason that attraction dies down is that couples neglect the very things that build and maintain attraction in the first place: friendship, fun, and so forth.

But before we focus on the sensual and sexual side of things, we have some exercises to help you break the fun barrier.

## Exercises

We'd like you to go through the steps we discussed in this chapter. Here they are again:

1. Brainstorm a list of fun things. Be creative. Anything goes, so have fun coming up with ideas.

2. Write these ideas out on three-by-five cards to make your fun deck. It will come in handy when you don't have much time to decide what to do but are ready for some fun.

3. Set aside time. Pick from the deck three things you'd enjoy doing. Hand these three to your partner. Each of you should take responsibility for making one of your partner's three things happen in the time you've set aside. Go for it!

Now we move on to the area of physical intimacy. It can be a great way to have fun together, but it's much more. Physical intimacy is one of the most fundamental ways a couple have of building and keeping a positive bond in their marriage.

# 13

# Sexual Healing

Remember Marvin Gaye's songs "Sexual Healing" and "Let's Get It On"? For their time, songs of that kind were controversial because they were such an open presentation of sexuality. They made us publicly think about our sexuality. For many, the first thought when someone mentions sexuality is of intercourse and all the pleasurable acts that may come before and after. Anything else? What about thoughts of what is arousing to you or your partner, or feelings you have when you want to make love with your partner?

Now think about sensuality. What comes to mind? Usually, some pleasant experience that involves touching, seeing, smelling, or feeling, such as walking on the beach or being massaged with sweet-smelling oil. How about the roughness of a beard or curliness of hair? The smell of your partner after a shower? Chocolate? You get the idea.

These sensual experiences are not necessarily goal-oriented or connected with sexuality. Sensuality includes physical touch or other senses but is not always associated with making love. We include hugging, affectionate cuddling, nonsexual massages . . . all acts that lend physical pleasure in a nonsexual way. This distinction between sensuality and sexuality is important as we go along in this chapter.

In the early stage of a relationship, touching, holding hands, hugging, and caressing are common. Unfortunately, over time many couples tend to bypass the sensual and move exclusively to goal-oriented sexual behavior. Less time is spent on the kind of touching and sensing that was so delightful before. This leads to problems in a marriage because such touching is a basic, pleasurable part of your overall intimacy.

For example, Adonna and Charles have been married for eight years. Like most couples, they used to spend a lot of time just cuddling and caressing each other. As time went by, they got busier with kids, work, home, and extended kin, as most of us do. After a year or two of marriage, they settled into a pattern of having sex about twice a week. Given time pressures and other cares of life, less and less time was devoted to sensuality. At night, in bed, one or the other would initiate sex and they'd quickly have intercourse, usually finishing in about ten minutes.

Adonna and Charles have become quite efficient about making love—or rather, having intercourse. They don't have or make a lot of extra time, so they make do. In fact, they are "making do" rather than making love. Their focus on sexual intercourse rather than sensuality leads to dissatisfaction for both. "What happened to all those times we'd lay around for hours together, just caressing and laughing?" she wonders. "It seems like she used to be a lot more responsive when we made love," Charles muses. We'll come back to them in a bit.

The fact is, there needs to be a place for sensual touching in your relationship, both in and outside the context of making love. This is similar to the distinction between problem discussion and problem solution. Just as the pressures of life lead many couples to problem solving prematurely, too many couples shortchange the sensual and prematurely focus on just sex. This leads to sex without the overall context of touching. But what people really value, both men and women, is sensual touching.

Therefore it's important to make sensual experience a regular part of your relationship, apart from sexuality. Furthermore, sensual experience sets the stage for better sexual experience. Even when making love, couples can forget the sensual side of things. The whole climate for physical intimacy is better when you keep the sensual temperature. Talk together about what is sensual for each of you. What do you enjoy? Wayne and Belinda communicate a lot as to what they like about what the other does. Belinda tells Wayne, "I like it when you touch my stomach; for some reason that's a real sensitive spot for me." Wayne shares with Belinda, "There is something about putting your hands on my face when you kiss me that gets me going." Make the time for sensual experience that doesn't necessarily lead to sex—simple things, from holding hands to a massage.

It's also important to keep sensuality as a regular part of your lovemaking. When you keep a focus on a variety of touching, it preserves and elevates the importance of the whole sensual experience. Most couples prefer this broad sensual focus to a narrow focus on sex. It offers a fuller expression of intimacy in your physical relationship.

## Protecting Physical Intimacy from Anxiety

Arousal is the natural process by which we are stimulated to sensual or sexual pleasure. It's a state of pleasurable excitement. Just about everyone is capable of being aroused; however, this pleasurable feeling can be short-circuited by anxiety. Numerous studies suggest that anxiety is the main inhibiting factor to arousal.

There are two major kinds of anxiety that we'd like to discuss in this context: performance anxiety and the tension from conflict in your marriage.

### The Barrier of Performance Anxiety

Performance anxiety is anxiety about how you're "performing" when you make love. Regularly asking yourself questions such as *How am I doing?* or *Is my partner enjoying this?* reflects performance anxiety.

When you're keeping an eye on your performance, you put distance between yourself and your partner. You're focused on how you are doing rather than on being there with your partner. Many people report feeling distant when making love, as if they're just watching what's going on instead of participating. This kind of detachment is believed to lead to a variety of sexual problems. The focus is no longer on the pleasure you're sharing. Instead, your self-esteem feels at stake. It's as if the event of making love has triggered issues of acceptance and the fear of rejection.

The focus on performance interferes with arousal because you are distracted from your own sensations of pleasure. This distraction leads to many of the most common sexual problems people experience: sexual disinterest, premature ejaculation, problems in keeping an erection for men, and difficulty lubricating or having orgasms for women. You can't be both anxious and pleasantly aroused at the same time. And you can't be relaxed and enjoy being with your partner if you are concentrating on not making mistakes.

Consider Charles and Adonna again. Charles has become aware over time that Adonna is less and less pleased with their lovemaking. Because a focus on sensuality and touching has been largely absent throughout their relationship, Adonna is beginning to feel that Charles is just using her sexually. This feeling is intensified because he has orgasms every time they make love, but hers are less frequent. As dissatisfying as their lovemaking is for both of them, it seems to Adonna that it is still better for Charles. So her resentment grows.

Charles is becoming aware of her resentment and wants to make things better. But instead of talking it out and working on the problem together, he decides he'll just do a better job of making love to Adonna. This isn't all bad, as ideas go. However, it leaves him more and more focused on performing—and his anxiety grows. Thoughts about performance become his constant companion during their lovemaking: *How's Adonna doing? Is she getting excited? Does she like this? I wonder if she thinks I'm doing this right? Man, I'd better try more of this for a while; I'm not sure she's ready.*

Pretty soon he is pleasing Adonna somewhat more, but he is growing tenser about what he's doing when they make love. Sure, he is meeting some of her needs, but he doesn't feel at all connected with her or satisfied in their lovemaking. He is performing! Adonna knows there is some change in Charles's attention to her arousal, which does please her to some degree. But she has this growing sense that Charles is somewhere else when they make love. She is having more orgasms, but she doesn't feel they are sharing a sensual experience.

The key for Adonna and Charles is to rediscover the sensual side of their relationship and make it more of a priority. They have to talk out loud about what's going on. Adonna and Charles have a lot of love and respect for each other, so once they start dealing with the issues, their relationship quickly gets better.

In the PREP approach, we emphasize that you can *prevent* problems from developing in the first place if you are willing to do so and you know what to do. This is especially true for your sex life. You can do a lot to keep a problem like Adonna's and Charles' from ever developing. For some of you, their story is very familiar; for many it is much worse. For others, your physical relationship hasn't deteriorated, and that's great. The goal? Learn to keep things that way.

## The Barrier of Relationship Conflict and Anxiety

Mishandled conflict can destroy your physical relationship by adding tension, both in and outside the bedroom. Let's face it: when you've been arguing and angry with each other, you don't often feel like being sensual or making love. Although for some the sexual relationship is temporarily enhanced by making up following the conflict, for most people poorly handled conflict adds a layer of tension that affects everything else in the relationship.

Tension isn't compatible with enjoyable, intimate lovemaking for most people. In fact, there may be no area of intimate connection that's more vulnerable to the effects of conflict and resentment than your physical relationship. If you are experiencing conflict in other areas of your relationship, it can be difficult to feel positive about sharing an intimate physical experience. Worse, these conflicts too often erupt in the context of lovemaking.

Touching sensually or making love is a powerful way to connect, but destructive conflict builds barriers. If you can protect your times for physical intimacy from conflict, you can do a great deal to keep your physical relationship alive and well. To do this, you must work to handle conflict well—for example, by using the ground rules and other techniques we've been stressing. It's critical to agree to keep problems and disagreements off limits whenever you have the time, or are making the time, for just touching and making love.

## Communicating Desires

It's critical to communicate about your physical relationship in a way that protects and enhances this important means of being intimate. That goes not only for handling potential conflict around physical intimacy but also for telling each other what you desire. We're talking about real communication, not mind reading. Mind reading can cause many serious conflicts throughout a relationship, including issues of sensuality and sexuality. The problem is that people too easily assume they know what their partner wants, and when.

### You Should Know What I Like!

It's a mistake to assume that your partner likes whatever you like, or that you can read each other's minds. Would you go out to a restaurant and order for your partner without talking about what was desired? Of course not.

It's also too easy for some people to assume that their partner doesn't like the things they like. Either way, you're making assumptions. Since many couples have trouble communicating about their physical relationship, it's really easy for these assumptions to take control. You don't know what your partner's expectations are until you ask, and vice versa.

Of course, on the basis of previous experience together, you can often assume correctly, and things can work out fine from those assumptions. However, keep in mind that people change, so checking in with each other about desires and expectations is valuable for having a good sexual relationship.

We can't tell you how many partners we've talked with seem to expect the other "to know" what they like most when making love. It's as if people believe that "it just isn't romantic or exciting if I have to tell you what I want; you *should* know!" This is an unreasonable expectation. If you hold this fantasy, you should probably challenge it, for the health of your relationship.

Couples who have the best sensual and sexual relationships have ways of communicating verbally and nonverbally about what they like. Furthermore, there's usually a genuine unselfish desire to please one another. There's a strong sense of teamwork involved, even in lovemaking, where each gives to and receives from the intimacy they share. The giving combined with the direct communication leads to great lovemaking.

We recommend that you communicate clearly about what feels pleasurable to you while you are touching or making love. Your partner doesn't know unless you say something. We're not suggesting that you have a speaker-listener discussion in the middle of lovemaking (although if the idea really excites you that much, let us know how it goes!).

Finally, look for ways to give to your partner in your physical relationship. If you're keeping conflict out of the bedroom, handling conflict well in the rest of your relationship, and taking the time and energy to preserve sensuality, this kind of communication is much easier to do.

## Taking a Risk

Communication is the key. It also helps to try some new ideas to break out of a rut. Read a book on massage or sex together. It might help you talk about these issues. Agree to surprise each other one night. Try something new, even if just once. Exploring the sensual and sexual side of your relationship may relieve many concerns about performance with one another and help you find even more pleasure.

We're not saying every couple can have a wonderful physical relationship. You both have to want it, protect it, and nurture it. If things are going well in your physical relationship, keep it that way. If some problems have developed, what we are emphasizing here can help you get back on track.

## Make It a Priority

Carmen and Enoch have what they consider a good marriage, but like so many couples they rarely have sex now. They both grew up in strict Baptist households where sex was not talked about in public. When they first got together, they took the development of their physical intimacy slowly. This was wonderful in that it gave them ample opportunity to really get to know one another without the context of sex. They abstained from sex till they got married. As newlyweds, they would have sex only once or twice a month if they were lucky (as they put it). When they did have sex, they said it went well, with both getting aroused and having orgasms (though Carmen was more often orgasmic through oral sex or when Enoch touched her than through intercourse). Their current lack of sex suggested problems other than specific sexual dysfunction.

Rather than focusing on whether they really love each other or are still really attracted to each other, we assumed in working with them that the issue is their falling into bad habits by not making their love life a priority. With our urging, they have decided they both want to increase their involvement in physical intimacy. Thus we developed this simple but powerful plan, which has worked for them and can work for virtually any couple. The key is that each person agrees to carry out the plan on his or her own, without any prompting from the other:

• Focus on being romantic and sensual (send flowers, romantic e-mails, whisper suggestive desires during dinner, touch your partner's leg under the table). Talking as friends and sharing fun times are aphrodisiacs; we hear this often from women, but we believe it's also true for men. Don't focus on orgasm or outcome; pressure is not an aphrodisiac.

• Focus on wooing your partner rather than taking his or her love for granted. The man should be her knight in shining armor, winning her love and affection daily.

• Be sensitive to your partner's rhythms, needs, and wishes. For example, so many couples say they don't have sex because "he's a night person and I'm a morning person." If this is the case, push yourself to be sensual during your partner's times.

• Be creative and take the initiative. Let your partner know you care and are attracted, and that you want him or her—but do so in a variety of ways. The possibilities are endless. You might be driving to work together and passing a motel and say, "Let's be an hour late. . . ." Even if this isn't possible that day, the message is that you're attracted to your partner and want him or her, and so you might do it some other time.

• Be a great lover. When having sex, kiss and touch sensual (not just sexual) spots that your partner enjoys, such as the earlobe or neck. Be creative and suggestive; remember that marital sex is the place to engage in virtually any mutually consented activity. Some research suggests that a couple's love life is best when the man and the woman both initiate, rather than only one person typically initiating. Flexibility is a good thing.

In this chapter, we've emphasized several factors for keeping your physical relationship growing and vibrant. Now it's up to you.

We don't intend for this chapter to be a substitute for sex therapy if you have a history of significant sexual difficulties. If this sounds like you, we want to encourage you to work together to overcome the problems. Working with an experienced sex therapist can usually accomplish a great deal when there are significant problems. Our focus here is to help couples who have satisfying physical relationships to keep things that way and to make it even better. Sometimes difficulty with sexual intimacy exists because of physical problems. We strongly suggest that if problems persist, see a urologist or gynecologist.

To close this chapter, we offer exercises that can help you enhance your ability to connect physically. They are exercises that have been tried successfully for years with many couples. If you're ready for sensual and sexual enhancement, read on.

## Exercises

1. Sensate-focus. Years ago, William Masters and Virginia Johnson began studying how sexual relationships develop problems. They developed an exercise that has benefited many couples, whether or not they have struggled in their physical relationship. It's called the sensate-focus. The purpose is twofold: to keep you focused on sensuality and touching in your physical relationship, and to help you learn to communicate openly and naturally about what you like and don't like in your lovemaking.

This isn't the time for sexual intercourse. That would defeat the purpose, since we want you to focus on sensuality. Don't be goal-oriented (other than on the goal of relaxing and doing this exercise in a way that you each enjoy). If you want to make love following the exercise, that's up to you. But if you've been having a lot of concerns about feeling pressured in sexuality, we recommend you completely separate out these practice times from having sex. In fact, you shouldn't have sex unless both of you fully and openly agree to do so. No mind reading or assumptions.

The general idea is that you each take turns giving and receiving pleasure. The first few times, you are either the *giver* or the *receiver*, until you switch roles half-way through the exercise. When in the receiver role, your job is to enjoy the touching and give feedback on what feels good and what doesn't. Your partner doesn't know this unless you tell him or her. You can give either verbal or hand-guided feedback.

Verbal feedback means telling your partner what actions feel good, how hard to rub or what areas you like to have touched. Hand-guided feedback consists of gently moving your partner's hand around the part of the body being massaged to give feedback about what really feels good.

As the giver, your role is to give pleasure by touching your partner and being responsive to feedback. Ask for feedback as often as necessary. Be aware of changes in how your partner is reacting; what feels good one minute may hurt the next. You are to focus on what your partner wants, not on what you think would feel good.

Choose roles and give a massage of the hands or feet for about ten to twenty minutes, asking for and giving feedback. For the first few times to get the hang of the technique, we recommend massaging areas such as the hands, back, legs, feet, and so on. This also helps you relax if there are some issues about sexuality between you. Then switch roles. Repeat as often as you like. Also practice the giver and receiver roles in other aspects of your sensual and sexual relationship.

We recommend that you try the sensate-focus exercise over the course of several weeks, several times a week. As you work on the exercise, there are some variations of the technique to work in over time. Assuming all is going well in your exercises, begin to move to other areas for touching. Wherever you want to be touched, including the sexual areas, is great.

Over time, you can drop the rigid emphasis on the giver and receiver roles and work on both of you giving and receiving at the same time, while still keeping an emphasis on sensuality and communication of desires. Or you can vary the degree to which you want to stay in these roles as you wish. If you practice this regularly, it becomes easier for you to communicate openly about touch. It is also easier for you to work together to keep physical intimacy vibrant and alive.

2. Exploring the sensual. In addition to the sensate-focus exercise, set aside a specific time for sensual activity together. This works for all couples, regardless of whether they are engaging in sexual activity. Be sure you will not be interrupted (this is the time for baby-sitters and answering machines).

At the start of this exercise, talk about what's sensual for each of you, and what you'd like to try doing to keep sensual experience in your relationship. Here are some ideas:

1. Give a massage to your partner, using the sensate-focus technique.

2. Share a fantasy you've had about your partner.

3. Cuddle and hug as you talk to your partner about the positive things you love about him or her.

4. Plan a sensual or sexual activity for your next encounter.

5. Plan a wonderful meal together. Prepare it together, and sit close together—really share the meal.

6. Wash your partner's hair.

7. Spend some time just kissing.

This chapter seeks to help you maintain and grow in physical intimacy. As with so many other areas we've discussed, working on this aspect of your marriage wisely can produce great benefits. Physical intimacy isn't all that marriage is about, but it's one of the areas—along with fun and friendship—where you can really develop a lasting, satisfying ability to connect.

# 14

# Keeping It Together

We've covered many concepts in this book: communication and conflict management, commitment, forgiveness, friendship, fun, sensuality, and the impact of core belief systems and social support on your relationship. We're confident that these ideas and techniques of the PREP approach can go a long way toward helping you keep your African American marriage strong.

My great-grandmother cooked soup during the Great Depression and shared it with everyone in the neighborhood. What was interesting was that everyone would try to tell what the secret ingredient was that made each soup so special. Of course, she would never let her secrets out. She said that was for my family to know.

You can think of this book as being a recipe for a good soup. The ingredients are your love and attraction, commitment to working together, use of the skills outlined in our approach, and so forth. Now, what you have to do is to take the ingredients for a relationship and cook them up in your own kitchen. It's your own individual soup, whatever works best for you and your spouse. Remember that it takes some time to get the ingredients of every good soup just right. It's the effort and the persistence of the cooks in doing it right that makes a great soup.

The key for you now is to blend these ingredients to make a great marriage happen. From our experience with couples, we've suggested recommendations for how to keep your relationship strong and vital for years to come. Now we have some final and important points to make.

## You Are Not Alone

When people have problems in a relationship, the mistakes they make are fairly predictable: escalation and withdrawal, invalidation, and negative interpretation. In contrast, there are actually many, many ways to have a good relationship. Happy, healthy couples have many different qualities that contribute to their strength. In short, couples who are struggling look more alike than the diversity that characterizes couples who are doing well.

In the course of developing this book, we have talked to numerous couples about what is going on in their relationships. We see their frustration about the negative patterns that are going on from time to time. It is deeply satisfying to confirm to them that what they have as issues is not uncommon among other African American couples we speak to.

You're in good company if you encounter some of the negative patterns and attitudes discussed throughout this book. We all do. They're common. But divorce is common, too. So it's important to be concerned about the negative patterns. It's even better to do something with your concern.

Fortunately, the news is good. There's hope for couples who are invested in stopping negative patterns and preserving all the great things in marriage. Our research shows that you can prevent such problems from building up and harming your relationship; you can restore greatness to a relationship in trouble—but you have to invest in your marriage to make it all it can be. This means hard work and making play a priority. It means being there for the other person and avoiding becoming defensive. It means really, really talking about your issues in the way we have suggested.

Sometimes we are like a train on a track. We know only how to go where the track leads us. To work on and change things in your marriage that aren't how you want them to be, you have to find a way to create another track and direction to go in. This is hard to do. People tend to do what they have done before unless there is a really good reason for change. This leads us to the issue of motivation.

## Motivation

All of our principles, our knowledge base, our research and techniques aren't going to work for you unless you're motivated to do what it takes to have a good relationship. Sometimes it's hardest to motivate the couples who can do the most to prevent serious problems from developing in the first place: engaged and newlywed couples. There's just too much else going on. When you're still early in the relationship, it's hard to imagine having serious trouble later on. If this is your situation, please keep in mind that working to implement the kind of strategy recommended here can do a lot to keep your relationship vibrant.

If you have been together for some time, you probably fall into one of three categories:

1. Those who are doing great and want to keep it that way

2. Those having some struggles and in need of a tune-up

3. Those who are having significant problems and are in need of major changes to get back on track

Now might be a good time to go back to the quiz you took in the Introduction and see what things have changed regarding how you now think about issues or try to approach issues in your relationship.

Wherever you are at, you can't get the most out of this approach with a half-hearted effort. Even though we emphasize relatively straightforward techniques and ideas, it still takes effort to make any kind of meaningful change in life.

## But My Partner Won't Try These Things

What if your partner isn't motivated to learn some of the things we've presented? This can be a frustrating problem if you really like the ideas. Don't lose faith; there are things you can try.

### Work on Yourself First

It's wisest to begin working on what *you* can change about how you handle yourself in the relationship, regardless of what your partner is willing to do. It's too easy for all of us to get focused on what our partners can do. Instead, focus your attention on what you have the most control over—yourself!

Do you have a tendency toward negative interpretation? Do you tend to withdraw from talking about issues? Do you bring up gripes when you are out to have a fun evening with your partner? You can make substantial changes in such patterns no matter what your partner is doing. There are many ways you can work on maintaining and demonstrating your dedication without your partner ever reading this book.

You can also demonstrate some of the ground rules without necessarily working on them together. For example, you might be out together and begin to get into conflict; simply say: "You know, we're out to have fun tonight. Let's deal with that tomorrow when we have more time so we can focus on relaxing together this evening." Most partners get the idea even if they've never heard of PREP or ground rules. It's really pretty basic, yet powerful to make some of these changes.

Although all the things we've suggested work best when you're working together, you can accomplish a lot on your own so long as you're willing to try and your partner isn't actively working to damage the relationship.

### PREP Lite: Tastes Great, Less Filling

You can try getting your partner interested in some of the lighter topics we've discussed, such as fun or friendship. There are ideas in Chapters Eleven and Twelve that you could suggest to your partner as a start. This could get some potent and positive changes going, which can open up interest in other features of this program. As you may have noticed, many of the key ideas about fun and friendship don't depend on knowledge of other key concepts in this book. It is rare for both people in a marriage to have exactly the same level of desire to work on a relationship or see problems in the same areas as the partner does. This is OK and part of what makes us individuals on the same team.

### There's More Than One Way to Skin a Cat

If these ideas fail to spark interest in your partner, then you have a choice to make. Give some thought to the significance of your partner's reluctance. It could simply mean that your partner is less interested than you are in a particular approach to strengthening your marriage. If this is the case, it's a serious and inaccurate negative interpretation to assume that your partner isn't as interested as you are in keeping your marriage strong.

In fact, we often talk to couples where one partner—usually the woman—thinks the other isn't doing enough for the marriage and the other—the man, generally—brings up all sorts of things that he feels he's doing because he does care for the relationship.

One couple we saw in counseling had a big problem with this kind of thinking. She loved to read self-help books and he didn't. She interpreted his lack of interest as lack of motivation in the marriage. Yet he was doing all sorts of other things that showed his investment: agreeing to active involvement in counseling, wanting to go out and be together, and being a reliable provider for the family.

So be careful how you interpret things. Either way, perhaps you can talk together about how you each think you can make progress as a couple. Your partner may have different ideas about what's best for the marriage and how to get there. Listen up!

*But My Partner Really Isn't Interested*

If, by contrast, you're pretty convinced that your partner is substantially less motivated than you are to work on the relationship in any way, you have a tough situation. What you choose to do is up to you, but to give your relationship the best chance we still recommend that you do the best you can to strengthen your marriage according to principles of the sort we advocate here.

As we said earlier, one person can cause substantial changes in a marriage; it's just a lot easier and more fun when you're working together. If you value your marriage, your own positive investment gives you the best chance of bringing about the changes you desire. Just keep in mind that sometimes the most positive investment you can make is to confront any problems you see head-on. You might need to ask your partner to sit down and then say something to him or her like this: "I've been worried about where we're headed. I'm really committed to making this a great marriage, not just one where we get by. I'm willing to do what it takes to make that happen. I'm hoping we can work together, and I want you to know that I'll be trying hard. Let me know if you want to try some of the same things."

## When Help Is Desired

We think most couples can benefit from the educational approach we've outlined. But there are times when couples can benefit from professional help—times when motivation alone isn't enough to get you on a better path. As African Americans, we have a history of not going to mental health professionals. Much of this comes from not wanting others to think of us as crazy. Some of this resistance also comes from who we are as a people. We have survived in the face of slavery, discrimination, and bigotry. We have survived every attempt to extinguish us as a people. We have survived in part because we have a rugged individual spirit about ourselves. This has benefited our survival, but the idea of not being in control or not being able to fix what's wrong on our own is an untenable proposition that contributes to our avoiding mental health professionals.

We have long needed assistance but historically had few African American counselors we could turn to for help. We have also noted that there is little material out there that approaches solutions to marital problems with African Americans in mind. We are happy to say that this book is one exception.

We wish everyone could work on *preventing* serious problems from developing. But as marriage therapists as well as researchers, we recognize there are times when couples can really benefit from a professional's skill. We hope that reading this book breaks down some of the barriers you might think of when it comes to seeking a therapist's help.

We are not intending the PREP approach to be a substitute for therapy if that's what is really needed. There are many reasons a couple or individual might wisely seek professional guidance: physical abuse, substance abuse, depression, ongoing conflict that is never resolved, and so forth. These are danger signs that indicate the educational approach might not be enough.

The most common reason couples seek professional help is that they feel stuck, wanting or hoping for some significant changes to occur but not being able to make them happen. For example, you might both be reading this book, love the approach, and try some of the techniques but still find that you're having trouble changing ingrained patterns.

A good therapist can help such a couple in numerous ways. He or she can give you a new perspective on a problem. The therapist can offer a structured, safe place to talk about difficult issues, much like the structure given by some of the techniques we recommend. The professional can hold you accountable for making certain changes happen. He or she can coach you in learning skills you may be having trouble with on your own. He or she can also help you explore the various effects of family background and expectations on your relationship.

If you decide that getting professional help may be something for you to consider, seek help sooner rather than later. Studies show that people endure as much as seven years of stress before they start seeking help. That's a really long time to wait. It's easier to change patterns earlier than later—especially easier than waiting until one of you has given up.

Once you have decided to get professional help, where do you go to find it? The first place you might consider is the church. Clergymen and clergywomen of many churches have training in counseling and can combine the spiritual and religious traditions that may be important to you. Some people worry about others in the church finding out that they are in counseling, so they avoid going to clergy for help. You might consider at least starting with your clergyman or clergywoman because he or she may be able to refer you to other sources in your city. You may also want to ask a friend you can trust.

In seeking someone to talk to, one of the biggest problems for African American couples is finding a counselor who is sensitive to your specific issues and to those related to being an African American. It is often hard to find an African American counselor who is in private practice. You may feel that counselors from other ethnic backgrounds won't know enough about the African American experience to really help. We suggest that you ask any counselor you talk to about their style and approach to working with couples as well as whether he or she has worked with African American couples before. There may be a therapist from another ethnic background who has experience with African American couples. If you're at a point where you think professional help might be useful, see the additional tips at the end of this book for finding a competent couples counselor.

# What to Do Now

Bill Coffin, a colleague and prevention specialist who works for the U.S. Navy, suggests that couples think about relationship fitness as they might think about physical fitness. Just as physical fitness experts recommend that you work out three or four times a week for twenty to thirty minutes, a couple should devote at least that much time to working on the relationship. This doesn't mean just having meetings as a couple, but planning fun times together, having friendship talks, making love, giving a back rub, hanging out together or reading a book in the same room, listening to music, or playing with the children. Make the time for your relationship to be regularly renewed in these ways.

If you're serious about putting some of these key ideas into practice, here are some important points to keep in mind.

## Looking Back to Move Forward

To get the most out of what we have presented here, be sure to review the material. We all learn better when we go over key concepts again and again. Perhaps you've highlighted key sections in this book as you read them. Go back and read those sections again. For example, this would be a great time to go back to Chapter Five and review the ground rules. Are you using them? Have you kept at it? How is your fun and friendship going?

It would be especially valuable to review the rules for the speaker-listener technique, problem solving, and principles on forgiveness. These rules and ideas aren't all that complicated, but you want to master them to get the greatest benefit in your marriage. Better yet, read through the whole book again, together.

## Practice

The PREP approach is, in part, a skills-oriented model for building a solid relationship. The key to such an approach is to practice the specific skills and ways of thinking we've recommended. It's not enough to just review the ideas; you need to make them part of your life.

Practice the techniques and strategies so that you can put them into practice. We know they feel artificial at first; they're not like the behaviors you naturally act out. But if you practice enough, the solid skills, techniques, and ways of thinking that we emphasize become regular habits in your relationship.

At the same time, the PREP approach is a set of attitudes and a way of thinking about your relationship. We are relationship optimists who believe you can have a great relationship if you invest in it and make it a major priority in your life.

## Rituals and Routines

One way to think about the PREP approach is that every couple can benefit from the patterns that work for happy couples and that help unhappy couples fix problems. Too many couples are controlled by relationship problems. We want couples to take control.

A ritual is a well-organized habit that guides people in life. A colleague of ours, Bob Weiss at the University of Oregon, refers to the benefits of this as being under *rule control* rather than *stimulus control*. To be under stimulus control means you're constantly reacting to the things happening around you—the stimuli of your life.

We've given you some pretty good rules, but it's up to you to make them habits. In effect, we're suggesting that you not fall into a pattern of reacting to events, but instead build rituals into your lifestyle that give you as a couple control over important aspects of your life.

Many rituals take place during important life transitions. This is because transitions are stressful; think of birth, wedding, leaving the nest, and death. Rituals and routines can reduce stress by providing some structure during these times of change. For example, most cultures have ritualized ways of dealing with death and mourning. Rituals offer a map or structure to help in handling these transitions. But the daily conflicts that come up in life are stressful, too. Rituals and routines can give stress-reducing benefits.

There are many rituals that you can create as a couple. One that my wife and I (KEW) do when things get stressful is to go to our bedroom and, behind closed doors, sing songs about how we are feeling. Sometimes we sing "Hey, Hey, the blues are all right." Sometimes we try to sing a rap song that doesn't make any sense to us, but we like the beat and it makes us smile.

You may already have rituals in your relationship: a simple routine for getting ready for bed, or how you handle a special meal for a holiday. Clearly, young children benefit from routine for family life. But it's not just kids who benefit from structure. For example, if you are having weekly meetings as a couple to deal with issues in your relationship, you've begun a ritual that we believe has a positive payoff over the long run. Meeting regularly helps prevent destructive conflict and enhance intimacy. It gives you a routine for anticipating predictable issues, such as those around an upcoming holiday or in child rearing.

We're not suggesting that you get weighed down by all sorts of rules. We suggest that some solid, commonsense skills can make all the difference in the world in how the tough issues affect your relationship. When such skills and ways of thinking become routine, you get the greatest benefit. Here are some of the powerful rituals we recommend:

1. Using the speaker-listener technique
2. Separating problem discussion from problem solving
3. Working through the forgiveness model when you need to
4. Having a weekly couple's meeting
5. Agreeing to keep fun and friendship times off limits for argument and issue discussion
6. Making time to practice the skills that help you keep your marriage strong

Preserve spontaneity and creativity in the wonderful aspects of your relationship. Structure conflict; let loose with fun.

## Engaging the Skills

As you consolidate your skills through practice and developing positive rituals, the most important thing is for you to be able to engage the skills when you need them. Knowing how to use the speaker-listener technique or the problem-solving model is great, but the real benefit comes from using these skills when they are most needed. Unfortunately, the time when you need a skill the most may be the same time it's hardest to use it, so being able to make the shift to engage more skill is critical. This is where practice and good habits really pay off.

It's hard to engage the skills the first few times. For example, as you work on ground rule number one (time out), it is more difficult to do so at the start than after using it a few times. It can seem like avoidance to start using time outs, but the habit gets stronger as you see that this works. Your relationship benefits from the increased control over how and when you deal with difficult issues.

## Reinforce, Reinforce, Reinforce

When we train other professionals and paraprofessionals to work with couples, we emphasize over and over the need to be active in reinforcing the positive steps couples make in learning the skills we teach. It's important to reinforce new skills, as well as reinforcing the positive things that are already happening.

We make the same suggestion to you. As you work on learning new patterns and ways of thinking, reinforce each other. Praise your partner for trying things out, for listening well, for working with you to handle issues well, for being committed, and so forth. Don't take each other for granted. Show your appreciation for positive effort. Also, don't dwell on the past. In other words, don't say to your partner (or to yourself), "Why couldn't you have done this seven years ago?" Instead, focus on reinforcing the positive changes that are occurring now.

When was the last time you said, "Hey Baby, I sure like how you do that?" Or, "I really felt great the other night when you dropped what you were doing and spent time just listening to me talk about my problems at work." It's not hard to say "Thanks" or "Great job!" or "I really appreciated the way you did that." The effects on your relationship can be dramatic. We are often too focused on the negative. Instead, try looking for how to reward the positive. This is the best way to encourage more positive behavior in the future.

In general, our entire culture greatly underestimates the power of verbal reinforcement. Maybe that's because we are so focused on attaining economic success. Don't succumb to the tendency. Positive verbal reinforcement is the most potent change agent ever devised. Use it. If you like some things you see going on, say so. Reinforce, reinforce, reinforce.

## In Closing, We'd Like to Say. . .

If this society can train the best army in the world (sure, we're a bit biased), you'd think we could train couples to have good marriages. But, in fact, marriage is in trouble among African Americans just as it is for the rest of the people in the United States. We don't think it has to stay this way. If you have the know-how and the will to have a great marriage, you stand a good chance of making it happen.

We wouldn't pretend to know everything about marriage and relationships, but we think the material in this book gives you a good start. We started off wanting to write this book because there is so little out there on the African American marriage. We wanted to write something that African Americans could identify with, something with examples that are uniquely representative of the African American experience and that demonstrate the common, day-to-day situations that people of every color experience.

You can't prevent marriage from being hard work at times. But if you work together, you can make your relationship the kind that deepens and grows over the years, whatever comes your way. We've detailed our approach in this book. We've tried to give you tools you can use to build a relationship that brings long-term fulfillment, and to protect your relationship from naturally occurring storms. But like anything else, once you have the tools what you do with them is really up to you. Take these tools and have fun with them. Make them your own by figuring out how they work best in your relationship. Be patient, and know that it may take a couple of tries to find out what works best for you. The most important thing, as the ad says, is to just do it.

# Selected Research and Resources

Amato, P. R., & Rogers, S. J. (1999). Do attitudes toward divorce affect marital quality? *Journal of Family Issues, 20*(1), 69–86.

Arp, D., & Arp, C. (1997). *10 great dates to energize your marriage.* Grand Rapids, MI: Zondervan.

Arp, D., & Arp, C. (1998). *Love life for parents.* Grand Rapids, MI: Zondervan.

Arp, D., Arp, C., Stanley, S., Markman, H., & Blumberg, S. (2000). *Fighting for your empty nest marriage.* San Francisco: Jossey-Bass.

Baucom, D., & Epstein, N. (1990). *Cognitive behavioral marital therapy.* New York: Brunner/Mazel.

Beach, S. R., & O'Leary, K. D. (1993). Marital discord and dysphoria: For whom does the marital relationship predict depressive symptomatology? *Journal of Social and Personal Relationships, 10*(3), 405–420.

Behrens, B., & Halford, K. (1994, August). *Advances in the prevention and treatment of marital distress.* Paper presented at the Helping Families Change Conference, University of Queensland, Brisbane, Australia.

Birchler, G., Weiss, R., & Vincent, J. (1975). Multimethod analysis of social reinforcement exchange between maritally distressed and nondistressed spouse and stranger dyads. *Journal of Personality and Social Psychology, 31,* 349–360.

Bradbury, T. N., Beach, S.R.H., Fincham, F. D., & Nelson, G. M. (1996). Attributions and behavior in functional and dysfunctional marriages. *Journal of Consulting and Clinical Psychology, 64,* 569–576.

Call, V. R., & Heaton, T. B. (1997). Religious influence on marital stability. *Journal for the Scientific Study of Religion, 36,* 382–392.

Center for Marriage and Family. (1995). *Marriage preparation in the Catholic Church: Getting it right.* Omaha, NE: Creighton University.

Cherlin, A. J., & Furstenberg, F. F., Jr. (1994). Step families in the United States: A reconsideration. *Annual Review of Sociology, 20,* 359–381.

Christensen, A., & Heavey, C. L. (1990). Gender and social structure in the demand/withdraw pattern of marital conflict. *Journal of Personality and Social Psychology, 59,* 73–82.

Clements, M., & Markman, H. J. (1996). The transition to parenthood: Is having children hazardous to marriage? In N. Vanzetti & S. Duck (Eds.), *A lifetime of relationships* (pp. 290–310). Pacific Grove, CA: Brooks/Cole.

Clements, M., Stanley, S. M., & Markman, H. J. (under review). *Predicting Divorce.* Unpublished Manuscript.

Cowan, C. P., & Cowan, P. A. (1992). *When partners become parents: The big life change for couples.* New York: Harper Collins.

Crohn, J., Markman, H. J., Blumberg, S. L., & Levine, J. R. (2000). *Fighting for your Jewish marriage.* San Francisco: Jossey-Bass.

Cummings, E. M., & Davies, P. (1994). *Children and marital conflict.* New York: Guilford.

Eidelson, R., & Epstein, N. (1982). Cognitions and relationship maladjustment: Development of a measure of dysfunctional relationship beliefs. *Journal of Consulting and Clinical Psychology, 50,* 715–720.

Fincham, F., Grych, J., & Osborne, L. (1993, March). *Interparental conflict and child adjustment: A longitudinal analysis.* Paper presented at the biennial meeting of the Society for Research in Child Development, New Orleans, LA.

Fincham, F. D., Beach, S. R., Harold, G. T., & Osborne, L. N. (1997). Marital satisfaction and depression: Different causal relationships for men and women? *Psychological Science, 8*(5), 351–357.

Fincham, F. D., Garnier, P. C., Gano-Phillips, S., & Osborne, L. N. (1995). Pre-interaction expectations, marital satisfaction and accessibility: a new look at sentiment override. *Journal of Family Psychology, 9,* 3–14.

Floyd, F., Markman, H., Kelly, S., Blumberg, S., & Stanley, S. (1995). Prevention: Conceptual, research, and clinical issues. In N. Jacobson & A. Gurman (Eds.), *Handbook of marital therapy* (second edition). New York: Guilford.

Forthofer, M. S., Markman, H. J., Cox, M., Stanley, S., & Kessler, R. C. (1996). Associations between marital distress and work loss in a national sample. *Journal of Marriage and Family, 58,* 597–605.

Fowers, B. J. (2000). *Beyond the myth of marital happiness.* San Francisco: Jossey-Bass.

Fraenkel, P., Markman, H., & Stanley, S. (1997). The prevention approach to relationship problems. *Sexual and Marital Therapy, 12*(3), 249–258.

Giblin, P., Sprenkle, D. H., & Sheehan, R. (1985). Enrichment outcome research: A meta-analysis of premarital, marital, and family interventions. *Journal of Marital and Family Therapy, 11*(3), 257–271.

Glenn, Norval D. (1998). The course of marital success and failure in five American 10-year marriage cohorts. *Journal of Marriage and the Family, 60,* 569–576.

Gottman, J., Notarius, C., Gonso, J., & Markman, H. (1976). *A couple's guide to communication.* Champaign, IL: Research Press.

Gottman, J. M. (1993) A theory of marital dissolution and stability. *Journal of Family Psychology, 7,* 57–75.

Grych, J., & Fincham, F. (1990). Marital conflict and children's adjustment. *Psychological Bulletin, 108,* 267–290.

Guerney, B. G., Jr. (1977). *Relationship enhancement.* San Francisco: Jossey-Bass.

Hahlweg, K., & Markman, H. (1988). The effectiveness of behavioral marital therapy: Empirical status of behavioral techniques in preventing and alleviating marital distress. *Journal of Consulting and Clinical Psychology 56,* 440–447.

Hahlweg, K., Markman, H. J., Thurmaier, F., Engl, J., & Eckert, V. (1998). Prevention of marital distress: Results of a German prospective longitudinal study. *Journal of Family Psychology, 12,* 543–556.

Halford, K., & Bouma, R. (1997). Individual psychopathology and marital distress. In K. Halford & H. J. Markman (Eds.), *Clinical Handbook of Marriage and Couples Intervention* (pp. 291–321). New York: Wiley.

Halford, K., & Markman, H. (Eds.). (1997). *Clinical handbook of marriage and marital interaction.* London: Wiley.

Heaton, T. B. (1984). Religious homogamy and marital satisfaction reconsidered. *Journal of Marriage and the Family, 46,* 729–733.

Holtzworth-Munroe, A., Markman, H. J., O'Leary, D. K., Neidig, P., Leber, D., Heyman, R. E., Hulbert, D., & Smutzler, N. (1995). The need for marital violence prevention efforts: A behavioral-cognitive secondary prevention program for engaged and newly-married couples. *Applied and Preventive Psychology, 4,* 77–88.

Hood, R. W., Spilka, B., Hunsberger, B., and Gorsuch, R. *The psychology of religion.* New York: Guilford Press, 1996.

Jacobson, N. S., & Christensen, A. (1998). *Acceptance and change in couple therapy: A therapist's guide to transforming relationships.* New York: Norton.

Johnson, M. P. (1995). Patriarchal terrorism and common couple violence: Two forms of violence against women. *Journal of Marriage and the Family, 57*(2), 283–294.

Johnson, M. P., Caughlin, J. P., & Huston, T. L. (1999). The tripartite nature of marital commitment: Personal, moral, and structural reasons to stay married. *Journal of Marriage and the Family, 61,* 160–177.

Jones, W., & Adams, J. (1999). *Handbook of interpersonal commitment and relationship stability.* New York: Plenum.

Jordan, P., Stanley, S., & Markman, H. (1999). *Becoming parents.* San Francisco: Jossey-Bass.

Karney, B. R., & Bradbury, T. N. (1995). The longitudinal course of marital quality and stability: A review of theory, method, and research. *Psychological Bulletin, 118,* 3–34.

Kiecolt-Glaser, J. K., Malarkey, W. B., Chee, M., Newton, T., Cacioppo, J. T., Mao, H. Y., & Glaser, R. (1993). Negative behavior during marital conflict is associated with immunological down-regulation. *Psychosomatic Medicine, 55,* 395–409.

Kurdek, L. A. (1993). Predicting marital dissolution: A 5-year prospective longitudinal study of newlywed couples. *Journal of Personality and Social Psychology, 64,* 221–242.

Larsen, A. S., & Olson, D. H. (1989). Predicting marital satisfaction using PRE-PARE: A replication study. *Journal of Marital and Family Therapy, 15,* 311–322.

Laumann, E. O., Paik, A., & Rosen, R. C. (1999). Sexual dysfunction in the United States. *Journal of the American Medical Association, 281,* 537–544.

Lehrer, E. L., & Chiswick, C. (1993). Religion as a determinant of marital stability. *Demography, 30,* 385–404.

Levenson, R. W., & Gottman, J. M. (1985). Physiological and affective predictors of change in relationship satisfaction. *Journal of Personality & Social Psychology, 49*(1), 85–94.

Levinger, G. (1980). Toward the analysis of close relationships. *Journal of Experimental Social Psychology, 16,* 510–544.

Lindahl, K., & Markman, H. J. (1990). Communication and negative affect regulation in the family. In E. Blechman (Ed.), *Emotions and families.* New York: Plenum Press.

Mahoney, A., Pargament, K. I., Jewell, T., Swank, A. B., Scott, E., Emery, E., & Rye, M. (1999). Marriage and the spiritual realm: The role of proximal and distal religious constructs in marital functioning. *Journal of Family Psychology, 13*(3), 321–338.

Margolin, G., John, R., & Gleberman, L. (1988). Affective responses to conflictual discussions in violent and nonviolent couples. *Journal of Consulting and Clinical Psychology, 56,* 24–33.

Markey, B., Micheletto, M., & Becker, A. (1985). *Facilitating open couple commu-*

*nication, understanding, and study (FOCCUS)*. Omaha: Archdiocese of
Omaha.

Markman, H., Floyd, F., Stanley, S. & Jamieson, K. (1984). A cognitive-
behavioral program for the prevention of marital and family distress:
Issues in program development and delivery. In K. Hahlweg &
N. Jacobson (Eds.), *Marital interaction*. New York: Guilford.

Markman, H., Floyd, F., Stanley, S., & Storaasli, R. (1988). The prevention of
marital distress: a longitudinal investigation. *Journal of Consulting and
Clinical Psychology, 56,* 210–217.

Markman, H. J. (1981). The prediction of marital distress: A five year follow-up.
*Journal of Consulting and Clinical Psychology, 49,* 760–762.

Markman, H. J., & Hahlweg, K. (1993). The prediction and prevention of marital distress: An international perspective. *Clinical Psychology Review, 13,*
29–43.

Markman, H. J., & Kraft, S. A. (1989). Men and women in marriage: Dealing
with gender differences in marital therapy. *The Behavior Therapist, 12,*
51–56.

Markman, H. J., Renick, M. J., Floyd, F., Stanley, S., & Clements, M. (1993).
Preventing marital distress through communication and conflict manage-
ment training: A four and five year follow-up. *Journal of Consulting and
Clinical Psychology, 62,* 1–8.

Matthews, L. S., Wickrama, K.A.S., & Conger, R. D. (1996). Predicting marital
instability from spouse and observer reports of marital interaction. *Journal
of Marriage and the Family, 58,* 641–655.

McCullough, M. E., Worthington, E. L., Jr., & Rachal, K. C. (1997). Interpersonal forgiving in close relationships. *Journal of Personality and Social Psychology, 73,* 321–336.

McManus, M. (1993). *Marriage savers*. Grand Rapids, MI: Zondervan.

Miller, S., Wackman, D. B., & Nunnally, E. W. (1976). A communication training program for couples. *Social Casework, 57*(1), 9–18.

Noller, P. (1996). What is this thing called love? Defining the love that supports
marriage and family. *Personal Relationships, 3,* 97–115.

Notarius, C., & Markman, H. J. (1993). *We can work it out: Making sense of marital conflict*. New York: Putnam.

Ooms, T. (1998). *Toward more perfect unions: Putting marriage on the public
agenda*. Washington, DC: Family Impact Seminar.

Parrott, Les, & Parrott, Leslie. (1995). *Saving your marriage before it starts: Seven
questions to ask before (and after) you marry*. Grand Rapids, MI: Zondervan.

Pasch, L. A., & Bradbury, T. N. (1998). Social support, conflict, and the development of marital dysfunction. *Journal of Consulting and Clinical Psychology, 66*, 219–30.

Peck, M. S. *The road less traveled*. New York: Touchstone, 1985.

Pistole, C. (1989). Attachment in adult romantic relationships: Style of conflict resolution and relationship satisfaction. *Journal of Social and Personal Relationships, 6*, 505–510.

Prado, L. M., & Markman, H. J. (1999). Unearthing the seeds of marital distress: What we have learned from married and remarried couples. In M. Cox & J. Brooks-Gunn (Eds.), *Conflict and cohesion in families: Causes and consequences*. Mahwah, NJ: LEA.

Renick, M. J., Blumberg, S., & Markman, H. J. (1992). The Prevention and Relationship Enhancement Program (PREP): An empirically-based preventive intervention program for couples. *Family Relations, 41*(2), 141–147.

Rusbult, C. E. (1983). A longitudinal test of the investment model: The development (and deterioration) of satisfaction and commitment in heterosexual involvements. *Journal of Personality and Social Psychology, 45*, 101–117.

Rusbult, C. E., Zembrodt, I. M., & Gunn, L. K. (1982). Exit, voice, loyalty, and neglect: Responses to dissatisfaction in romantic involvement. *Journal of Personality and Social Psychology, 43*, 1230–1242.

Sanders, M. R., Halford, W. K., & Behrens, B. C. (1999). Parental divorce and premarital couple communication. *Journal of Family Psychology, 13*(1), 60–74.

Silliman, B., & Schumm, W. R. (1989). Topics of interest in premarital counseling: Clients' views. *Journal of Sex and Marital Therapy, 15*(3), 199–204.

Silliman, B., Schumm, W. R., & Jurich, A. P. (1992). Young adults' preferences for premarital preparation program designs. *Contemporary Family Therapy, 14*, 89–100.

Silliman, B., Stanley, S. M., Coffin, W., Markman, H. J., & Jordan, P. L. (in press). Preventive interventions for couples. In H. Liddle, D. Santisteban, R. Levant, and J. Bray (Eds.), *Family psychology intervention science*. Washington, DC: American Psychological Association.

Smalley, G. (1996). *Making love last forever*. Dallas: Word.

Spilka, B., Hood, R., & Gorsuch, R. (1985). *The psychology of religion: An empirical approach*. Englewood Cliffs, NJ: Prentice-Hall.

Stahmann, R. F., & Hiebert, W. J. (1997). *Premarital and remarital counseling: The professional's handbook*. San Francisco: Jossey-Bass.

Stanley, S. (1998). *The heart of commitment: Compelling research that reveals the secrets of a lifelong, intimate marriage*. Nashville: Thomas Nelson.

Stanley, S., Trathen, D., McCain, S., & Bryan, M. (1998). *A lasting promise*. San Francisco: Jossey-Bass.

Stanley, S. M. (in press). Making the case for premarital training. *Family Relations*.

Stanley, S. M. (1997). What's important in premarital counseling? *Marriage and Family: A Christian Journal, 1*, 51–60.

Stanley, S. M., Blumberg, S. L., & Markman, H. J. (1999). Helping couples fight *for* their marriages: The PREP approach. In R. Berger & M. Hannah, (Eds.), *Handbook of preventive approaches in couple therapy*. New York: Brunner/Mazel.

Stanley, S. M., Bradbury, T. N., & Markman, H. J. (2000). Structural flaws in the bridge from basic research on marriage to interventions for couples: Illustrations from Gottman, Coan, Carrere, and Swanson (1998). *Journal of Marriage and the Family, 62*(1), 256–264.

Stanley, S. M., Lobitz, W. C., & Dickson, F. (1999). Using what we know: Commitment and cognitions in marital therapy. In W. Jones & J. Adams (Eds.), *Handbook of interpersonal commitment and relationship stability* (411–424). New York: Plenum.

Stanley, S. M., & Markman, H. J. (1992). Assessing commitment in personal relationships. *Journal of Marriage and the Family, 54*, 595–608.

Stanley, S. M., & Markman, H. J. (1997) *Marriage in the 90s: A nationwide random phone survey*. Denver, CO: PREP, Inc.

Stanley, S. M., & Markman, H. J. (1998). Acting on what we know: The hope of prevention. In *Strategies to strengthen marriage: What we know, what we need to know*. Washington, DC: The Family Impact Seminar.

Stanley, S. M., Markman, H. J., Prado, L. M., Olmos-Gallo, P. A., Tonelli, L., St. Peters, M., Leber, B. D., Bobulinski, M., Cordova, A., & Whitton, S. (2001). Community-based premarital prevention: clergy and lay leaders on the front lines. *Family Relations, 50*, 67–76.

Stanley, S. M., Markman, H. J., St. Peters, M., & Leber, D. (1995) Strengthening marriages and preventing divorce: New directions in prevention research. *Family Relations, 44*, 392–401.

Stanley, S. M., & Trathen, D. (1994). Christian PREP: An empirically based model for marital and premarital intervention. *The Journal of Psychology and Christianity, 13*, 158–165.

Stanton, G. (1997). *Why marriage matters*. Colorado Springs, CO: Pinon Press.

Storaasli, R. D., & Markman, H. J. (1990). Relationship problems in the early stages of marriage: A longitudinal investigation. *Journal of Family Psychology, 4*(1), 80–98.

Sullivan, K. T., & Goldschmidt, D. (2000). Implementation of empirically validated interventions in managed-care settings: The prevention and relationship enhancement program. *Professional Psychology: Research and Practice, 31,* 216–220.

Sullivan, K. T., & Bradbury, T. N. (1997). Are premarital prevention programs reaching couples at risk for marital dysfunction? *Journal of Consulting and Clinical Psychology, 65*(1), 24–30.

Thurmaier, F. R., Engl, J., Eckert, V., & Hahlweg, K. (1993). *Ehevorbereitung— ein partnerschaftliches lernprogramm EPL*. Munich, Germany: Ehrenwirth.

Thurmaier, F., Engl, J., & Hahlweg, K. (1999). Eheglück auf Dauer? Methodik, Inhalte und Effektivität eines präventiven Paarkommunikationstrainings—Ergebnisse nach fünf Jahren. Zeitschrift für *Klinische Psychologie, 28,* 54–62.

U. S. Bureau of the Census (1992). *Marriage, divorce, and remarriage in the 1990s* (Current Population Reports, P23–180). Washington, DC: U.S. Government Printing Office.

Van Lange, P.A.M., Rusbult, C. E., Drigotas, S. M., Arriaga, X. B., Witcher, B. S., & Cox, C. L. (1997). Willingness to sacrifice in close relationships. *Journal of Personality and Social Psychology, 72,* 1373–1395.

Van Widenfelt, B., Hosman, C., Schaap, C., & van der Staak, C. (1996). The prevention of relationship distress for couples at risk: A controlled evaluation with nine-month and two-year follow-ups. *Family Relations, 45,* 156–165.

Weiss, R. L. (1980). Strategic behavioral marital therapy: Toward a model for assessment and intervention. In J. P. Vincent (Ed.), *Advances in family intervention, assessment and theory* (Vol. 1., pp. 229–271). Greenwich, CT: JAI Press.

Weiss, R. L., & Dehle, C. (1994). Cognitive behavioral perspectives on marital conflict. In D. D. Cahn (Ed.), *Conflict in intimate relationships* (95–115). Mahwah, NJ: Erlbaum.

Whitehead, B. D. (1997). *The divorce culture*. New York: Knopf.

Whitton, S. W., Stanley, S. M., & Markman, H. J. (in press). Sacrifice in romantic relationships: An exploration of relevant research and theory. In Reiss, H.T., Fitzpatrick, M. A., & Vangelisti, A. L. (Eds.), *Stability and change in relationship: Behavior across the lifespan*. Cambridge University Press.

Worthington, E. L. (1990). *Counseling before marriage*. Volume 23 of the Resources for Christian Counseling series edited by Gary R. Collins. Dallas: Word.

# More Information on the PREP Approach

The authors of this book have a variety of resources available. We also conduct workshops both for couples and for those who work with couples. We have included the following section for those of you who may wish to go further, either as couples, or as counselors who help couples make great marriages.

## The PREP® Approach

### Books

In addition to this book, we have the following titles in this series. Each represents the same basic approach for helping couples build their marriages, but each is adapted and developed for a special audience. All are published by Jossey-Bass, Inc.

> *Fighting for Your Marriage* (1994), by Howard J. Markman, Scott M. Stanley, and Susan L. Blumberg.
>
> *A Lasting Promise: A Christian Guide to Fighting for Your Marriage* (1998), by Scott M. Stanley, Daniel Trathen, Savanna McCain, and Milt Bryan.
>
> *Becoming Parents: How to Strengthen Your Marriage as Your Family Grows* (1999), by Pamela L. Jordan, Scott M. Stanley, and Howard J. Markman.

*Fighting for Your Jewish Marriage: Preserving a Lasting Promise* (2000), by Joel Crohn, Howard J. Markman, Susan L. Blumberg, and Janice R. Levine.

*Fighting for Your Empty Nest Marriage: Reinventing Your Relationship When the Kids Leave Home* (2000), by David H. Arp, Claudia S. Arp, Scott M. Stanley, Susan L. Blumberg, and Howard J. Markman.

These books can be ordered from PREP, Jossey-Bass, Inc., or from any book store. Books or tapes can be ordered from PREP at the number below or from Jossey-Bass at (415) 433-1740.

## Audio and Video Tapes

*Fighting for Your Marriage* audio and video tapes are available from PREP Educational Product, Inc. Please call 800-366-0166 or write to us at the address below to order.

## Workshops

We conduct workshops for mental health counselors, clergy, lay leaders, and other marriage educators who desire to be more fully trained in the PREP Approach. For information about these instructor workshops, please call (303) 759–9931 or write to us at the address below. We will be glad to give you information about seminars or products to help you in your ministry to other couples.

We also have a list of counselors who have been trained in this approach and who do either workshops or counseling using aspects of this model. To obtain that list, you can either write to us at the address above and request the referral list, or you can visit our website.

You can write us at:
PREP
P.O. Box 102530
Denver, Colorado 80250-2530
E-Mail: PREPinc@aol.com
Website: www.PREPinc.com

# Finding a Counselor
# When You Need One

There are so many potential therapists and counselors to choose from in most areas, it's hard for couples to know how to find the best help. How do you find a good couples' therapist out of all the psychologists, marriage therapists, professional counselors, psychiatrists, social workers, and so on and so forth that are listed in the Yellow Pages?

The best way to find a couples' therapist is to get names from some source you trust: a friend, a physician, a clergyperson. If all else fails, you can write to us for referrals to people who have been trained in the PREP approach in your area. If you want to do that, send a self-addressed, stamped envelope to us:

**PREP, Inc.**
**1780 S. Bellaire St., Suite 621**
**Denver, CO 80222**

Or you can write to the American Association of Marriage and Family Therapists:

**1100 17th St. N.W., 10th Floor**
**Washington, DC 20136**

Ask them to send you a list of certified marriage and family therapists in your area.

You can also call your state's marriage and family therapy association, psychological association, or social work association. You might even have a trusted radio talk show psychologist or therapist in your area. These commentators usually know of some of the best resources in their community because they have to be prepared to refer a lot of people for help.

Look on the World Wide Web by keyword "marriage counselors" for information on what questions to ask a potential counselor, what expectations you should have for counseling, and other important issues in trying to find a good counselor.

Getting two or more names is a good idea. Then be an active consumer and call them up; ask about their training, experience, approach, fees, license, and billing policies. If you really like the kind of approach taken in this book, you might ask for a therapist who specializes in what is called the cognitive/behavioral approach. You can and should ask a potential therapist directly about such things, and anything else that's important to you, such as religious or cultural background, viewpoint on codependency issues, or experience with a specific issue such as the effect on a marriage of having a seriously ill child. You get the idea.

Most important, you should ask if the therapist specializes in working with couples rather than as an individual therapist. Many individually oriented therapists gladly do marriage therapy, but this doesn't mean they're skilled at it. There are members of all the professions we mentioned just above who specialize in marriage or couples' work. Again, you are a consumer, and in many locations there are loads of therapists you can consider seeing. If you don't like the answers to your questions, move on and try another name.

If you begin to see a therapist, keep these issues in mind. If, after a few sessions, you don't feel that this person can help you, you may be right. You're going to spend a lot of money with a therapist, so don't persist long with someone you don't feel right about.

It's vital to get a sense of the connection and the fit you may have with the potential therapist. One of the best predictors of success in couples' therapy, as with all other therapy, is the quality of the relationship that you have with the therapist. Do you think this is someone you can trust and respect?

Last of all, what if you want to get professional help but your spouse isn't interested? Here's what psychologist and colleague Andrea Van Steenhouse often suggests on her radio call-in show. Say something like this to your partner: "I've been concerned about some of the issues in our relationship, and I think we could benefit from some help. I've made an appointment with a therapist for Wednesday at 4:00 P.M. I'd really like you to come with me. I want to do this together. But if you don't want to, I want to let you know that I plan to go anyway. I want to do what I can to get this situation turned around, for the sake of both of us."

This kind of strategy shows your positive intent. It also shows how serious you are about getting help. This strategy may not work; but then again, it just might. It takes some courage to get help. If you need help, we hope you'll be brave. Know we are behind you!

# Some Thoughts on Domestic Violence

Since PREP (and therefore this book) deals with communication and conflict between partners, questions about domestic violence arise at times. Domestic violence is a very complex topic and not the subject of this book. Nevertheless, we have a few key points we would like to stress on the matter:

- PREP (and this book) is not a treatment program for domestic violence.

- There are some couples who can reduce their chances of becoming physically aggressive by learning techniques such as those taught here. These are couples who are at risk for conflicts becoming physical as a result of difficulty handling conflict well *together*—not couples in which the man is using aggression to dominate or control his partner.

- Domestic violence of any sort is unacceptable, wrong, and dangerous.

- There is an alarming level of domestic violence (at various levels) taking place in families in our society.

- No matter what the nature of the violence, when a man strikes a woman, the woman is in greater danger and will likely suffer long-lasting and negative after-effects. Of course, many women strike men, too, and that is just as unacceptable.

- *With any kind of domestic violence, the preeminent concern should be safety.* That means you should seek the necessary services to assure that neither partner is in danger. That could mean seeking counsel from a Christian therapist or a pastor *who has experience in this area,* or a community shelter for battered women in cases where the woman is in significant fear and danger.

- We recommend that those who work with couples be aware of the complex issues around domestic violence and also be fully aware of local resources for help in dealing with domestic violence in ways that can increase safety (such as law enforcement access and shelters).

For more reading about the controversies surrounding domestic violence, we recommend the following:

Gelles, R., and Loseke, D. (1993). *Current controversies on family violence.* New York: Sage.

Johnson, M. P. (1995). Patriarchal terrorism and common couple violence: Two forms of violence against women. *Journal of Marriage and the Family, 57*(2), 283–294.

# About the Authors

*Keith E. Whitfield* is an associate professor of behavioral health at the Pennsylvania State University in the College of Health and Human Development. He received his Ph.D. in 1989 from Texas Tech University in Lubbock in life span developmental psychology. He conducts research on African American twins and families, in work supported by the National Institute on Aging. He has more than 120 publications, presentations, and invited lectures to his credit and is actively involved in more than $1 million in research funding for his various studies of African Americans; one focus of his research is successful aging among families. His work has been featured in various magazines, among them *Essence* and *Heart and Soul*.

*Scott M. Stanley* is codirector of the Center for Marital and Family Studies at the University of Denver, an adjunct professor of psychology, and president of PREP Educational Products. He has published numerous research reports and writings for couples. He is internationally known for his work on the PREP (Prevention and Relationship Enhancement Program) approach to reducing the risks of marital distress and divorce, as well as research and theory on marital commitment. Stanley is the coauthor of *A Lasting Promise* and *Becoming Parents*, and author of *The Heart of Commitment*. He contributes extensively to print and broadcast media as an expert on marriage.

*Howard J. Markman* is one of the world's leading experts in the field of couples research and intervention. He is a professor of psychology at the University of Denver and president of PREP. He frequently appears in the national media (including "The Oprah Winfrey Show," "The Today Show," "20/20," and "Nightline") and is invited to give talks on relationships around the United States, Europe, and Australia. He is coauthor of *Why Do Fools Fall in Love?* (Jossey-Bass, 2001) and *The Clinical Handbook of Marriage and Couples Intervention*. He is the codeveloper of the PREP approach and the author of more than one hundred scientific articles and chapters.

*Susan L. Blumberg* is a licensed clinical psychologist in private practice in Denver, working with children, families, and couples. She presents regularly on topics related to communication and conflict management skills to professional and public audiences. She leads PREP workshops for couples and works with families and businesses interested in improving communication skills.

# Index